D11193813

A ROVING RECLUSE

TO

ALICE AND ARTHUR GANNON

1920–1945.

A ROVING RECLUSE

More Memoirs

By

PETER F. ANSON

With Illustrations by the Author

1946
THE NEWMAN BOOKSHOP
WESTMINISTER
MARYLAND

First Published, March, 1946.
Second Impression, May, 1946.

Written and Illustrated by Peter F. Anson:

Illustrations only:

PRINTED IN IRELAND BY CAHILL
AND CO., LTD., PARKGATE
PRINTING WORKS, DUBLIN.

FOREWORD

After the publication of *Harbour Head* in the autumn of 1944, otherwise appreciative readers pointed out, quite correctly, that my roving career had not been exclusively connected with the sea, ships and sailors. They thought that there was more than sufficient non-maritime material to make an even more interesting volume of reminiscences. So I have tried to keep the sea well in the background of these pages, although, as the reader will discover, it has not been so easy to do so! These memories may not be maritime in subject matter, but they are not unlike a long voyage on a choppy sea. My ship has been tossed about like a shuttle-cock for many a long year, until at last it came home. I have described, not only the voyages, but also the shipmates, i.e., the people of all types and circumstances, personalities and professions; rich and poor, priests, monks, and ordinary layfolk, Catholic, Protestant, and without religion, who have gone out of their way to help me in countless ways. Each had some gift of heart or mind which they offered. Some were famous, others unknown, but what does it matter? Yet the portrait gallery is far from complete. Many persons who ought to have been immortalised have been left out, not so much because they are forgotten, but because the decks were already far too crowded!

A special word of thanks is due to the Rev. Ivor Daniel for his drastic revision of the original manuscript. Many useful suggestions and criticisms by the Rt. Rev. Mgr. Clapperton, Rev. A. V. Hauber, Dr. J. F. Milne, Mr. J. M. D. Smith, Mr. Alex John McKay, and the Benedictines of Prinknash and Millichope must also be acknowledged. I must likewise thank the editors of *Pax, The Father Mathew Record, The Catholic Herald, Franciscan Annals* and *The Universe* for allowing me to incorporate material which has already appeared in these publications.

Perhaps it should be pointed out that the use of such expressions as " Mass ", etc., with reference to the Church of England services has no ulterior significance. It is merely employing the usual terminology of a certain section of Anglicans whose sayings and doings occupy a considerable portion of this book.

ILLUSTRATIONS

CONTENTS

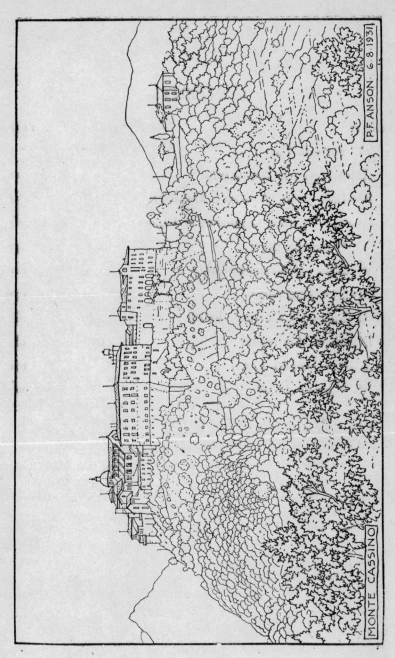

MONTE CASSINO.

CHAPTER I

BOYHOOD DAYS

A little old lady, who looked very tired, sat in an open carriage drawn by four stately high-stepping grey horses through the streets of Windsor on a sultry June evening in the year 1897. Wisps of silver hair peeped out beneath her violet bonnet. Her head nodded from side to side with the clockwork-like regularity of a china mandarin or a mechanical doll. In fact, she might have been an over-dressed doll: one was not quite certain if she was human. The windows of every house that commanded a view of the streets were crowded, and spectators lined the pavements. Perspiring policemen were on duty, trying to keep the crowds in order. As the carriage moved on, a roar of cheering drowned the music of a brass band in the background. On one of the balconies stood a red-haired boy, about eight years old, dressed in a sailor suit with a white jumper: the latter showing black marks across the chest and sleeves as the result of leaning heavily against the iron railings.

When I revisit Windsor and look up at the balcony at the corner of High Street and Sheet Street, I recall the Diamond Jubilee of Queen Victoria. It must have made a great impression on my imagination. Mixed up with the memories of the Little Old Lady is a mental picture of a fair-haired girl, rather older than myself, who was sitting in another of the many carriages that made up that long procession. I enquired who she was, and was told that her name was Princess Ena, and that her mother was Princess Beatrice. The future Queen of Spain became my first sweetheart—quite correctly my first blonde, to use the current phrase. For many months after I was on the look-out for the little golden-haired Princess—whom I loved from afar. More than once she drove past me, but I doubt if she returned my bold glances, or even noticed my copper locks—for, of course, I had taken off my cap in honour of royalty!

*   *   *

Looking back over half a century, the days of my boyhood tend

B

to become a sort of kaleidoscope, made up of flashes of colour, ever changing and shifting. Two photographs on the mantelpiece of the room in which I write help to bring back the looks of my father and mother. The former wears the uniform of a Naval Officer and two stripes of gold lace on his sleeves—one broad, the other narrow, indicate that he was a rear-admiral when the photograph was taken. It is a kindly face, with a firm chin. The eyes, with overhanging lids, look curiously like my own. The latter shows a woman in early middle-age; black hair, already streaked with grey, done in the fashion of the nineties. She sat for this photograph in 1902, when she was thirty-nine years of age, and it is interesting to note that she has not changed her mode of hair-dressing to that which had become fashionable; though she has discarded the out-moded Leg of Mutton sleeves for the tight-sleeved bodice, with a tall lace collar, supported by whalebone, and adorned with much lace. A rather sad face, indicative of pain and suffering—the eyes make one wonder what she was thinking about that summer afternoon when she posed to Sarony at Scarborough.

Then there is another picture of a dear old lady, wearing a white lace cap with four curious little bunches of black ribbon surmounting the forehead. She is seated in a low chair in a garden; over the shoulders of her black silk dress is a black lace shawl. Hanging from her waist by a silver chain are a spectacle case and a reticule— the small bag worn by Victorian ladies and used instead of a pocket! This is my grandmother—Caroline Maria Vernon (1826-1918), who married Frederick Anson and became the mother of fourteen children, among whom was my father, Charles Eustace. During her later years I have been told that she was often mistaken for another Old Lady who, for part of the year, also resided at Windsor, but, as Granny drove about in a hired one-horse cab and not in a royal carriage and pair, I am inclined to discredit this legend!

The walls of my grandmother's house at Windsor were hung with many a gilt-framed engraving of paintings by Winterhalter, depicting Queen Victoria, the Prince Consort and their children—the latter in swelling crinolines with frilly drawers peeping out beneath. My great-uncle, George Anson, had been Private Secretary to the Prince Consort as will be recalled by all who have read Laurence Housman's play, Queen Victoria, or seen the film. Other near relatives were Ladies in Waiting to the Queen. In 1845 my grandfather, Frederick Anson, became Canon of St. George's, Windsor, and for the next forty years divided his time between his country parish in Derby-shire and his duties in the royal chapel.

After his death an alabaster font was erected to his memory in the south-west corner of the nave of St. George's Chapel, with an inscription at its base. On October 7th, 1889, a six-week-old baby was carried to this same font and baptised by Canon Capel Cure. He was given the names of Frederick Charles, and duly recorded in the baptismal register with those of other babies of more illustrious lineage. The baby was myself, and this was his first appearance in a place of worship. I doubt if the godparents, or their proxies, foresaw what a roving and restless career lay ahead of the tiny bundle in their arms. They had undertaken a greater spiritual responsibility than they realised.

This book is largely made up of ecclesiastical memories, inter-spersed with recollections of people of all classes of life who have influenced or helped to shape my career. Bright blue hassocks, adorned with yellow fleur-de-lis, happen to be almost the first mental picture associated with a church after a more remote and hazy recollection of a Harvest Festival coinciding with the baptism of my elder sister, Edith, in what is now the Anglican cathedral at Ports-mouth: so that the font was decorated with a profusion of pumpkins, apples and vegetable marrows! It surprises me to discover, on checking the date, that I must have been nearly ten years old when the blue hassocks fixed their shape and colour in my brain. It is a proof how little interest I took in religion as a child. I doubt if the blue hassocks would have been in that pew if my father, always a devout Anglican of the old-fashioned type, had not returned from a long commission with the Australian squadron and started to take me to church on Sunday mornings. My mother had shown me how to find the places in the *Book of Common Prayer*. She explained, tactfully, that he might be surprised if I could not discover the whereabouts of the psalms, litany, collects, epistles, gospels and hymns in a hitherto seldom opened leather-bound volume. So my first lesson in Liturgy was given me by a mother who had never taken me to church, for it was either a nurse or a governess who had been in charge of me on the rare occasions when I assisted at an afternoon Children's Service. Whether those blue hassocks were already in our pew in the north aisle of St. John's, High Park, Ryde, on that first Sunday when I attended Mattins with my father, I cannot be sure. Anyhow, they appeared soon after. The only other feature

I recall about this little Gothic-revival church is a stained glass
window, depicting Our Lord walking on the waters. I always
wondered how that tiny ship, overladen with apostles, could withstand the buffeting of the choppy sea.

Maybe it was due to that same fascination in colour and pageantry
that caused me to imprint on my memory the details of the Diamond
Jubilee procession of Queen Victoria that accounts for the precocious,
and, in my father's opinion, highly dangerous interest in everything
to do with the theatre at about the age of nine. It began soon after
we went to live in the Isle of Wight. But he was sensible enough not to
forbid me buying *The Stage* every week, and sometimes *The Era,*
when I could afford an extra sixpence. I carefully preserved all the
back numbers of these two theatrical journals, and spent hours
browsing over them. I could have told you the name of every provincial theatre and music-hall from Aberdeen to Dover; what company
was playing in them each week, and the names of all the leading
actors and actresses. The first show to which I was taken by my
parents was *The Geisha,* soon after it went on tour in 1897 at the
old Theatre Royal, Portsmouth. After that I was taken to Christmas
pantomimes and to other musical comedies, such as *The Greek Slave*
and *Floradora.* I started building model theatres (kept in my bedroom), which, so far as possible, were reproductions more or less to
scale, of buildings I had visited. To assist my memory of the
decorations of the interiors, I would take a sketch-book, and make
notes during the intervals—with sketches of the scenery and costumes
during the performance. These model theatres were made of toy
bricks, cardboard and paper, the roofs being arranged to take off so
that I could get my hands inside. They were complete with façade,
auditorium, bars, and even dressing-rooms for the paper actors. The
lighting was always a difficulty, and more than once they caught
fire. My passion for correct detail even led me so far as to paint
sets of posters. These were pasted outside week by week and were
copies from those which I saw on the hoardings. I used to rebuild
these models from time to time, but, for a long period, I was satisfied
with the Theatre Royal and Princes' Theatre at Portsmouth, or the
Theatre Royal, Ryde. But having discovered in a French almanack
some plans of Parisian theatres, I built models of the *Folies Bergères,*
the *Comédie Française,* and *Palais Royal.* I even subscribed to the
Matin for a while in order to know what was actually being played
at them! One year I constructed models of Covent Garden Opera

House and the Wagner Theatre at Bayreuth, complete with all the boxes. These were, perhaps, the most ambitious efforts.

Then I began to collect theatre programmes. Friends and relatives (especially my Hardcastle cousins) used to save them up for me. Before long I had gathered together an interesting and what would now be a valuable collection; but I destroyed them all later on.

My love of music was diverted into theatrical channels. I bought the piano scores of musical comedies and comic operas, playing them right through from beginning to end at a sitting, reading the *libretto* at the same time so as to create the illusion that I was taking part in an actual performance. I cannot recall all the operas of which I had the music by the end of 1902, but I remember *The Belle of New York, The Shop Girl, The Runaway Girl, La Poupée, Floradora, The Silver Slipper, The Prince of Pilsen, The Belle of Cairo, The Geisha, The Greek Slave,* and most of Gilbert and Sullivan. My favourite composer of this style of music was Leslie Stuart. The only objection to his work was its difficulty, due to the curious rhythm, changes of key, and intricate harmonies.

I had a rival interest in the sea, which the counter-attractions of the stage never altogether supplanted. My bedroom was also littered up with large fleets of paper battleships and cruisers of my own handi-work. The walls were decorated with lists of weekly sailings of the pleasure steamers from Ryde and Southsea, in addition to the theatrical bills which I would beg from the box-offices.

* . * *

I have devoted rather much space to this juvenile interest in the theatre because it was the first definite proof of a life-long instinct to regard " all the world a stage, and all the men and women merely players ", with exits and entrances; to see men in their time playing many parts; their " acts being seven ages ". A tremendous interest in life, yet a critical detachment from it. That toy theatre build-ing was my initiation into architecture! The programme-collecting was the birth of a habit of storing up data which could be diverted into other channels in after years, but the motive behind it was pre-cisely the same. At the age of fifty-five I have not outgrown my love of opera. Even those faded musical comedies of half a century ago can still thrill me if I hear them on the radio! Following the vocal score, I have sat through *Tosca* (on the air) over forty times! Before the war I had done Wagner's *Ring* at least half a dozen times from Berlin or Vienna when sitting by my own fireside. So the child

was the father of the man as regards the stage! I still like playing
with toy theatres!

*   *   *

I became a day boarder at Little Appley, a small preparatory school
about ten minutes' walk from our house, soon after we went to live
at Ryde in the summer of 1898, and here I remained until 1902. I
was a tiresome and difficult pupil. I remember many rows with my
masters, and conduct reports, which nearly every term were headed,
"Frivolous and volatile." I was good at music, drawing, history
and geography, but mathematics were, and always have been, beyond
my intelligence. The mention of geography reminds me that even
then I had a passion for maps and guide-books. I asked for no better
birthday present than a new guide-book. How I used to pore over
them, visiting in imagination all the places they described! In 1900
I bought a Ward Lock's *Guide to Paris* (it was the year of the
exhibition) and soon mastered the topography of that city. About
the same time my uncle, Frank Hardcastle (who married my mother's
elder sister, Ida Ross), used to encourage this hobby of mine. One
Xmas he presented me with an Appleton's *Guide to the United
States.* So before long I became just as much at home in the cities
of New York, Chicago, Boston, and New Orleans. When I landed
in San Francisco twenty-six years after, I was able to find my bear-
ings without having to ask my way, and the same applies to almost
every other great city in the world.

Bradshaw's *Railway Guide* and Cook's *Continental Handbook*
were other favourite reading, for I loved to plan out complicated
journeys across Europe or more remote continents. All these interests
are very much alive, even to-day!

With the exception of football, which I thoroughly enjoyed, both
indoor and outdoor games bored me; they seemed such a waste of
time when there were far more interesting things to be done. Cricket,
in particular, I detested as a futile occupation for a summer afternoon.
Butterfly and moth collecting was a hobby for some years, for I
enjoyed the long walks and, later on, the cycle rides over the Isle of
Wight in search of rare specimens.

When it came to examinations I was a failure, except in music and
drawing. I lacked the patience to attend to any subject which did not
interest me, and so my school career was neither brilliant nor
creditable.

I do not remember making any special friends during my four

FORT AUGUSTUS ABBEY.

years at Little Appley. I left the school with no great regret, despite
the fact that both the headmasters had always shown a greater interest
and kindness than their undoubtedly exasperating pupil deserved.

The incidents of the Boer War are still clear in my mind. It was
great fun to follow up the movements of the troops by means of
flags pinned on the map in my father's smoking-room. Every morning one or two changes had to be made. I saw the famous C.I.V.s
in their khaki uniforms and rakish hats, going off to Africa from
Southampton, and I learnt to play " Goodbye, Dolly, I must leave
you," and Leslie Stuart's " Soldiers of the Queen."

At school it was the correct thing to decorate oneself with
innumerable pins, each bearing the portrait of a British
general. Needless to say, " B.P." was the favourite. Mafeking
Day was the occasion of a whole holiday at school, and
we were marched around Ryde. Our jackets bristled with generals
on pins, and we, each of us, waved one or more Union Jacks.
I was not specially patriotic, I felt that perhaps the Boers might be
in the right after all, but wisely kept such heterodox views to myself.
In this case it was quite amusing to behave like my companions, but
more often than not my defiance of school-boy conventions roused
their antagonism.

I had had a last glimpse of Queen Victoria, whom I had
often seen in earlier years. I was driving back to Ryde from
Osborne, where my father and mother had gone to leave cards,
since his position as captain of a royal yacht demanded these attentions
from time to time. We were not far from Whippingham Church
when suddenly our coachman pulled into the side of the lane to
allow another carriage to pass. We looked out and saw that the
occupant was the Old Lady herself. It was a cold raw January day,
yet the carriage was open. A few days later we read in the paper
that she had caught a chill. Within a week, if I remember rightly,
she was dead. How Noel Coward's *Cavalcade,* at Drury Lane,
brought back those far-off times!

My mother had now decided that Eton was the only possible public
school for me, since she wished me to enter the diplomatic service.
At that time, Mr. Arnold, a nephew of Dr. Arnold of Rugby, was
headmaster, and Wixenford had few rivals among the preparatory
schools in England. The fees were as exclusive as the clientele, most
of whom could be found in Debrett and Burke, or, at least,
in *Who's Who.* If some had not already secured that social dis-

tinction, it was merely a matter of time. The school buildings had been specially designed for their purpose. They were surrounded by large gardens and playing fields. A wooded park provided ample space for a private golf course. There was every convenience and comfort, but no superfluous luxury. There were about sixty boys and a large staff of masters. In these days I do not suppose that the fees of that time at Wixenford would be regarded as anything out of the way, but, in 1902, it was one of the most expensive preparatory schools in England. But the parents got their money's worth. I spent two years there, and my education must have been a serious matter for my father, who, at that time, had not much more than his captain's pay. However, my mother, having made up her mind that Wixenford was the only school in England that was good enough for me, insisted that I went there no matter what it cost. I enjoyed my two years, and was much happier than at Little Appley. On the day I arrived at Wixenford with my mother, there was a boy of about my own age sitting in the drawing-room as we were ushered in. He had fair hair, and I recollect that he was wearing a pale blue tie that matched the colour of his eyes. The headmaster's wife introduced him to us as Alfred Duff Cooper. No doubt the present British Ambassador in Paris, and the husband of Lady Diana Manners, has long since forgotten this meeting and the violent friendship that sprang up between us soon afterwards. Duff Cooper and I shared a common love for the stage, and he seemed to be on intimate terms with nearly all the leading actors and actresses of the day. I thought it wonderful to have a friend who had talked to George Alexander and Herbert Beerbohm Tree, Henry Ainley, and many lesser stars in the theatrical firmament. When he went home for the next holidays he sent me his complete collection of theatre programmes. No present could have given me greater satisfaction. We kept up a regular correspondence until he went on to Eton. After that we drifted apart. But when I read his books I can still picture the boy I knew; the same rather precocious brilliance and over-developed cynicism: that then found an outlet in sarcastic comments on masters and pupils. I detected these qualities in Duff Cooper's *Life of Talleyrand;* the charm that accounted for our juvenile friendship in his utterly different biography of David. When I listen to his voice on the radio I form a mental picture of that boy who shook hands with me in an Edwardian drawing-room on a September afternoon over forty years ago.

Among my school mates were many others who have become
famous in after life. There was Piers Legh, who rose to be equerry
to the King, and whose Cheshire home, Lyme Park, was adjacent
to Poynton Towers where dwelt my cousin, Lord Vernon. Some of
the boys were representatives of the American millionaire families of
Morgan and Astor, while Greek finance and Irish brewing figured
in the Rodocanachies and Guinnesses. There were several Sturts
and Butlers—the latter the sons of the fourth Marquess of Ormonde,
at that date Lord Arthur Butler. I shared a small dormitory with his
two sons during my first term. Another congenial companion was
the chubby-faced Roger Wodehouse, who, even at fourteen, had begun
to take an interest in Anglo-Catholicism, to find expression in after
life as in transforming St. Paul's, Oxford, into such a perfect imitation of a Roman church that it could deceive visitors into believing
that it was the genuine article! I have a vivid recollection of Roger
rushing up to me in the playground and informing me that Pope
Leo XIII was dead, a bit of news which failed to arouse any interest
at that date. As captain of another dormitory I had to keep in order
the present Lord Lisburne, and the next desk to mine in the chief
classroom was occupied by a somewhat argumentative and quarrel-
some boy named Archie Sinclair, whose future career as a politician
had already begun to be obvious. But neither of us could have
prophesied that forty years later he would rise to be Secretary of State
for Air in the National War Cabinet, or that Duff Cooper would be
British Ambassador in Paris.

The religious teaching at Wixenford was vague and colourless. We
had to memorise the Catechism in the *Book of Common Prayer,* and
were examined in it on Sunday mornings before church. The more
musical of us were armed with bags, containing a Bible, Prayer Book,
Cathedral Psalter, Hymns, Ancient and Modern, and the particular
musical setting for the *Te Deum* and *Benedictus* that had been chosen
by the organist. As a keen musician I quite enjoyed those Sunday
morning services, although I much doubt if they had the least religious
influence.

Yet I owe a great debt to Wixenford for the good training it gave
me in music and drawing. We had a fully-equipped school of art
in which I spent much time. As one of the " star turns " at school
concerts I was featured on one programme with two of the more
difficult of Bach's Preludes and Fugues ("the 48") and a Chopin
Nocturne and Polonaise, so I must have been somewhat above the

average in music for a boy of fourteen. There was serious talk of my taking up music professionally. However, it came to nothing. At this school my dislike for cricket was not lessened by my being made to score for the first eleven one summer term when, owing to a weak heart, all violent exercise was forbidden. To make matters worse, when the autumn term came round, instead of playing football I was forced to spend my afternoons walking round our private golf links with the headmaster. He did his best to rouse my enthusiasm for the Royal and Ancient Game. But the only result was to make me hate golf ever since. Dancing was a social accomplishment made much of at Wixenford. We were taught by a mistress who came down from London every week. It was the moment when the two-step had begun to invade ballrooms, and was threatening to oust even the well-entrenched Valse, Lancers and Barn-dance. This new transatlantic measure was looked upon with a certain disapproval, and regarded by nice people as "rather vulgar" especially when the dancers imitated the more unrestrained movements of the Cake Walk. Accordingly there was great excitement when one afternoon our mistress announced that she was going to teach us a new dance called the Two-Step, which we had already heard of or seen performed. I can still remember the spectacle of our tall, good-looking, grey-haired headmaster giving an exhibition of this new dance with Madame (we boys often debated whether her golden hair was a wig) as his partner, prancing and parading around the gymnasium to the strains of the rag-time rhythm of Down South, while old Mrs. Arnold, plump and smiling, looking on with benevolent approbation, beat time with her feet.

School parties at the end of term, cricket matches and sports, were occasions for a great gathering of parents, some of whom came down from town in their cars, for the motor had just begun to supersede the train as a means of locomotion for those who could afford it. They were not many, and the motor-car was still regarded as something of a novelty. Among that fashionably-dressed crowd of mothers and sisters I recall the Lady Alington, Lady Newton, the Dowager Countess of Lisburne, and, above all, the Countess of Plymouth, whose picturesque frocks, suggestive of the wan women in Burne Jones' paintings, were in startling contrast to the other ladies in their thick veils and dust cloaks, donned to protect the ravishing Edwardian fashions beneath—huge flower or feather-decked hats, long rustling skirts that swept the ground, and lace adorned parasols.

Like butterflies emerging from chrysalises, these great ladies hid their glories until they appeared in the sunshine of the cricket field. And none of the fathers would have thought it decent to arrive unless wearing a frock coat and silk, or perhaps grey felt topper.

During the spring term of 1904 I had a bad attack of influenza, followed by rheumatic fever. The doctors said there would be a grave danger to my health if I went on to Eton, owing to its damp climate. The merits of Harrow on its hill were discussed—it would be more bracing, perhaps—but nothing came of these discussions, except that I never went to any public school, and left Wixenford shortly before my fifteenth birthday.

CHAPTER II

ASPECTS OF ANGLICANISM

I must have been about sixteen years of age when my interests were suddenly diverted from maritime and theatrical affairs to the problems of religion. Because I was essentially an artist by temperament, my approach to these problems was mainly on visual lines rather than subjective. What interested me most was the external presentation of religion, that is, *worship* rather than a system of morals. Again, even in my youth, I was intensely critical and would never accept facts unless I had proved their authorities by brutal process of analysis and dissection. I would never accept statements on their face-value, for I was too much of a sceptic! I might be attracted by externals, but my love of logic, and impatience with what seemed to be an incorrect use of argument, soon led me to doubt the credentials of that system of religion in which I had been brought up.

A friend who read the original draft of this chapter remarked that he felt sure that the mass of apparently irrelevant details would merely bore the average person! He advised me to make drastic cuts and to condense the material. On further reflection I maintained my conviction that the general effect of the picture depended on the building up of detail rather than on a vague impression. Nobody has quite the same method of finding his or her way into the Catholic Church, which was the eventual goal I was seeking.

The following pages record experiences between the ages of sixteen and twenty-one that hastened this spiritual journey to Rome.

It was during the nine months I spent at Eyke Rectory, Suffolk, as one of four or five pupils boarded at the rectory, that my interest in religious matters was aroused for the first time. My tutor, Mr. Darling, later on Archdeacon of Suffolk, was an old-fashioned Evangelical in doctrine as well as being a typical " sporting parson ". He was more keen on shooting and gardening than on theology. It was beneath his roof that my curiosity about the Catholic Church was first aroused, due in no sort of way to any encouragement on the part of my tutor or his wife, who belonged to an out-and-out North of Ireland Orange family. She would often talk of the ignorance, poverty and superstitions of the " poor Irish Roman Catholics ", and of the domineering influence of the priests, in and around her old home at Omagh. I have sometimes wondered if it had not been for Mrs. Darling's denunciations of Popery if I should ever have become a Papist—who can tell? Anyhow, it was on the shelves of her husband's library that I discovered the *Secret History of the Oxford Movement, Priests and People in Ireland,* also several revelations of escaped monks and nuns. The effect of this rather unsavoury literature was just the opposite to that intended by the authors. The religious system they attacked with such violence seemed to possess something lacking in the Church of England, and which attracted me. It might be decadent and superstitious, but I felt it would appeal to me much more than the type of services which I was obliged to attend in that neglected, dreary, musty-smelling Suffolk church, erected for Catholic worship more than four centuries ago.

Early in 1906 I went to stay with my grandmother at Windsor, to be prepared for Confirmation by the Rev. J. C. Ellison, then vicar of the parish church. His instructions and friendly talks did not help me very much, and I fear he must have found me rather a problem. Neither was I inspired by the very moderate but hearty services in his church, which I used to attend with my relatives on Sunday morning. I had already developed a distaste for Anglican chants, and hymn-singing made little appeal to me.

A middle-aged convert who looks back on the Church of England, after more than a quarter of a century as a Catholic, is able to view the religious world in which he was brought up with a certain detachment. Any bitterness which he may have felt at the time of his reception into the Catholic Church has long since vanished. Old wounds have been healed, and he realises that there were many features of Anglicanism which, in themselves, ought not to be judged with the same harshness as he felt they merited as a raw neophyte, with the water of conditional baptism still wet on his brow. Yet, at the same time, it is almost inevitable that with the clearer vision of middle-age, a convert cannot help being more alive to the inconsistencies of Anglicanism as a religious system, due, as he now sees, to that comprehensiveness which is inherent in the very nature of the Church of England, and which—to others—is an almost infallible mark of its true catholicity.

It was my lot to be brought into contact with almost every aspect of Anglicanism during boyhood and youth—from extreme Evangelicanism to extreme Anglo-Catholicism. A puzzling diversity of belief and practice whose only link was to be in communion with the See of Canterbury and established by law. These recollections of the Church of England cover a period between 1895 and 1913—the date of my submission to the Holy See.

It is not easy for the wrongly called "born Catholic" to realise how the infinitely subtle shades of Anglicanism merge into each other with no clearly defined outlines. True, there are the three main divisions —High, Broad, and Low—but there is an infinity of sub-divisions, and the temperature of each may rise and fall for no obvious reason. One is never sure if a particular church which was "Low" yesterday may not be High to-morrow, although such violent changes are safeguarded to a large extent by the system of patronage, especially in the case of parishes which have been acquired by Evangelical or Anglo-Catholic Trusts, which ensures a definite continuity of faith and practice.

It was among the more moderate Anglicans that I was brought up. My father's family was definitely clerical, my grandfather having been a Canon of St. George's Chapel, Windsor, and his father Dean of Chester—both of them having been Rectors of the parish of Sudbury, Derbyshire. Then there was that great-great-uncle, Edward Vernon, Archbishop Vernon-Harcourt of York, who must have been a prelate of almost Renaissance dignity, who drove to his cathedral with six horses to his carriage. He was a great sportsman, too; kept a pack of hounds, and never failed to attend the York races in state. Three of my father's brothers—Alfred, Harold and Hugh— were Anglican parsons; the only now living survivor, Canon Harold

Anson, is Master of the Temple. There were numerous cousins who were clergymen or parsons' wives. One of these Anson cousins became a missionary bishop in Canada. This is enough to prove that I can claim to have more than a superficial knowledge of the Church of England, even if it came to an end at the age of twenty-one. On the other hand, to counteract the clerical influence of the Ansons, most of my mother's family appeared to take very little interest in religion, she herself never attending any place of worship so far as I can remember. She called herself a Presbyterian, but this, I am inclined to think, amounted to little more than one of her many manifestations of Scottish Nationalism! Her attachment to the religious opinions of John Calvin was purely negative.

How rare is it to-day to find oneself in a household—Catholic or Protestant—where Family Prayers are a regular part of the life. Forty years ago nearly all my father's relatives held family worship, either before or after breakfast. To have absented oneself from these corporate prayers would have been regarded as most peculiar, except if one happened to be ill. At Carfax, Windsor—that typical mid-Victorian square box-like house with the Doric porch over the front door and a conservatory built on to one side, my grandmother's home for the last twenty years of her long life, where I stayed so often during my boyhood and youth, family prayers took place after breakfast. My grandmother got up from the table before the rest of us and went off to her study to look up the portion of the Bible she would read that morning, select the hymn and prayers. When she was ready she would ring a bell, to warn the maids and the members of the family who were still sitting at the breakfast table (and what sumptuous meals they were!) that they must join her. Along one side of the study there was a row of chairs for the six or more domestics. They entered in procession, according to rank, the elderly cook leading the way, the kitchen-maid following last. Vested in clean aprons over their well-starched print dresses, they presented an almost hierarchic appearance. Members of the family or visitors occupied chairs; the dog took possession of the hearth-rug. My grandmother sat on the sofa behind her writing table, on which were arranged a Bible, prayer book, and *Hymns, Ancient and Modern*. Her eldest daughter—my Aunt Laura—took up her position at a small portable harmonium. Then everybody knelt down, leaning over their chairs—the back view of that row of maids —of all shapes and sizes, presented an interesting contrast of con-

tours. This homely little service, consisting of prayers, reading from
the Old or New Testaments, and a hymn, occupied from ten minutes
to a quarter of an hour. Sometimes, just when everybody would be
on their knees, their faces buried in the seats of the chairs, a military
band would strike up—Guardsmen from the neighbouring barracks
out for their morning exercise and on their way to the Great Park.
The dog would jump up from the hearth-rug, start barking furiously,
and have to be let out into the garden by the kitchen-maid, whose
chair was always close to the door. Should my aunt happen to be
away from home, it was my duty to accompany the hymn. I used
to dread this ordeal, for the harmonium had a tiresome way of slipping across the carpet as one pedalled with one's feet. I never
managed to control the erratic movements of that nasty little
instrument.

In some houses family prayers took place in the dining-room
before breakfast, where the smell of kidneys and bacon or fried fish
provided a sort of domestic incense and gave atmosphere to the worship. But no matter where and how these prayers were conducted,
they were utterly spontaneous and genuine, and it is a pity that this
external manifestation of Christian ideals has now vanished from the
average household. Night prayers in common were less frequent,
at least in the houses of my Anson relatives, though I am told they
had formerly been customary—I do not know why they had been
abandoned before my time.

On more than one occasion my grandmother and Aunt Laura
mentioned in the course of conversation—and with a certain disapproval—the High Church goings-on at St. Stephen's, Clewer,
situated in a suburb of Windsor. One Sunday evening I summoned
up my courage and slipped out of the house after tea, having decided
that I would like to sample this particular church. A raw fog hung
over the valley of the Thames, and rain dripped from the trees along
Osborne Road. I hurried past St. Edward's Catholic Church—at
that date I had never dared to enter its doors—and over the roofs
of the houses the tall flèche of St. Stephen's beckoned me. Once I
had got inside this rather drab-looking yellow brick Gothic Revival
building, I was in another world. Six candles flickered on the
gradines of the high altar, backed by a lofty reredos; red lamps were
suspended above the sanctuary, and in the semi-darkness of the Lady
chapel I noticed a blue light twinkling. There was a curious, not
unpleasant, bitter-sweet smell, which I realised must be incense.

Black-robed nuns hovered about and piloted school girls into the front benches. Pious women curtsied to the altar before going to their seats, making elaborate signs of the cross before they began to pray. Men and boys bowed profoundly, and sat apart from the female members of the congregation—I was thankful I had slipped into a bench on the left and not on the right! I gazed at the great rood screen with its crucifix and figures of Our Lady and St. John, glancing sideways at the Stations of the Cross on the walls of the aisles. A lady organist began to play a voluntary; the vestry door opened, and in walked the clergy and choir. To my astonishment the former were wearing odd-shaped black caps with little tufts on top. Evensong proceeded on normal lines, but when the moment came for the psalms, I was surprised to find that the congregation did not stand up, but remained seated. Instead of the bright, cheerful Anglican psalm tunes with which I was familiar, the organist gave out a few notes of an unharmonised minor theme—I now know that it must have been the *Tonus Peregrinus*. A cantor intoned the first line, and the choir took up the rest of the verse. Such was my initiation into Plain Chant. I do not remember much else about my first Evensong at Clewer, St. Stephen, except that it ended with a procession—crucifix, lights, cope, banners, and clouds of incense, and that the hymn sung was *Shall We Not Love Thee, Mother Dear,* which would indicate that my visit must have been on the feast of the Annunciation or during the Octave, for it is not likely that there would have been a procession in honour of Our Lady on any other Sunday in Lent. My Anglican confirmation having been performed by the Bishop of Oxford, Dr. Francis Paget, in the parish church at Windsor, a few days before Palm Sunday, I made my First Communion in the Church of England on Easter Sunday, 1906, in the not very inspiring surroundings of St. Mark's, Windsor. That same morning I attended my first Choral Eucharist at St. Stephen's, which I found was far more satisfying than Solemn Evensong, what with the celebrant wearing a chasuble, the deacon and sub-deacon vested in dalmatics; even more incense, acolytes in scarlet cassocks and lace-trimmed cottas, and bells rung at the consecration. Whenever I hear *O filii et filiæ, Alleluia,* I always think of that Easter morning procession.

* * *

The churches patronised by most of my father's family were of the moderate type—neither High nor Low—where the usual Sunday

c

morning service consisted of Choral Mattins, followed by the Litany
or Ante-Communion service. Some of my more devout relatives
usually attended Early Service every Sunday morning, i.e., went
to Communion, but I cannot recall that any of the family or the
servants felt it necessary to fast before Communion, and the regular
morning cups of tea and thin bread and butter were brought up to
the bedrooms on Sunday as well as on weekdays. I doubt if any of
my relatives, except two of my parson-uncles, and maybe one aunt,
had ever been to Confession, for I vividly recall the alarm and distress when it was discovered that I had started this practice. My
grandmother and Aunt Laura spoke of it with bated breath as if
it were some secret vice which must be nipped in the bud.

When staying with my maternal grandmother I had to attend
churches of a definitely Evangelical type—or what Anglo-Catholics
would describe as Protestant. In these, anything that savoured
of either Rome or Ritualism was regarded with horror, although all
of them had a peculiar and very remarkable ritual of their own.
I can still recall the interior of St. Simon's, Southsea, or St. John's,
Sandown, Isle of Wight—both of them bright and spacious buildings
in a mild form of Early-English-Gothic-Revival. I remember the
texts that adorned the chancel arches and aisle walls, and which also
served as decorative features at the back of the Holy Tables—for the
word altar was never used by the Low Church party. In these,
and in other churches of the same category, the table itself was
invariably vested in a stiff frontal of crimson cloth, usually with lilies
or passion flowers embroidered in the centre, or perhaps an I.H.S.
There was neither cross nor candlesticks, and unless a particular
church had advanced so far as flower vases, the only ornament displayed was a brass alms dish. Whether flower vases were permissible
or not always remained a matter of controversy. Like one Scots
Presbyterian minister of my acquaintance, most Evangelical parsons
and lay-folk regarded them as maybe the first step on the road to
Rome. The white linen cloth was generally removed from the Holy
Table except on such Sundays as there happened to be a celebration
of the Lord's Supper, which in the more rigid strongholds of
Evangelical Anglicanism took place in the evening, though in some
churches there would be a Communion service once a month after
Morning Prayer. Great importance was attached to the clergyman
taking what was known as the North End when administering
the Lord's Supper, for the Eastward Position was regarded as a

superstitious relic of medieval Mass, and therefore forbidden by the rubrics of the Book of Common Prayer.

I cannot remember taking part in any Communion service in this type of church which was not conducted with real reverence and devotion, even if the ceremonial was reduced to a minimum. Indeed, the very infrequency of Communion tended to make it a solemn occasion for most of the congregation. They regarded it with much the same kind of awe as do the strongly conservative Catholics even to-day in the north-east of Scotland, where Jansenist traditions are not quite extinct. On great festivals, such as Christmas and Easter, when there were large crowds, the words of administration were often said over a rail-full of communicants instead of to each individual. Ordinary white bread was used, sometimes being cut up into small pieces before the service for the sake of convenience.

Morning and Evening Prayer, otherwise Mattins and Evensong, were hearty services with rousing hymn singing, something which many of our own congregations might well learn to copy! The most popular hymn book in Evangelical churches was the *Hymnal Companion,* for *Hymns, Ancient and Modern,* and much more the recently published *English Hymnal,* contained far too many references to Our Lady and the saints, and some of the hymns associated with the Holy Eucharist were looked upon as definitely superstitious in doctrine. Acts of reverence, such as bowing at the name of Jesus, making the sign of the cross, or turning to the east during the recitation of the Creeds, were frowned upon by the Evangelicals. It needed some courage to indulge in these outward marks of ritualism if one happened to be worshipping in an Evangelical church.

I have a vivid recollection of being taken to a stirring parochial Mission, on the lines made popular about forty years ago by the then famous American evangelists, Torry and Alexander. A special hymn book was distributed, and the tunes were of a lively and rather secular nature. The sermons, so I seem to recall, were tinged with strongly Calvinist doctrine. Although the conductors of such Mission services would have been horrified at the idea of anybody going to confession, yet they encouraged those who were conscious of sin to have a heart to heart talk in the vestry, where they could unburden their souls in private.

The *Record* and the *English Churchman*—then as now—were the two most popular weekly journals read by Evangelical Anglicans.

The former was a well-edited and serious paper, typical of the best traditions of the Low Church party, whereas the latter specialised in lurid revelations of ritualistic illegalities and fulminations on the errors of Rome. I must confess that I used to enjoy reading the *English Churchman,* just because it contained such vivid and detailed descriptions of services in Anglo-Catholic churches—not always very accurate, it must be admitted. It was really quite useful, for it informed me of the existence of many a church which proved to be worth a visit, if only for the sake of its ritualistic fittings and decorations.

I may be wrong, but I think I am right in stating that as late as 1910 only three Anglican cathedrals had started a daily celebration of the Eucharist, and a daily Communion was far from common in parish churches of the moderate type. In none of them were Eucharist vestments worn, so far as I am aware, but on certain festivals the celebrant in a few cathedrals wore a cope, as was ordered in the First Prayer Book of Edward VI. The usual *horarium* of Sunday services in cathedrals and moderate parish churches was an early celebration at 8 a.m., followed by Choral Mattins, Litany and sermon at 10.30 or 11 o'clock. When a celebration of the Communion followed Mattins, the Litany gave place to the ante-Communion service, otherwise the Book of Common Prayer version of the Mass of the Catechumens. This would be rendered chorally, but as a rule the choir and the majority of the congregation dispersed after the sermon, and the Liturgy of the Faithful was continued without music.

Even forty years ago there were not many cathedrals or parish churches where what is known as Cathedral Worship was in vogue without two candles on the altar, but in some of them the candles were only lit at the early celebrations of the Communion, lest the more Protestant-minded of the congregation should take offence. In other places they were never lit, and were purely unfunctional ornaments. In most cathedrals there was no recognised position for the celebrant. It was left to individual choice, and depended on the theological point of view of the dean, canons and minor-canons, among whom there might be a sprinkling of Evangelicals, Broad or moderate High-Churchmen, or very rarely a parson who had been promoted from one of the less extreme Anglo-Catholic parishes. Such clergymen would be obliged to tone down their sermons and modify their accustomed method of celebrating the Eucharist, and to conform, more or less, to the level of the rite of the particular cathedral of which they now formed one of the Chapter.

There were already in the days of my youth a few quite "moderate" churches, both in towns and in the country, where white linen vestments had been daringly introduced in order to prepare the way for coloured vestments later on. But these linen vestments were usually displayed only at early celebrations. They might have offended the less Catholic-minded worshippers who stopped behind for the mid-day Communion when the majority of the Congregation at Mattins had departed homewards. I remember noticing advertisements in *The Church Times* in which "linen vestments, mixed chalice and lights" were held out as a bait for applicants for curacies. But sometimes there would be the proviso: "No Extremes", lest some too-advanced Anglo-Catholic parson should be moved to apply.

Processions, either before Mattins or after Evensong, had long since become popular in quite "moderate" churches, and were a special feature on holidays. But they somehow missed fire, so to say, for a procession without lights and incense makes a poor show, which a gay display of banners and even a celebrant in cope cannot make up for. My first introduction to a cope took place at Ufford in Suffolk. My curiosity had been roused as to the strange practices at the neighbouring parish to Eyke, by the rector's wife remarking that she'd "heard that the man at Ufford wore a cope"—he might have been living in a state of mortal sin, to judge by the tone of her voice. So the following Sunday I slipped off to the Ufford, and was rewarded by the sight of the mysterious garment, so full of sinister significance.

Mattins and Evensong, together with the Litany on Wednesdays and Fridays, were said publicly in a large number of churches where the ceremonial was quite moderate in character. As I look back I am filled with admiration at the loyal way in which so many clergymen used to fulfil what they believed to be an obligation imposed on them by their ordination's promises. I can remember countless churches in the depths of rural England where the rector or vicar often said his daily offices with no congregation, especially on cold winter mornings. Very frequently these devoted country parsons would have to toll the bell themselves. More likely than not, his Catholic confrère would have fulfilled the obligation of getting through *his* office in a comfortable armchair before the fire!

This custom of reciting the offices publicly was part of the Tractarian tradition, handed down by the leaders of the Oxford Movement—a relic of pre-Reformation times when it was usual for priests to perform the Work of God (to use St. Benedict's expression) in church. Only when seriously ill did such parsons feel able to dispense themselves from the obligation of holding daily public worship, even if nobody assisted at it. Week-day celebrations of the Communion service were less frequent, apart from red letter saints' days, for which there are special collects, epistles and gospels in the Book of Common Prayer.

How much I have often missed not being able to join in the public recitation of the Breviary offices in church since I became a Catholic! After all, what are Mattins and Evensong but a most ingenious attempt to cut down and fit together the essential parts of the Breviary into two vernacular offices of such brevity that they can be got through in about twenty minutes? "Vernacular Devotions" at present in use among English speaking Catholics are, to myself and possibly to other converts, a poor substitute for the *Te Deum,* the *Benedictus,* the *Magnificat,* and *Nunc Dimittis!*

From 1905 to 1908 my home was at Bournemouth, where I came in touch with another type of Anglicanism which is difficult to explain to anybody not familiar with the Church of England. It was elusive, slowly rising in temperature as those who adhered to it became more " Catholic " in their ideas. Many clergymen in this rapidly-growing holiday resort believed in the motto *" festina lente ",* and were gradually training their congregations to appreciate their full Catholic heritage, whetting their appetites with attractive morsels of doctrine and ceremonial until they were able to digest a little more. So one would find congregations, for instance at St. Peter's, St. Ambrose's, St. Swithin's or St. Aldhelm's, climbing higher and higher by easy stages, so gently that the gradient on the spiritual road was not sufficient to involve a change of gear, or even to be conscious of any sensation of devotional vertigo with the rise of altitude!

Similar conditions prevailed at other seaside resorts on the south coast, where it was common to find an eclectic and constantly changing body of worshippers. The clergy had to exercise tact and prudence, for it would have been unwise to offend visitors with strange doctrines or ceremonial. They took care to provide services to satisfy the mentality of almost every grade of churchmanship, except the

BUCKFAST ABBEY.

two extreme groups of Anglicans. The result was that they attracted big congregations by being more or less all things to all men.

So there would be early celebrations where vestments—white linen or coloured silk—were worn. There was usually a Sung Eucharist at 9.30 or 10, which ended in good time for the more Catholic-minded congregation to disperse before the church filled up again for Choral Mattins at 11 or 11.30. I seem to remember at least one church in Bournemouth where Mattins was followed at least once a month by what the notice board described as a Plain Celebration, some- times stating that it was for invalids. I presume that the emphasis on invalids was made lest those who were not in a weak state of health should take advantage of this service and have breakfast before Communion? The plain epithet was due to the fact that the celebrant wore a surplice and stole instead of Eucharist vestments, lest the more conservative invalids—and others—should be upset by any visible sign of unfamiliar ritualism. For a similar reason, incense was seldom used at the Sung Eucharist, for the fumes hanging about the church would have doubtless driven away many a retired admiral, general, or colonel from Mattins, and such elderly gentlemen were often influential members of the congregation, and even church- wardens. Yet, at St. Peter's, Parkstone, incense was used in a " non- ceremonial manner " on the greater festivals; also, I think, in St. Clement's, Boscombe—neither of these two churches having then reached such heights of Catholic ceremonial as is now general. The scent of the elaborate floral decorations on the altars and elsewhere in the building mingled with that of stale incense, so that the latter could not always be detected after an hour or so. Besides, there was time to ventilate the place between the Sung Eucharist and Choral Mattins! Talking of incense reminds me that one visitor to St. Peter's, Bournemouth, told me afterwards that there were " seven censers before the altar ". He was quite annoyed when I explained to him that they were merely lamps. Most of the clergy who served churches of this type had received their training at Cuddesdon or Ely, and it would be quite wrong to suggest that they lacked a strong sense of their sacerdotal responsibilities or priestly vocation. Many were celibates, at least while they remained curates. But it was not regarded as a lapse from Catholic discipline if they availed themselves of the Sacrament of Matrimony. Once they had taken this step they generally began to look out for preferment, usually in the shape of a country parish, for the salary of the average curate was hardly enough to provide for a wife and family. I can remember instances of a gradual—sometimes sudden—slowing down of zeal for spreading the " Full " Faith on the part of a once eager young curate in a parish that boasted of its Catholicism, once he was faced with the obstacles of trying to convert his rural congregation to what he had been accustomed during the first years of his ministry. He grew wiser and older in the ways of the world, and ended up just a typical country parson.

There was an often puzzling diversity in the manner of celebrating the Communion service in churches of what I may call the comprehensive type. In one such church at Bournemouth, where I often used to serve Mass as a youth, there was a choice of missals to suit all tastes, from the authorised rite for Administration of the Lord's Supper according to the Book of Common Prayer to an almost literal translation of the Roman Rite or the Sarum Liturgy. It was disconcerting to serve a strange celebrant, for one never knew beforehand what rite he would follow. One had to be prepared to make the responses to preliminary prayers at the foot of the altar, or not to be surprised if he began his Mass straight away with the Lord's Prayer as is laid down in the Prayer Book rite. One never knew if he would mix the chalice before the service or at the Offertory; say the *Gloria* at the beginning or the end of the Mass; recite the Ten Commandments or the *Kyrie Eleison;* take the ablutions after the final Blessing or immediately after the Communion of the people—despite the rubric in the Prayer Book ordering that " what remaineth of the consecrated Elements " be covered with " a fair linen cloth ". Sometimes the celebrant would indulge in long private devotions before and after the Prayer of Consecration, or he would interpolate the greater part of the Roman Canon, omitting bits of the authorised rite as the spirit moved him. At the consecration he might either genuflect or make profound bows. The actual prayer of consecration might be quite inaudible, or recited so that it could be heard at the back of the church.

There would often be recommendations about going to confession in sermons—with appeals to the First Exhortation of the Communion Service or Canon 113, which lays down that private confession is not contrary to the mind of the Church of England if anybody feels moved to " unburden his conscience " and wishes to receive spiritual consolation from a Minister. For reasons of discretion, the times for hearing confessions in churches where it was a regular custom were sometimes announced in the following manner: " The clergy will be in the vestry " at such and such a time—followed by a list of names and hours. Confessional boxes were non-existent except in a few very advanced strongholds, and in most dioceses were forbidden by the Bishops. The penitents either knelt at a prie-dieu, hidden away mysteriously in some secluded corner of a side-chapel. In St. Peter's, Parkstone—where I made my first confession as an Anglican—one used to retire to the ambulatory behind the high altar. In other churches where I occasionally unburdened my conscience I did so in the Vestry—just as I have so often done in more recent years in Italy, where in some parts of that country, no man ever goes to confession in the body of the church, the confessionals being reserved to women. But in Anglican days one always had a subconscious feeling that one was guilty of a criminal offence which had to be carried out as stealthily as possible. Making one's confession was a far more serious business than it is as a Catholic. I shall never forget that first Church of England confession when the late Canon Dugmore, vicar of St. Peter's, Parkstone, kept me on my knees for at least half an hour and gave me a terrific penance. One was usually told to write out the matter for confession on a slip of paper, lest one forgot every sin and omission. In some dark churches there would be a candle and matches at the prie-dieu to be lit in cases of loss of memory!

Few Anglican parsons forty years ago, except those of the more advanced type, had made any serious study of Moral Theology, for it did not form part of their regular training in any of the theological colleges. They had to rely more on their instincts and intuition when giving advice or direction to penitents. It would be quite untrue to say that all those clergymen to whom I laid bare my soul did not do their best to be helpful and sympathetic, but what strikes me on looking back is their lack of any clear conception of the difference between mortal and venial sins as understood by any Catholic priest or layman. Their readiness to give absolution depended more or less on an individual outlook on life, and not on the hard and fast rules laid down by the Church. The majority of parsons, so I now feel, were inclined to over-strictness, even Jansenism. The penances imposed were often long and elaborate; the recitation of the seven penitential psalms being not infrequent, and the period over which they had to be recited might extend to the following week. Churches where the full Catholic Faith was taught and practised without any attempt at compromise were far less numerous than is the case to-day. I came across them in London, Brighton, Birmingham, and in a few other towns, but I remember well how different it was in Manchester, Liverpool and Sheffield. There was a great diversity of ceremonial at the leading strongholds of Anglo-Catholicism in London which I got to know between 1908 and 1910. Some were out and out Roman, others tried to be loyal to what they believed to be Sarum, others invented peculiar rites of their own which were a mixture of Rome, Sarum and post-Reformation Canterbury. With a change of incumbent, the church might switch over from one type of ceremonial to another; go back a little or plunge forward. An instance of this took place at All Saints, Margaret Street, soon after I got to know this famous church. Even after the late Prebendary Mackay became vicar and made considerable changes in the ritual, the result was far below the level of recent years.

Quite a number of very advanced London churches were banned by the Bishop who refused to visit them or to license curates. Yet in the days of my youth I cannot recall one of them which had thrown overboard the Book of Common Prayer, even if they added much to the services laid down in this volume. Loyalty to the Prayer Book was still part of the High Church claim in opposition to the Low or Moderate parties which, as the Anglo-Catholics were never tired of pointing out, constantly ignored rubrics that did not appeal to them.

In the extreme Anglo-Catholic churches the principal Sunday morning service was a Choral Eucharist (seldom, if ever, described as Mass on the notice boards either within or without the building, although almost always referred to as such from the pulpit or in conversation). There were often two or three Low Masses earlier in the morning, maybe a Children's Eucharist about 9.30. Mattins would be recited without music before the Choral Eucharist. Evensong, with the celebrant vested in a cope, was the regular service at night, and had not given way to Vespers or Compline as is now the case in some churches. Incense was always used " ceremonially " at High Mass and Evensong, i.e., during the *Magnificat*. The high altars in such churches were usually backed with rows of gradines upon which were displayed many candlesticks and brass flower-vases, giving the impression that the Forty Hours " Exposition " was about to be held. The higher the church, the greater the number of candles—such

was the general rule! But no extra-liturgical devotions, such as
Exposition or Benediction, were indulged in, at least not publicly, so
far as I am aware, though they were held in secret in a few convent
chapels to which the general public were not admitted. There were
very few parish churches, even the most advanced, which had started
continuous reservation of the Sacrament, and if they had done so, the
tabernacle, hanging pyx or aumbry, was hidden away out of sight in
a chapel, often locked and only accessible to the clergy and more
devout members of the congregation for private devotion. Such was
the case, for instance, at St. Matthew's, Westminster, and St. Mary
Magdalene's, Paddington, but at St. Cuthbert's, Philbeach Gardens, I
seem to remember that the place of reservation was on the rood loft.
To-day there must be about fourteen hundred Anglican churches
where reservation of the Sacrament is to be found, including several
cathedrals. But forty years ago reservation was still regarded as a
spiritual privilege which might be gained with patience and not as
a matter of course.

The influence of Modernism had not begun to be felt among
Anglo-Catholics to any great extent. Taken as a whole, I imagine
that they were more orthodox in their theology and they would have
been horrified at being regarded as liberal, though a number of
the more advanced clergy were inclined to be what was then called
Socialists. Their attitude towards the Roman Claims differed
greatly. Some were as bitterly opposed to the Papacy as were the
most extreme Evangelicals. They gloried in the fact that the *Ecclesia
Anglicana* had broken away from Rome at the Reformation, though
they would maintain that the Church of England still formed a part
of the Western Patriarchate, which involved the obligation of
observing Western ceremonial. Seldom, if ever, did I hear such
violently anti-Roman sermons as at St. Stephen's, Clewer, near
Windsor, where its vicar—the late Canon Nicholas—was in all other
respects uncompromisingly Catholic. Clergymen of this particular
school of thought would denounce the Italian Mission as schismatic and might refuse to give absolution to penitents who confessed
that they had assisted in the worship of a Roman church in this
country. On the other hand, if one was travelling on the continent
of Europe, it was regarded as schismatic to attend the Anglican
chapels in foreign countries, and, consequently, an obligation to
frequent churches in communion with Rome. I never discovered
what would be the correct thing to do if one happened to be staying

in Jersey, Guernsey, or the other Channel Islands; and the position regarding Malta or Gibraltar was quite puzzling.

There were other parsons who held quite opposite views on Rome. They were never tired of reaching Corporate Reunion and maintained that they were only held back from making their submission to the Holy See by the firm conviction that they possessed valid Orders, which it would be sacrilege to deny. While accepting the judgment of the Holy See in all other points of faith and morals, they believed that the Papal decision on Anglican Orders would be revoked sooner or later and that a Uniate Church would be established in England.

Another party among the Anglo-Catholics was enthusiastic about Reunion with the East, and felt that Moscow and Constantinople had far more in common with Canterbury than Rome, and that they could well afford to ignore the Papacy altogether. The only thing that mattered was to achieve reunion with the Eastern Churches, regardless of the heresies they might or might not stand for. It was always a great delight to some clergymen if they could induce some wandering archimandrite who happened to be in England, usually for the purpose of collecting money, to visit their Churches. He would be invited to assist at High Mass and given a prie-dieu in the sanctuary or a stall in choir, where he would be censed with the correct number of swings as laid down in Roman ceremonial.

Then there was a small but ardent group which did its best to spread the cultus of St. Charles the Martyr—otherwise King Charles I—the only saint which the Church of England has added to its calendar since the Reformation, and whose special proper had been since removed from the Book of Common Prayer some time during the last century, if I remember rightly. In at least two Anglo-Catholic churches in London—usually St. Cuthbert's, Philbeach Gardens, and St. Margaret Pattens—High Mass was celebrated on the anniversary of the martyrdom of St. Charles, and his devotees would lay wreaths and bouquets at the foot of his equestrian statue in Whitehall.

In most Anglo-Catholic parishes there was an intensive round of special services, Guilds, Confraternities, Retreats and Quiet Days. In all of them one would be certain of finding at least one daily Mass. Evensong and Mattins were recited regularly, usually in a side chapel. But I cannot recall any church where it was the custom forty years ago for each clergyman to say Mass daily. They usually took it in turns.

To return to the subject of confessions: it was quite common, in a number of London churches, for all the clergy to hear them on Saturday evenings. They generally sat behind low screens or grilles in the side-aisles, separated from their penitents but both being visible. In such popular churches as St. Matthew's, Westminster, St. Alban's, Holborn, or All Saints', Margaret Street—which I knew best—the crowds on a Saturday afternoon or evening were almost as great as one would find in any Catholic church in London. Going to confession was a far more business-like affair than in the more moderate places of worship already described. In fact, the whole thing was carried out efficiently, and one was not kept waiting or given long penances.

I never had much experience of extreme Anglo-Catholicism in country parishes, but among the few churches of this type which I used to attend was Hickleton in Yorkshire, where the local squire happened to be the late Lord Halifax. I loved to cycle over to Hickleton from the neighbouring village of Badsworth, where my uncle Harold Anson was then rector and whose services were of a much less advanced character, even if he did have to wear linen vestments rather against his inclinations, just because the patroness of the living liked them! In the dim, dark, incense-laden Perpendicular Gothic interior of Hickleton Church, one was transported into another world. The Sung Mass went on mysteriously behind the rood-screen, with much genuflecting, twinkling of lights, ringing of bells and clouds of incense. In a side chapel one got a glimpse of the white-headed leader of the Anglo-Catholic party and President of the English Church Union. Such a pilgrimage was well worth making in the opinion of a susceptible youth of eighteen or nineteen!

The lure of incense, more than of vestments, drew me to other churches in the country, even if it involved a long and often tiring cycle ride on a Sunday morning. When living with a private tutor at Swanage in Dorset I would climb the steep road that leads to the little Norman church at Worth Matravers; while in Yorkshire, North Elmsall and South Kirkby drew me for the same reason. I often stayed in the Isle of Wight, and thought nothing of cycling ten miles to escape from Evangelical Mattins at Sandown for Mass with incense at Swanmore. At Portsmouth, there was the choice of St. Michael's, St. Matthew's, or St. Agatha's; at Bournemouth, forty years ago, I had to do without the fumes of gum olibanum and other ingredients except on the greater festivals when they pervaded the interiors of St. Peter's, Parkstone, or St. Clement's, Boscombe, at Choral Eucharist. During my first years in London as an architectural student I sampled in turn, St. Alban's, Holborn; St. Barnabas', Pimlico; All Saints', Margaret Street; St. Mary's, Graham Street; St. Matthew's, Westminster; St. Mary Magdalene's, Munster Square, and other churches, before I discovered St. Mary's, Primrose Hill, which became my final mecca.

At this church I first realised that the details of worship must be ordered by authority, and that the only authority which one could accept in the Church of England was the Book of Common Prayer. I can still recapture the thrill of the first service I took part in at St. Mary's—Choral Evensong on the Saturday before Advent Sunday, 1908—coming in out of a thick, yellow London fog into the dimly-lit, white-washed interior of a not specially interesting example of French medieval Gothic architecture, adapted to 19th century Anglican requirements. Every year when Advent arrives I always think of Primrose Hill, for it is linked up with the fourth mode plainchant melody of the office hymn, *Creator Alme Siderum,* which on that evening I heard for the first time, sung by the choir under the direction of Dr. Martin Shaw. I can see that stately but dignified high altar, with riddel posts and low dossal, standing beneath the Bodley reredos in the apse. Two candlesticks and no more rested on the *mensa* and there were no flower vases. I can recall the typical Sunday morning service which consisted of sung Mattins, processional Litany and Choral Eucharist; the latter always with a deacon and sub-deacon—or epistoler and gospeller as they were termed. The vestments worn by the ministers were of a shape then almost unknown—very long and ample. The music was strictly liturgical, mostly Plain Chant. Never before or since have I heard better congregational hymn singing or Gregorian music than during my twelve months at Primrose Hill. There was a generous though nonceremonial use of incense. The Prayer Book rite was carried out to the letter, with no interpolations or verbal additions. Dr. Percy Dearmer, to whose genius all this was due, could produce authorities for every detail of ceremonial he had introduced. He would maintain that nothing was in any way illegal or contrary to episcopal or Privy Council legislation. This was one of the reasons, quite apart from the purely æsthetic grounds, why St. Mary's, Primrose Hill, attracted me in comparison with other strongholds of various shades of Anglo-Catholicism. Even at nineteen I had begun to suffer from " Roman Fever " and this church acted as a temporary antidote, since it convinced me that it was possible to be a loyal member of the Church of England and yet indulge in as elaborate and satisfying forms of ceremonial as anybody could reasonably wish for. It was a perfect manifestation of Anglican worship.

It was soon after I went to Primrose Hill I became one of the regular servers at the week-day Eucharists, celebrated in the side chapel. A month or two later I was promoted to be an acolyte—or taperer in Dearmer idiom—at the Choral Eucharist and solemn Evensong on Sundays and Saturday nights. I enjoyed dressing up in an amice and alb—adorned with " apparels "—" so beautiful a feature in the English ceremonial that it is the more regrettable that some clergy should have discarded them ", so Percy Dearmer wrote in his *Parson's Handbook;* nowadays an almost official manual for the ordering of such Anglican services. Finally, to my great delight, I was put on the list of thurifers. The famous Lambeth Opinion of 1899 on the subject of the liturgical use of processional lights and incense implied that incense could not be used in, and as a part of public worship in the Church of England, but merely " to sweeten the church, and outside the worship altogether". But this " Opinion " was not adopted by every Bishop, with the result that nobody was really quite clear what was permissible or not. So far as I can remember, there was no censing of " persons or things " at St. Mary's; we rather liked to boast that we followed the original liturgical use of the Church of Rome down to the 9th century! What a long time one used to spend in church on a Sunday morning, nearly two and a half hours from the beginning of Mattins to the end of the Sung Eucharist, at which the sermon was preached. But I never recall finding it wearisome, either as a member of the congregation or as a minor-performer in the liturgical rite. I remember delightful Rogation processions through the streets of South Hampstead and Primrose Hill, with its grassy slopes looking fresh and green on a May evening.

To quote from reminiscences which I contributed to Mrs. Dearmer's *Life* of her husband (Cape, 1940): " For the whole of the year which followed my settling in Adelaide Road, there was seldom a day when I did not meet the Vicar. He was always in and out of the offices and workrooms of the St. Dunstan Society—a picturesque figure in his cassock and gown, with a square cap sometimes covering his shock of rather untidy hair. On other occasions his hair blew about in the wind. P. D. always maintained that the correct outdoor dress of Anglican clergymen was the cassock, and gown, and I cannot recall any occasion when I ever saw him in coat and trousers at this period. . . . He seldom touched on controversial matters in the sermons he preached nearly every Sunday. He generally contented himself with expounding Christianity on lines after the heart of F. D. Maurice and Bishop Westcott. One of the things I can still remember vividly is his reading of the lessons. I doubt if any other person was such a perfect reader of English, especially Elizabethan English. He was a convinced Anglican and really did believe in his Church, unlike so many Anglo-Catholics who try to turn it into a feeble imitation of the Roman article, merely emulating features which some of us Romans most deplore! On looking back I can see the difference in his conception of his official status and that of certain other neighbouring clergy. There was much more of the Lutheran about him, and I think he would have revelled in Scandinavian Lutheranism, with its ceremonial and liberal theology, had he discovered it as a young man. The first time I went to Denmark I thought to myself how like the religion was to what I recall at Primrose Hill."

The reference to Plain Chant at Primrose Hill reminds me how the music in extreme Anglo-Catholic churches varied as much as the ceremonial. In some of them one could listen to the florid Masses of Gounod, Mozart, Beethoven or Schubert—on the great festival with orchestral accompaniment. All Saints', Margaret Street—then as now—was famous for its elaborate Sung Eucharists, rendered exquisitely by boys of the resident choir school. The psalms at Even-song—those at Mattins were usually recited—were generally sung to Gregorian tones, either in the Mechlin or Ratisbon versions, with loud rumbling harmonies on the organ. There may not have been much rhythm (in the Solesmes sense) about these Gregorians, but they were lusty and virile. I have a sort of feeling that people would not dislike Plain Chant half so much if we could return to the Mechlin and Ratisbon books—but this I know is sheer heresy! At the Cowley Fathers' church at Oxford, the editions of the Plainsong and Medieval Music Society had already been adopted when I first attended Evensong there in 1908. This was the first occasion when I heard Plain Chant sung quietly and rhythmically by boys—a revelation of pure beauty.

I would like to transport some of my Catholic friends to a Sunday

D

morning Sung Eucharist at St. Matthew's, Westminster, about forty years ago. Here the congregation were provided with books that contained the chant in modern notation. It may not have been very correct, but how one enjoyed singing it! One may find the same type of music sung in some village churches in France. These books contained many of the 17th century French office hymn tunes—which go with a swing and suggest baroque angels floating up to Heaven.

The *English Hymnal* had been published in 1906 and I well remember the sensation it caused. It was a marked improvement in every respect on the older editions of *Hymns, Ancient and Modern*. Very soon its bright green binding could be seen in many Anglo-Catholic churches, although it was banned by some bishops because it contained direct invocations of Our Lady and the saints. So an expurgated, or rather an abridged, edition was brought out to pacify episcopal scruples about Mariolatry. Strange to say, it was the otherwise High Church Bishop Gore who was among the most bitter opponents of this hymnal, based, so it seemed, on the subtle distinction between public and private invocation of saints. He admitted that the latter was permissible, but maintained that only indirect invocation could be allowed in church!

CHAPTER III

LIFE IN AN ANGLICAN MONASTERY

A large water-colour in my spare bedroom is a constant reminder of the next important phase of my roving career. It is painted on David Cox paper, and shows a small island, viewed from the mainland; a vivid ultramarine sea, broken with purple shadows from cumulus clouds that float over a cerulean blue sky. Closer inspection reveals the presence of a group of white buildings on the island; a line of dark trees; a lighthouse and a small spire which indicates a church. The indented coast-line is rocky, with high cliffs against which blobs of Chinese white convey the impression that, although the sea is calm, there must be a big swell rolling in from the ocean. Here is the Isle of Caldey that lies off the coast of Pembrokeshire in South Wales, and was to be my home—more or less—for about fourteen years.

*　　　*　　　*

One afternoon early in the year 1906 I was looking for a book in
Boot's Library at Bournemouth, and I noticed a big blue bound
volume among the travel and biographical section, entitled *The
Life of Father Ignatius, Monk of Llanthony*. I took it out and
glanced at the illustrations. It looked interesting, for my curiosity as
to monks and nuns had already been aroused. I admit that I lapped
up this flamboyantly-written biography with relish, in fact I decided
to buy a second-hand copy as soon as one was available, and placed
an order with the librarian. This was my introduction to Anglican
monasticism, and until I got into touch with the Benedictines of
Painsthorpe about six months afterwards, all my interests centred
round that strange community which an eccentric Anglican deacon
and famous mission preacher had tried to establish in a remote valley
of the Black Mountains in South Wales.

That summer I came across an advertisement in the *Church Times*
stating that a new issue of *Pax*—the quarterly magazine of the
Benedictine Community of Painsthorpe—was on sale and could be
obtained for the sum of 8d. The *Life of Father Ignatius* had briefly
referred to the existence of these monks, but told me little more than
that they were Olivetans, whatever this might mean. I immediately
wrote off for the seven back numbers of *Pax* and when they arrived
a few days later, provided me with more than enough material to
satisfy my seventeen-year-old enthusiasm for monasticism. From
these green and gold covered magazines I found out that this
community had been founded by Benjamin Carlyle, a medical student
at St. Bartholomew's Hospital. In 1894, having gathered round him
a small group of like-minded young men and youths, he took a house
at Ealing, and thus began community life. Then the Brothers
migrated to the Isle of Dogs, and, after a series of ups and downs,
had managed to find a home at Painsthorpe, thanks to the help of
Lord Halifax. The Notes on the History of the Community,
which were appearing in serial form, also told me that Brother Aelred
Carlyle had been solemnly professed in 1897 on the written authority
of Archbishop Temple of Canterbury; a notable event as being the
first officially recognised profession of a monk in the restored Order
of St. Benedict in the Church of England. It was related how an
American Bishop, with the permission of Dr. Maclagan, Archbishop
of York, had blessed and installed Brother Aelred as abbot, and how
this same prelate of the Protestant Episcopal Church in the U.S.A.
had ordained him to the priesthood. From what I could gather from

the magazines, this community appeared to be far less heterodox than Llanthony, as described by the Baroness de Bertouch in her *Life* of its founder. Whatever might be its faults, the Benedictine community at Painsthorpe could show that it had the approval of the highest authorities in the Church of England.

Having absorbed and digested the contents of the seven numbers of *Pax* I felt there was nothing else to be done but join the Confraternity which had been founded to link up friends with the Community. I wrote to the Abbot, enclosing half-a-crown, and was thrilled when there arrived back an impressive-looking " Letter of Confraternity " signed by himself, together with a bronze medal of St. Benedict. I attached it to my watch chain, worn across my waistcoat, where it dangled aggressively, inducing one of my aunts to describe it as " your gastric cross "! Being in Yorkshire that summer, staying with my uncle Harold Anson, to-day Master of the Temple, I wanted to visit my newly-found monastic brethren. But this visit never came off, and two months later the Community left Painsthorpe for Caldey Island, South Wales. The next issue of *Pax* contained a romantic description of this " low, long island in the Bristol Channel, surrounded by the blue waters of the Severn Sea, and fragrant with the scent of flowers and the memory of holy lives ". It told how the monks had taken possession of their new home and of their plans for the future, how they intended to build a Guest House and later on a large abbey. Caldey Island must be an ideal spot, so I felt, and I vowed I would make a pilgrimage there as soon as possible. But it was not until three and a half years later that I was able to do so.

Meanwhile my enthusiasm for monasticism increased. I started to recite the Breviary offices, beginning with an Anglican translation, known as the *Day Hours of the Church of England*. I fitted up an oratory in a cupboard in the eaves off my bedroom, and furnished it with a Crucifix and candlesticks. Feeling that I wanted to recite the same prayers as the monks at Caldey I invested in a Latin *Horæ Diurnæ Breviarii Monastici,* and began to use it for the first time on the feast of St. Joseph Calasanctius, August 27th, 1908. A year later I spent two pounds on a morocco-bound, gilt-edged, four-volume *Monastic Breviary,* at which my father, on discovering the books, expressed indignation at such a waste of money. Finally I completed my liturgical library by buying a *Graduale* and *Antiphonale.*

As a member of the Confraternity of the Benedictines of Caldey I began to take my Catholicism very seriously. I was never much worried by scruples about attending what some of my Anglo-Catholic friends called Schismatic places of worship, and I loved to wander in to the Jesuit churches at Bournemouth and Boscombe or the humble little Italian Mission that had invaded the parish of Branksome. One summer afternoon I set out from Bournemouth on my bicycle, bound for the remote village of Martin on the borders of Dorset and Wiltshire, where so I had discovered from the *Catholic Directory* there existed a community of Cistercian monks. It was a long ride, but when at last I reached my destination I did not regret the dust and the heat of the journey. These good French monks, who had been driven into exile from the monastery of Bricquebec in Normandy, welcomed me with the utmost kindness. I was tired and thirsty and how I enjoyed that cider and bread and butter in the parlour, conversing with a monk who spoke English. Then I assisted at Vespers in their little chapel. Having read Huysmans' novel, *En Route,* I felt no stranger in these surroundings. I was so charmed with the simple and unaffected piety of these black-and-white habited monks that I resolved to pay them another visit, but for some reason or other never managed to do so. This was the first Catholic religious Community which I got to know.

On the afternoon of June 26, 1908, when in the Isle of Wight, I visited Quarr Abbey for the first time. Sitting at the back of the temporary wooden structure that served as a church before the present magnificent brick church, I listened enthralled to the incomparable Plain Chant of the exiled Benedictines of Solesmes, while they sang the Vespers of SS. John and Paul. The beauty of this music was different from anything I had ever known, and for days afterwards it haunted me.

Thanks to Huysmans again I already had a fairly clear idea of Benedictine life from *L'Oblat* before my first visit to Quarr, and that glimpse of nearly a hundred black cowled choir monks, and brown-cloaked lay brothers, with the late Abbot Delatte presiding over them like a white-haired general, very dignified and stately, made a tremendous impression on me. I became more eager to make the acquaintance of the Anglican Benedictines on Caldey Island, and wondered if they would fall short of the French monks in the Isle of Wight.

It must not be imagined, however, that my religious occupations were merely ritualistic and external. I was, in fact, sufficiently

enquiring after the metaphysical Truth to be badly bitten by the
claims of Theosophy (falsely so-called), for a time was an admirer of
Mrs. Besant and other writers of this queer sect. This did not affect
my attendance at High Anglican, or even Catholic churches, for
Theosophy was nothing if not comprehensive. A more healthy sign,
but less understandable in one of my upbringing, was the attraction for me of the great mystical writers (both Catholic and
Protestant) from the pseudo-Dionysius and Plotinus to Jacob Boehme,
Blessed Angela of Foligno, Dame Julian of Norwich and William
Law. Moreover, I read controversial works on the Roman claims,
for even at the age of sixteen my faith in Anglicanism had begun to
waver—if it ever existed—and needed constant bolstering up. Still, I
managed to find cogent reasons for remaining in the Church of
England, even when accepting the doctrine of the Primacy of Peter
and his successors, in the American magazine known as *The Lamp,*
published by the Society of the Atonement—a Franciscan community
in the Protestant Episcopal Church. This little buff-covered magazine
was quite the most pro-Roman publication I had come across, and I
decided that I must subscribe to it as a means of strengthening my
weakening allegiance to the Anglican body.

*   *   *

My other reading was more of a piece with that of other
" artistically-minded young men " of my generation. I had successive
phases of addiction to William Blake and Edgar Allan Poe;
devoured Walter Pater; and from D. G. Rossetti passed on as a matter
of course to Oscar Wilde. But my tastes did not lack solidity—or
broadness. I enjoyed Fielding, Smollett, and Marryat, had dipped
into most of the Restoration dramatists by my 18th birthday, and got
hold of every new novel about the sea and book of maritime history
as soon as it was published. I discovered Virgil, Horace and Catullus,
and read both French and German literature. Victor Hugo was my
Gallic favourite, and I treated myself one birthday to complete sets of
Schiller and Heine.

Mr. Stable, my tutor at Swanage, died suddenly at the close of
1907, so other arrangements had to be made for my sporadic education. For the next eight months I lived with my grandmother at
Windsor, and studied hard under several tutors, for I was due to sit
for Responsions at Oxford that summer as well as the entrance
examination for Christ Church, for which my name had been entered.
It was still supposed that I was cut out for a diplomatic career, and

consequently I had to specialise in foreign languages. I failed miserably in both exams. My tutors were surprised. I was not, for examination-rooms have always reduced me to such a state of nerves that memory and commonsense desert me. A month or two later I made a final attempt to get through, and was again ploughed. Thus I never became a member of the university or an undergraduate at "The House", which had been the home of so many of my father's family when at Oxford.

The whole matter of my career had now to be reconsidered, and there were long consultations and discussions with my relations. Finally I solved the problem myself by announcing that I wanted to study architecture, and within a week or two I found myself a student at the Architectural Association Schools in Tufton Street, Westminster, where I remained two years. The school has long since been removed to Bedford Square, in far more attractive quarters than the gloomy Gothic structure with its cast-iron galleries which housed a dusty and dirty collection of architectural casts of all periods. The buildings have now been turned into a library for the blind, and no longer are the gaitered bishops and deans on their way to Church House, or the staff of the Society for the Propagation of the Gospel in Foreign Parts, whose offices were in front of the school, disturbed by the crowds of noisy young men who then made up the pupils of the A.A. (girl students had not yet gained a footing in the ranks of British architecture. I don't quite know what we should have thought of the innovation of the charming young women in coloured smocks whom I now see in and out of the new A.A. in Bloomsbury).

I found the work tremendously interesting, and a welcome relief after several years' cramming at mathematics, classics, French and German . . . all except the purely constructional part of architecture. Here I was a failure and when it came to stresses and strains involving intricate calculations, I generally had to seek one of my companions to help me out while, in return, I would assist him with the artistic part of his perspective, in which, as a water-colour painter, I was more expert. Some of these students became distinguished members of this profession, especially George C. Wornum, Llewelyn Roberts, and F. M. Robertson.

At least once a week the students used to be taken on visits to places of interest—a new building under construction, a factory, brick kilns, timber works, and so on. We studied Byzantine domes on the

roof of Westminster Cathedral and penetrated into the triforium and
clerestory of the neighbouring Abbey to measure up Gothic mouldings.
We were taken as far afield as Stamford in Lincolnshire in order to
see what stone cottages could be like. We made sketches of brick
work at Hampton Court and Chelsea Hospital. We had more than
one afternoon in the then rising garden suburb of Golders Green,
and another on the North Downs near Reigate, which had been
chosen as the site for an imaginary church we had to design . . .
such were typical distractions from our routine work in the school.

Ecclesiastical architecture interested me more than any other.   I
developed an intense love and admiration for Augustus Welby Pugin,
visiting and sketching every church of his which I could find.   Other
architects whose work I greatly admired were Butterfield, Bodley and
Comper.   I was bold enough to write to Mr. Comper and was invited
to tea with him at his house in Norwood, where he showed me his
drawings and designs and gave me much-appreciated encouragement.

I got my first taste of foreign Catholicism during a fortnight's
cycling tour in Normandy during the summer of 1909, where I
revelled in the opportunities for assisting at Mass, above all the
Sunday High Mass and Vespers in Rouen Cathedral, and another
Sunday spent at Caudebec.   The distribution of *pain-bénit* among
the congregation in the lovely 15th century Flamboyant Gothic church
in this old world town enabled me to feel that I was at least in
spiritual communion with those around me.   On Sunday at Rouen I
felt it my duty to go to communion in the English church.   It proved
to be as Protestant in character as anything I had ever come across
at home, and I wished I had not been so conscientious.   I was certain
that the clergyman who administered the Lord's Supper had no conception that he was saying Mass like the Catholic priests in this
great city.   This service upset me terribly.   An hour or two later, when
following the High Mass in the Cathedral, with the aid of a newly-
purchased French *Paroissien*, complete with Plain Chant, I had an
uncomfortable feeling that under no circumstances whatever, could
the one type of worship be reconciled with the other, and that I had
to recognise the fact that I was a Protestant, or at least in communion
with Protestants.   Again, throughout that fortnight in Normandy, in
company with a dozen or so other young students from the Architectural Association, it was driven home to me how peculiar were
the religious opinions I upheld with such zeal.   So far as I can recall,
all of them were at least nominal members of the Church of England,

but it never occurred to any that they were Catholics. The churches we visited and sketched were just bits of interesting architecture, not places of worship. The Faith which had inspired the erection of these churches and which meant so much to me, was a closed book to my companions, and in their midst I felt like a fish out of water.

When I returned to London that same autumn I took up my residence at St. Edward's House, Westminster—the London headquarters of the Society of St. John the Evangelist, commonly known as The Cowley Fathers. I managed to obtain this rather rare privilege thanks to a life-long friendship of my uncle, Harold Anson, with the then Superior, Father Waggett, for it was not usual for a layman to be allowed to stay with the Community as a permanent guest. I shared in the life of the Fathers, had meals in their refectory, where silence was observed and a book read at dinner and supper, and was allowed to occupy a stall in chapel. Every morning I joined in the recitation of Prime which preceded the daily Mass. Whenever possible I assisted at other offices, and was seldom absent from Compline. I was allotted a big, barely-furnished cell overlooking Dean's Yard, with a view of the twin towers of the Abbey. I swept and dusted the room and made my own bed—a good training for the life I already looked forward to with the Benedictines of Caldey. I enjoyed this semi-monastic atmosphere, and look back on those nine months at St. Edward's House as perhaps the happiest period of my youth. Needless to say, my retirement to a monastery caused much comment and harmless jokes from my fellow-students, and I could not keep my residence secret, for it was situated exactly opposite the school.

During that last year in London my religious position became even more eclectic. Usually on a Sunday I would assist at the early celebration of the Communion service in the Community chapel, according to the rite of the Book of Common Prayer, together with the offices of Prime and Terce (said in English), before and after breakfast. Then very often I would make my way to Bayswater, where, in the Greek Orthodox church, I would follow the Liturgy of St. John Chrysostom from the gallery which commanded an unbroken view of the iconostasis. Some other Sunday I might attend the Old Slavonic version of this same liturgy at the Russian Embassy chapel then in Welbeck Street. As an alternative I would accompany Fr. Robinson, an elderly American member of the Cowley Community, to the church of Nôtre-Dame-de-France, off Leicester Square, where a French sermon was preached at the 11 o'clock Mass. Fr. Robinson explained to me that although it would have been an act of schism to have gone to Westminster Cathedral, this particular church was in a different category, for it primarily existed for the spiritual benefit of foreigners, even if, unfortunately, it was under the jurisdiction of a rival hierarchy which ought not to have been established in this country! These hair-splitting distinctions as to Roman Catholic places of worship were not shared by most of the other Fathers at St. Edward's House, and I don't think they quite approved of their confrère's attendance at Nôtre-Dame-de-France.

After dinner in the refectory, followed by recreation with the Community, ending up with the office of None, I would hurry off to Westminster Cathedral for Vespers and Benediction—disregarding Fr. Robinson's view that I was guilty of schism if I worshipped in that building. To complete this full Sunday more often than not I attended Solemn Evensong at the neighbouring Anglican church of St. Matthew, the day's worship concluding with Compline in the chapel at St. Edward's House. My tastes were sufficiently broad-minded to allow me to assist at the ornate liturgy at the Catholic Apostolic Irvingite Church in Gordon Square, but only occasionally. I might vary my Sunday morning pilgrimages by going to High Mass at some of the better-known Anglo-Catholic strongholds, such as St. Barnabas', Pimlico; St. Mary's, Graham Street; St. Cuthbert's, Phil-beach Gardens, or St. Cyprian's, Dorset Square. After I went to live with the Cowley Fathers I seldom went back to St. Mary's, Primrose Hill—it was too far off. All this sampling of churches may sound like mere religiosity, but I am convinced that I was seriously trying to discover a *point d'appui* for a goodly, righteous and sober life which ultimately I found in that doctrine of the union in Christ's mystical body of all *bona fide* Christians which has full, coherent and consistent expression in the Catholic and Roman Church alone.

By the early spring of 1910 I had become convinced that my mind would not be at peace until I had tested my vocation at Caldey, so I decided to write to Abbot Aelred Carlyle to ask if he would allow me to enter the novitiate. "I have been thinking over your letter," he replied on February 10th, "and feel that if you are so drawn to the form of the Religious Life that is lived on Caldey, I should like to see you before giving any definite opinion as to your best course. Can you therefore arrange to come and see us soon after Easter, and spend a week or so on the Island? We shall then be able to talk over your desires and prospects at leisure."

Meanwhile I had informed my father of what I wanted to do, and he wrote to the Abbot, requesting more detailed information about a manner of life which was completely beyond his comprehension. The Abbot's answer—which I have before me—makes quite clear to my father that " every precaution will be taken to make sure of the reality of the Vocation "; with the concluding assurance: " I will do all I can to help your son to a manly and right decision." So I obtained my father's permission to visit Caldey, and what is more he agreed to pay for this expedition. Not many convinced Protestant parents would have behaved in such a generous and disinterested manner if their eldest son had announced that he intended to become a monk! At the time I don't think I realised how much it must have cost him to give his blessing on what must have seemed such a futile career.

*   *   *

It seems only yesterday that I made my first journey from Paddington to Tenby instead of more than thirty-five years ago. I can recall the thrill of that morning of the Tuesday in Holy Week, 1910; the sense of setting forth on a great adventure into a new and unknown world. It was a bright spring day, and as the train passed along the coast between Kidwelly and Carmarthen, I beheld Caldey Island rising out of the sea away to the west. I crossed over to Caldey in the steamer *Firefly,* and having landed at the slip, made my way up the rough road between gorse bushes to the Guest House, where I was welcomed by the Warden—Br. Denys Prideaux—in after years well known as Abbot of the Anglican Community of Benedictines at Nashdom.

Here I spent my first week, moving into the monastery after Easter so that I could learn more of the life of the Community which I hoped to join. That fortnight was more than enough to convince me that there was nothing else in the world I wanted so much as to become a monk and it was decided that I was to come back at the end of July to test my vocation, by which time my course of studies at the Architectural Association Schools would have been completed.

So I returned to London. About a month later Abbot Aelred Carlyle wrote to me, saying that his letter was " going to be a little surprise and, I hope, a pleasant one ". He continued: " I have decided to send Brother Wilfrid to Quarr to hear the music before we move

into our new chapel.   Do you think you could possibly spare the time
to take charge of him (!) and see him to Ryde and back? . . . Br.
Wilfrid will, of course, be in his Habit, but he will go to the abbey
services as an ordinary visitor, and does not want to give the monks
any opportunity of being unkind to him!   This will also give you
the opportunity of becoming acquainted with your novice prefect."

It is almost needless to add that I did manage to spare the time.
I secured lodgings about a mile away from the abbey, for it would
have been embarrassing both for my future Novice Master and the
monks of Quarr if he had asked to be received at the Guest House,
for no matter how perfect French hospitality and politeness can be,
even in the most awkward situations, I think that Abbot Delatte and
his Community would have been puzzled at the correct way to welcome an Anglican monk.   I met Br. Wilfrid in London and travelled
with him to Portsmouth.   As he paced the deck of the steamer
crossing to the Isle of Wight the passengers stared at his shaven head
and black habit.   Our kind landlady—who informed me that she herself was a Methodist—was a bit mystified why a monk should stay
with her and not at the abbey.   We spent a long week-end at Quarr,
assisting at Sung Mass, Vespers and Compline every day.   Armed
with copies of the *Liber Usualis* we followed the Plaint Chant Masses
of SS. Philip and James and Rogation Sunday.   We joined in the
Rogation procession next morning and in the rear of the Community
helped to swell the response of the Litany of the Saints, with primroses
in bloom and blue-bells just coming into flower.   We noticed that every
night after Compline the Abbot always flicked the holy water brush
in our direction when he was giving the *Asperges*—did he think it
would drive out our heresy, we wondered?   We were not unconscious
of the discreet curiosity of the monks—of side glances at Br. Wilfrid's
habit and tonsure.   None of them spoke to us, so far as I can recall.
For myself I had always the feeling of an alien, no matter how much
I was enjoying the music and the ceremonial.

On Saturday night, as we were walking back to our lodgings after
Compline, Br. Wilfrid announced that he felt he must make his
Communion at Binstead parish church the following morning, explaining that this involved going without breakfast, for he did not want
to be late for High Mass.   I regret to say that I flatly declined to
accompany him.   The mental picture of assisting at an Anglican
Communion service in a church which was far from High—so
we had already discovered when we looked in one afternoon—and in

company with a tonsured monk, was more than I could face. So I stayed at home and, after a solitary breakfast, made my way to the Abbey; my future Novice Master slipping in beside me just as the Community were starting Terce. Many years later, when both of us had become Catholics and I happened to be staying at Quarr—this time in the monastery—I was told how, as the result of this strange monk having partaken of the Communion at Binstead, the story got around that one of the monks of Quarr had joined the Church of England! It appeared that Abbot Delatte had some difficulty in contradicting the report and was naturally annoyed.

If this week-end at Quarr did nothing else, it stimulated my enthusiasm for Plain Chant. When I got back to London I began to make a serious study of it, thinking that it would come in useful later on. I mentioned the fact to Abbot Aelred when next writing to him, and was just a little hurt to get the following reply: " I am interested to know that you are having some lessons in plainsong accompaniment; but whether or no such accomplishment is going to be useful to our Community is entirely dependent upon the sort of vocation you will prove to possess. It is conceivable that you might be so conceited about your powers of accompanist that you would never be allowed to touch the organ for the rest of your life." Then the Abbot went on to advise me " not to swallow Benedictine authors in too large a quantity, or you will certainly suffer from spiritual indigestion, from which you will take long to recover." He ended his letter with another mild rebuke for my precocious " questions about the Ordo " (I had asked him why certain saints did not appear). He explained that " Each Religious Congregation puts out its own Ordo Recitandi more or less arbitrarily. Both in theory and practice, we desire so far as possible to recite the Divine Office in accordance with the spirit of the rule of St. Benedict; the tendency of many Roman Religious and specialists is to get back more to ancient custom, and to drop a large number of Feasts with which the Calendar has gradually become overladen. Hence you will find that we exclude many Saints in favour of the Ferial Office."

The Cowley Fathers, with whom I was still living at St. Edward's House, Westminster, did not altogether approve of the Romeward tendencies of the Caldey monks, and some of them did their best to dissuade me from entering the novitiate. I can recall at least one long talk with Fr. Puller, and another with Fr. Conran, both of which took place on the roof of St. Edward's House on hot summer

evenings, where, against a background of the distant roar of traffic,
it was pointed out to me, very tactfully but quite clearly, that it was
extremely doubtful if the Caldey Benedictines had any real status
in the Church of England and that one must be prepared for anything
happening sooner or later.

But I did not take the well-meant advice of these good Fathers.
My mind was made up, and on July 31st, the feast of St. Ignatius
Loyola, I said good-bye to my family, with whom I had been staying
at Portland, where my father was King's Harbourmaster, and started
once more for South Wales. My father, although he was naturally
disappointed at my throwing up the chances of what might have been
a brilliant future as an architect—at least so it had been impressed on
him—and although he had no sympathy for this very different career
upon which I was embarking, most generously agreed to defray the
expenses of my novitiate.

So I found myself back again on Caldey Island after an interval
of three months. The community had finished supper when I
arrived at the monastery, and the bell was ringing for Compline
as I walked up from the steamer. The new chapel had been opened
since I was there in April, and I was much impressed by its sense
of spaciousness after the small room in which the monks and a few
visitors had crowded together at Easter. I went up the narrow stairs
and found myself in the gallery, where I looked down on the black-
cowled figures in the shadowy half-light of the choir stalls as they
chanted the already familiar and unchanging psalms of Benedictine
Compline. Once again I listened to the prayer " *pro famulo tuo
Frederico* "—the nightly commemoration of Archbishop Temple,
whom the community regarded as its founder, for he had granted the
original Charter and approved of the Blessing of the Abbot. I recalled what Mr. Athelstan Riley had written in the current issue of
Pax, referring to the " stupendous task " that Abbot Aelred had
accomplished in " reviving the Benedictine life within the Church
of England after an almost complete break of close on 400 years ".
I felt that Mr. Riley might well describe Caldey as " the greatest
phenomenon in the Anglican communion ". As I looked down on
the choir that July evening it did not occur to me as even a remote
possibility that in less than three years I should be kneeling on the
black marble floor below me, and, in company with twenty-three
of my fellow-monks, forsaking the communion of Canterbury for
that of Rome.

The Office ended, and when the long Night Prayers were over, concluding with the singing of *Salve Mater misericordiæ,* I made my way downstairs. Passing through the choir, I glanced up at the lofty reredos, bright with colour and gilding, with the image of Our Lady Star of the Sea enthroned in a niche at the top. Suspended from the overhanging tester was a white veiled pyx. Then I made my way to the dormitory, where each cell was divided from the other by curtains. Before I undressed I stood at the open window and watched the lighthouse casting its rays across the ocean. From the flower-beds beneath my window rose up a mingled scent of white nicotine and purple night-stock. Far away was the murmur of the sea breaking on the sandy shore of Priory Bay. " *Domine bonum est nos hic esse* "—" Lord, it is good for us to be here "—would have been the words I might have used had I expressed my thoughts. But it was now after Compline and I remembered that in the Rule of St. Benedict it is ordered that strict silence must be kept. So I got into bed.

*   *   *

I have already given a detailed description of the daily life in the Community in my *Benedictines of Caldey* (Burns Oates, 1940), so I must content myself with mentioning a few incidents of a more personal character. After I had spent three months as a postulant I was sent home for a brief visit before starting my novitiate. My loyalty to the Church of England was none too certain before I went to Caldey, and during my postulancy my doubts and misgivings had increased. In such a state of mind, was it right for me to enter the novitiate, was the question I kept on putting to myself during that fortnight I was back again at Portland. I decided that I must write to Abbot Aelred and lay bare my soul. I tried to make him understand that I was almost convinced that sooner or later *something* would force me to submit to Rome, but at the moment I felt it would not be right for me to make this submission—just *why* I was held back I could hardly put into words. It was a great relief when I received his reply dated All Souls, 1910. "You write on the very subject that I was going to deal with in your retreat," the Abbot stated, " and I do not think I need say more now than you have anticipated a great deal of what I was going to say to you, and that by your own researches you have formed an opinion of the position which is almost exactly my own! . . . I surmise that now you are out in the world again you are discovering how much you have changed during your three months at Caldey. Indeed I am glad to think Our Lord may be calling you to this work, and I believe He is giving you a true vocation to the Religious Life that you may be ready to fight among the 'cowled legions' in the battle that is sure to come."

During that fortnight out in the world I revisited Quarr Abbey and also spent an hour or two at Parkminster, for I was already smitten with what my Abbot used to refer to as Carthusian microbes! Later on they were to become a source of much worry, both to myself and my religious superiors. Anyhow, the effect of that first visit to St. Hugh's Charterhouse one stormy November afternoon was more than enough to make me feel that if I were a *Roman* Catholic, I would certainly consider joining the Carthusians rather than the Benedictines. But as there were no Anglican Carthusians I must put up with Caldey as the next best thing.

I was not sorry to get back to the island after this brief sojourn on the mainland, for once one had landed on Caldey it was possible to ignore, if not completely to forget, the infinite contradictions of Anglicanism—its puzzling comprehensiveness and lack of unity in faith and practice. During that fortnight I had been obliged to worship in at least one church where everything that we most cherished at Caldey was regarded as simple Popery. I had assisted at a celebration of the Communion service at which the clergyman would have been horrified if anybody described it as a Mass. Yet why should our version of the Communion service at Caldey be a valid Mass and this one be no more than a Protestant Lord's Supper, since both were carried out by priests of the same religious body? The doctrine of Intention did not seem to explain my difficulties.

On November 20th I "went into retreat" and on the Vigil of St. Andrew I was clothed as a novice and given the religious name of Richard, in honour of the martyred last abbot of Glastonbury, Blessed Richard Whyting. I had asked to be called Bruno—due to the effect of my recent visit to the only English monastery of the Carthusian Order. But our community had just been presented with a collection of bones which Mr. Bligh Bond, the architect who was in charge of the excavations then going on at Glastonbury, firmly believed were those of Abbot Richard Whyting. Since Anglicans, unlike Catholics, are not forbidden to venerate relics lacking episcopal authentification, there was nothing to stop us from accepting Mr. Bligh Bond's *testamur*. Neither did it seem illogical—at least to the majority of the community—to celebrate the feast of Blessed Richard with every

CALDEY ABBEY AND VILLAGE.

possible solemnity. The relics were enshrined in the midst of the choir; the feretory surrounded by every spare candlestick stored away in the sacristy. We sang the proper Office and Mass appointed by Pope Leo XIII, and I remember how I could not help feeling that it seemed somewhat inconsistent to pay such honour to a martyr for Roman supremacy and yet to withhold our obedience to the same spiritual authority for which he had laid down his life. How many of the brethren shared my misgivings I do not know, for the Roman Question was a forbidden subject of conversation at our brief recreations.

The Rev. Aidan Angle, to-day a Canadian Army chaplain, but at one time a member of the Caldey Community, has kindly sent me some recollections of life in that Anglican novitiate over thirty years ago. They refer to many little details which I had almost forgotten. He is quite correct in stating that all our training as novices was strict. Those who look back on the discipline and training received as Anglican novices at Caldey will count them as great blessings. Our instruction was thorough; especially the exegesis of the psalms and of the rest of the Bible. We were well grounded in Rubrics—I recollect how surprised Dom John Chapman was in after years when he discovered our easy familiarity in such complication as the Scripture occurring lessons in the Breviary. As to the Second Nocturns we early acquired a fine discrimination between fact and legend; and with regard to our pronunciation of Latin we were trained towards ideal " lingua Toscana in bocca Romana", although I fear that some of us found it hard to arrive at this high standard. In fact when hearing the stately Latin tongue voiced by Italian priests I have felt that had we ventured to so murder it in Rome as we did at Caldey we should have been worthy to be laid under interdict!

Not a few of the brethren were well advanced in the ways of mental prayer and even of contemplation. From the very first days of our postulancy we were taught the paramount importance of prayer. Anyone who reads the Abbot's Letters in Pax and the pamphlet The Benedictines of Caldey will realise this at once. And we were taught that the Divine Office was our supreme work and our supreme prayer—" nihil operi Dei praeponatur " to quote the words of St. Benedict's Rule. We were expected, moreover, to keep the quiet hour of prayer every evening as sacrosanct. Accordingly the hour between Vespers and Supper found us all in Chapel; and to absent oneself and to do other work of any sort, however important, during this time—except in extreme necessity—was regarded as a serious defection, in fact a fault to be confessed at Chapter.

Nearly all our spiritual books were Catholic ones, the chief authors we studied in the spiritual life being St. Theresa, Blosius, Père Grou, and Fr. Augustine Baker, also to a lesser degree, Mother Julian of Norwich, Père Caussade, Richard Rolle, and *The Cloud of Unknowing*.

The unique position of the community in the Church of England, about which so much used to be written, concerned us novices very little. In a very vague sort of way we probably felt ourselves to be among the privileged restorers of the waste places of monasticism, and that the poor old Church of England needed all the help she could get from the many religious communities flourishing in her bosom. But that was all. There was a vague sense of loyalty to the Church of our Baptism—we did not want to let her down. We were far more concerned with the immediate jobs to be done—to get our habits washed whiter, our floor scrubbed cleaner than that of any other novice, and to use our spare time to the best advantage —things like these left little or no time for thoughts about the " dry bones living ", or the " desert blossoming as the rose "—not even about the dew on Mount Hermon. Incidentally, the clumsiest of us became proficient in darning and repairing, and we were soon well up in all the best tricks for making a button stay put.

One of the little things in novitiate life which nevertheless was always a sense of pleasure and mild excitement was the weekly publication of the *Tabula,* as it was called: the list of officials for the week—Hebdomadary, Cantors, Reader in the refectory, and so on. There was great rejoicing if a novice saw his name down as reader for the coming week. Apart from such a low motive as showing off in reading aloud—this meant that we could get out of chapel immediately after Sext instead of waiting for the end of the three or four minutes' silence before the Midday Angelus. Those three or four minutes could seem a mighty long time especially to a hungry young man, whose thoughts, instead of being devoted to an examination of conscience, were much more concerned with speculations on what there might be for dinner. The reader's privilege, however, was but a " *frustulum* "—literally a crust of bread and a drink of water, but in practice a bowl of soup, and to a hungry young novice who had spent a long morning, much of it in hard manual work, this always tasted extremely good.

Talking in the refectory was only allowed on Christmas Day. For
the rest of the year, both at dinner and supper, we ate our food while
listening to biographies and books of travel at midday. In the evening
the reading was more ecclesiastical in matter. On reopening such a
book as Scott's *Voyage of the Discovery* after more than a quarter of
a century, one recalls that old refectory at Caldey, with the scents from
the garden coming in through the open windows, mingling with the
faint acrid smell, too, of soft soap and drying wood-work; for the
refectory tables and our bread platters were of plain wood, scrubbed
diligently and often. We covered a vast amount of literature dealing
with ecclesiastical history in the 16th century, a fact which has some
bearing on the enlightenment of our minds concerning the genesis
of the Church of England. How many lives of saints, written by
Catholic writers, were read in that old refectory at Caldey it would
be hard to count. Anyhow in the course of the year we imbibed solid
and interesting literary matter to our inestimable advantage. On
Sundays selected passages, marked with a blue pencil, were read from
The Church Times.

There was an exact code of ceremonial in the refectory, which often
proved a sore trial to a new novice. One had to forestall the needs
of one's neighbour at table should he require bread, salt, pepper or
water. The two-handled mug, supplied to us by an Austrian firm
in London, had to be raised to the lips with both hands. The utmost
quiet had to be observed, especially in unwrapping the wooden spoon
and fork, which with the knife were carefully folded up in the napkin
and kept on the table when not in use. A corner of this napkin had
to be tucked in over the front of the hood and inside the collars of
the tunic; the rest of it spread cornerwise, as a cloth, over the table.
We ate out of aluminium tins until 1914 when to us older monks
it seemed a sad retrogression in primitive observance when china
plates were adopted. Butter, measured out in a wooden mould, was
served to each one on little white china platters—a solitary touch of
daintiness. Any of it left over from supper we might keep till
pittance next morning, putting it for safe keeping under the inverted
mug on the folded napkin.

Yes! The ritual which embraced every part of our daily lives
was complicated, until one got used to it. Never to cross the knees.
Always, when seated, the hands under the scapular or in the sleeves
of the cowl, and when making a profound inclination, as during the
Pater Noster, to cross the arms, touching the knees with the hands;

and when wearing a novice's black cloak, hands always to be wrapped in the folds, even when holding a book. Hoods up when walking from one part of the monastery to another; and in the cloister and passages, juniors to walk close to the wall. When dressing, to step into the tunic, not to throw it over the head. When standing to drink or eat, as at pittance or tea, the front of the scapular to be thrown over the left and not the right shoulder. And the hood never to be drawn right forward over the head so as to cover the face, but its edges to come forward over the ears, and a dexterous tuck made, with one quick movement of the hand, in the peak. All these little details had to be acquired by degrees, and some novices found it a laborious business.

Before speaking, permission had to be asked from another by the phrase " Benedicite ", to which the reply, as granting the permission, was likewise " Benedicite ". The monastic necessity of Silence—it still comes natural to write it with a capital letter—was strictly insisted on, and we all realised that the tone of the Community rose or fell according to the degree to which this practice was observed. For some years before the conversion, Silence Books, as we called them, were in general use—little pocket books with shiny black covers, in which we wrote down any necessary messages to another Brother. A pity that these were not handed back when full, and preserved in monastic archives, for amid much that was of only momentary interest, a great deal was written which would have served as valuable material for reconstructing a fresh and vigorous picture of our daily life. Sometimes they came in useful for bits of gossip as well as strictly necessary messages. Previous to their introduction, there had been an elaborate sign system, based on the code of signals in use at Citeaux in St. Bernard's time, and still employed in Cistercian monasteries. It was wonderful how easy it was to break the spirit, if not the letter, of the rule of silence by this deaf and dumb language.

There was another notebook—much more important—the Chapter of Faults book. No gossiping here. We none of us looked forward to the weekly Chapter of Faults, held after Prime. There was little chance for a novice to get away with anything, for we knew pretty well everything that there was to be known about each other, and what every other novice was doing and was not doing at a given moment.

Although talking about food was one of the things which always had to be mentioned at the Chapter of Faults if one had been guilty of it, a few words more had better be said about our meals, which were always of a strictly vegetarian, or rather a non flesh-meat nature. A good and plentiful, well-cooked diet was provided and the general health of the community was far better in those days than when a modified flesh diet was introduced after 1913 in deference to the Catholic monks from Mardesous who were placed in charge of the community after the Conversion. All of us took our turn to work in the kitchen and scullery, either in the preparation of the vegetables or in washing up after meals.

We were encouraged to keep in close touch with our families, and weekly letters to friends or relatives were part of the novitiate routine. In theory our letters were given and received open. In practice, of course, our confidence was respected. What interesting pictures of Anglican monastic life would be recalled if some of those letters written about thirty years ago or more could be printed—pictures of an annual expedition along the coast of Pembrokeshire to Manorbier Castle in the steamer *Firefly*—picnics on Saturday afternoons or on great feasts in one or other of the bays—Sandtop, Drinkim or Bullums, where we would catch prawns, swim, collect firewood, light a fire and make tea.

The Sunday afternoon walks, followed by a general recreation at which all the community met together—novices and professed monks, and when we had the privilege of conversing with " seculars " staying on the island. The rock-climbing expeditions on the cliffs—dangerous but thrilling—in habits (usually tucked up into our belts). The sailing or rowing in our own boats, or fishing with mackerel lines, varied by an occasional oyster dredging in the *Firefly* along the south west coast of the island. Has the present Duke of Argyll forgotten how he helped us with the excavations on High Cliff in 1911, where we found nothing but old bones, but no buried treasure from Glastonbury as we had hoped?

Occasionally the weekly Chapter of Faults had its comical side, for it was the custom to hold up anything which might have been damaged by the culprit—the object being brought into the Chapter House before Prime, or hidden away just outside in a passage. Those of us who were present on a certain morning in 1911 will never forget how a certain novice, who always had to accuse himself of innumerable minor breaches of rule, drew out from his sleeve and displayed aloft, so that all could see, the handle and part of the rest of a lowly but useful and familiar article of bedroom furniture.

We were a community of non-smokers, but taking snuff was allowed as a compensation, and indulged in by many monks.

One could go on *ad infinitum* recalling those far-off days, which as one looks back seem almost as remote and unreal in some ways as the days of the stage coach or sailing ships. For those who lived them they are imperishable years, and their memories are among the things that grow not old.

* * *

As I look back over that twelve months' novitiate, so vividly described by Fr. Angle, I have happy recollections, in spite of periodical bad bouts of Roman Fever. Yet it was not altogether an easy time. I often got into trouble for my forgetfulness and carelessness in work, not to mention an incurable weakness for interfering in the private affairs of my fellow novices. I was too prone to give them what may or may not have been excellent advice in matters spiritual and intellectual, ignoring the fact that it is the business of the novice master to look after the souls of his flock and not the self-imposed task of one of themselves. I tried hard to play the organ, but without success, having no ear for improvising accompaniments for Plain Chant or transposing keys without warning. One morning, while seated at the organ during Prime, trying to pitch the psalm tones to suit the voices—not at their best at an early hour and before breakfast—I was making such a horrible noise that the Abbot could not endure the cacophony any longer. He darted out of his stall, ran up the stairs, and in a voice that must have been heard from the choir stalls below, ordered me to " stop making that infernal din!" I obeyed instantly and jumped off the organ stool. That was my last attempt to accompany plainsong. Peace and harmony were restored, and henceforth the organist was Dom Wilfrid Upson—the present Abbot of Prinknash.

The year 1911 was a busy time at Caldey, for building was going on without ceasing, the much needed additions to the original cottage-monastery, now so overcrowded, having been started. The plans for the so-called Gate House were abandoned and there appeared to be no immediate possibility of funds being raised to begin the great abbey that it was hoped to erect on the east side of the island overlooking Paul Jones Bay. The migration of the community of Benedictine nuns from West Malling, Kent, to Milford Haven, which took place about Easter, was a frequent subject of conversation at recreation. One bright sunny morning in April the nuns—who were still out of enclosure—came over from their new home and spent the day on Caldey. Later on, in company with other members of the community, I paid many visits to St. Bride's Abbey. Abbess Scholastica Ewart had been in close touch with Abbot Aelred from the beginning of his monastic career, and she became a loyal and devoted friend to me—or would it not be more true to describe her as a mother? Again and again she invited me to stay at Milford and latterly at Talacre, North Wales, whither she moved her nuns in 1920.

When I heard of her death in 1927, after many years of pain and suffering, there was a sense of loneliness, for there would be nobody who would quite replace her. To quote from an article written after her death: " She never really grew old, though she was seventy-five when she died. . . . She had the power of throwing herself into the interests of others as if there was nobody else in the world. She was essentially a mother and there was an atmosphere of home wherever she was, felt instinctively by all who came into contact with her. She was very quick and full of humour (how her eyes would twinkle when she told you an amusing story!). She was a most delightful companion." Dame Mary Scholastica Ewart seemed to sum up in herself all the requisite qualities of the ideal Benedictine abbess—a great lady, fully conscious of her status and position, yet withal intensely human and intensely spiritual.

In August, 1911, I was sent to Llanthony in the Black Mountains with the rest of the novitiate, where we spent a three-weeks' holiday in the monastery with which I had first become acquainted when I read *The Life of Father Ignatius*—my introduction to Anglican monasticism. It was also my first experience of mountain scenery, and I lost my heart to the place and its romantic surroundings. Yet there was something tragic about Llanthony: one never forgot that this grandiose scheme to revive Benedictine life in the Church of England had been a complete failure. The never completed abbey-church, with its towering reredos, was a reminder of dreams never realised. Ghosts of the many who had come and gone in the past fifty years seemed to haunt the dark, damp cloisters with their narrow lancet windows. The living rooms evoked memories of the seventies of the last century, being overcrowded with mid-Victorian furniture, ornaments, pictures, and what-nots—more in keeping with a theatrical lodging-house than a monastery. Altogether the whole thing was a perfect period piece of a certain phase of the Gothic Revival, over-laden with the by-products of already decadent Anglican ritualism. Fr. Ignatius wanted to establish a double-monastery—on the lines of the original Bridgettine foundations, and two old Sisters, the last survivors of the female branch of his double-monastery, were still living in the adjoining corrugated iron convent when we visited Llanthony that summer. They used to assist at Office and Mass in a tribune, practically invisible behind spiked wooden grilles. They crept down a narrow stair to make their Communions, and one got a glimpse of bright scarlet veils which they donned for the occasion. Otherwise we never saw the two old women. The Baroness de Bertouch had painted an almost unbelievable picture of this fan-tastic monastery in her *Life of Father Ignatius,* but the reality was even more incredible than the picture. I think it was largely due to the effect on me of this visit to Llanthony that I was finally con-vinced of the impossibility of trying to revive Benedictine monasti-cism in the Church of England. I could visualise Caldey develop-ing into something equally " *sui-generis* " and peculiar as time went on. But there was this vital distinction—I was certain that my own Abbot was fast moving on the road to Rome, maybe nearer than he realised, and so I had confidence in what might lie ahead of us. My fear was the danger of drifting into a similar position of pitiful isolation and of losing complete touch with any external authority, which had been the fate of Llanthony.

I made my simple profession on December 18th, 1911. I had managed to get through the novitiate without any great difficulty. My health seemed able to stand the life, a proof of which being that I was never absent from the Night Office as a novice. I did my regular share of hard manual work in the gardens, and soon after my profession I was appointed librarian—a most congenial occupation. The only illness from which I had suffered was a spiritual one— Roman Fever, resulting in periodical crises when I felt I could not remain in the Church of England. Heart to heart talks with my Abbot generally managed to soothe my brain storms—at least tem-porarily. His line of argument was that sooner or later the whole community would be faced with the decision of going over to Rome. He said that he would not put anything in my way if I was really convinced that it was my duty to leave Caldey and would make all arrangements to suit me. But was I really *quite* sure that the moment had come? Could I not hold on a little longer and take this highly probable step as one of the community of which I was now a professed member?

So I would pull myself together and make a fresh start, trying not to dwell on the intellectual and spiritual problems of the nature and organisation of the Catholic Church, but to throw myself into the everyday life of the community. The calm would not last long, and in a week or two my mind would be in a worse tangle than ever. As an antidote to Roman Fever, I started working on an article which was published in *Pax,* under the title of "*Negotiations for Reunion Between England and Rome since the Separation in the Sixteenth Century*". I tried to prove, for my own satisfaction, that there had always been a consciousness in the minds of many devout Anglicans of a supreme desire for reunion with the Holy See, without the necessity of denying that their own communion is part of the visible Catholic Church with valid orders and sacraments. What I tried to convince myself was that Canterbury and York were still two provinces of the Western Church, even if in a state of schism, the latter being material and not formal. Nearly thirty years later almost precisely the same arguments as I had used in this article were brought up again in a pamphlet entitled "*Anglican Papalists*", written by the Rev. Donald Hole for the Society for Promoting Catholic Reunion. We both maintained that the Church of England must not be regarded as a self-governing and independent Church, but merely as two provinces which, through no fault of their own, found themselves in a state of material schism during the sixteenth century. Like Mr. Hole, I deplored the condition of the Church of England, indicating that it was our duty to try to remedy its isolation by striving after corporate reunion. As the schism was corporate, so must the return to unity also be corporate. The only thing that could justify individual secession from the severed limb would be continued membership with actual heresy. My arguments, it seems to me, were plausible and specious, and I doubt very much if I really believed in them at the time. Rather do I think they were merely a sort of smoke screen put up to confuse the outline of the city set upon the seven hills which had grown too near for comfort. Still, I took no end of trouble to collect the historical data, and I managed to get hold of some curious and interesting facts.

By the beginning of Lent in 1912 our position in the Church of

England had become so uncertain that the Abbot announced that it was to be made a matter of individual prayer and study. So I arranged some shelves in the library with controversial books—both Catholic and Anglican. Perhaps the most popular was Fr. Maturin's *The Price of Unity,* which produced different effects on the readers. Some felt that it broke down all their remaining prejudices against Rome, others put it aside feeling that the whole business was so complicated that they had better stay where they were! Neither did a series of lectures given to the community by Fr. Puller, Dr. Langford James and Br. Denys—Warden of our Guest House—really help to clear our minds, for each of them held entirely different conceptions of the nature of the Papacy. Nevertheless, when Lent was over the community felt able to subscribe to a document drawn up by the Abbot, containing the assurance to friends, who were alarmed at the reports going around, that:

" after prolonged and careful consideration of the claim that the See of Rome makes upon the allegiance of all who would call themselves Catholics, we are convinced that severally, and as a community, we should be wrong to doubt our present position in the Church of England as true members of the Catholic Church of Christ. We believe the Church of England to have preserved, by the providence of God, the essentials of Catholic life; and we feel it to be the privilege of our Religious Vocation at Caldey to pray, to labour, and to suffer that the sin of the Schism between England and the Holy See may be forgiven and the separation ended."

This document, which was sent out to all benefactors and friends of the community, helped to pour oil on troubled waters, but I venture to think it was more like throwing dust in their eyes. Some of us were far from being " convinced that we should be wrong to doubt our present position in the Church of England as true members of the Catholic Church of Christ ", and I remember what misgivings I had when the moment came for me to add my signature to the paper. I cannot now recall how I cleared my conscience. For this is how one monk summed up our position : " Nominally we are Anglicans . . . a product of the Church of England, but in reality the community has been brought up on Roman Catholic food, if I may put it that way. Our Breviary, Missal and devotional books contain doctrines which are not compatible with the teaching of the

Church of England, e.g., the doctrine of Papal Supremacy. We have borrowed practically everything we have from the Roman Church, and now it may be that we shall have to look to Rome for that authority and recognition of our faith and practice which surely no Anglican bishop, true to his principles, can give us. And so we are face to face with the Papal claims; they are something which we cannot ignore and put aside."

The subsequent events which led up to our final submission to the Holy See have been related in detail in my *Benedictines of Caldey* (pp. 148-180), and also in the correspondence between Abbot Aelred and the Anglican bishops which was reprinted in pamphlet form. The whole thing began with a letter to Archbishop Davidson, dated December 13th, 1911, asking that official recognition of Abbot Aelred's ordination might be given so that his name could appear in *Crockford's Clerical Directory*. Technically our Abbot was a colonial clergyman and still needed specific licence to work in an English diocese; hence his request. We all felt that the time had come when some definite authority and guidance were an absolute necessity if we were to continue in the life we were leading. So this authority was sought, first from the Archbishop of Canterbury, and then, at His Grace's suggestion, from Dr. Gore, Bishop of Oxford. The latter sent two Anglican clergymen to Caldey to enquire into the faith, religious practices and worship of the community, and he found after careful investigation of their report that many of these were such that no Anglican prelate could sanction them. His decision was the providential means of opening our eyes at last to the full significance of our anomalous position.

To quote from the last letter in this Correspondence, a letter from Abbot Aelred to Bishop Gore, dated February 25th, 1913: "We had thought all along that our views were shared by many others, and could rightly be held in loyalty to the Catholic Church in England. But you have cleared up the matter, and have helped us to realise that we were in a false position, and could not honestly go on holding these views without at the same time being untrue to the teaching of the Church of England to whose authority, through you, we appealed. . . . Your remarks about accepting and rejecting the same Authority at different points were carefully considered by us, and helped largely to bring us to the conclusion that with our clear ideas of what we believe, we must take our stand upon the strictly Papal basis of Authority."

Looking back after thirty years, I wonder how on earth any of us could have been so blind as not to see that no Anglican bishop could have given even a tacit approval to the almost literal imitation of a particular form of *Roman* Catholic Benedictine life which existed at Caldey. For we were not content with following the Rule of St. Benedict, with its austere and dignified fifth century Roman spirituality and simple liturgical worship; on the contrary, we adopted practically every medieval and post-Tridentine accretion which subsequent centuries had engrafted onto primitive Benedictine life. We were trying to be twentieth-century Roman Catholic Benedictines yet at the same time demanding that we should be recognised by the bishops of the Church of England. I don't suppose that St. Benedict himself would have felt that he was being disloyal to the Catholic Faith if the Local Ordinary had ordered him to " eliminate the doctrine of the Immaculate Conception of the Blessed Virgin from the Breviary and Missal "—which Bishop Gore insisted on before he could become our Episcopal visitor. I venture to think that St. Benedict would not have felt it was a matter of life and death to celebrate the feast of the Corporal Assumption of Our Lady—her " Falling asleep " would have sufficed! I take it that he would have been rather surprised if his monks had wanted him to introduce Exposition of the Blessed Sacrament and the service known as Benediction. I doubt if he would have felt it of vital importance to make a stand for the Exposition of Relics and Benediction given with them. Most of the ceremonial to which we attached such significance would have been unfamiliar to him.

The monks at Subiaco and Monte Cassino did not celebrate the feast of Corpus Christi; they did not erect May altars in their oratories, and they might have found it difficult to recognise their simple form of Mass (only celebrated on Sundays and feast days) in the ceremonial details of modern *Missale Monasticum* which we followed at Caldey. It would have taken them some time to get accustomed to the manner in which we celebrated the Work of God; they would have been mystified at the vast number of saints whose festivals upset the regular recitation of the psalter, and a great many other things besides. Had we been content to revive primitive Benedictine monasticism and to stick to the letter of the Rule instead of interpreting it in the spirit of modern Roman Catholic monastic life, neither the Archbishop of Canterbury nor the Bishop of Oxford would have found any difficulty in giving full approval to the Community. But this is just what we were not prepared to do. We called ourselves " The Anglican Congregation of the Primitive Observance of the Holy Rule of St. Benedict ", but in so many ways we were very far removed from primitive; the greater part of the observances, ceremonial and devotional practices having been taken over *en bloc* from the Roman Catholic Benedictines at Buckfast, with whom our Founder used to stay before he embarked on his career as a Church of England monk. At the same time we were trying to revive the manner of life of the 12th century reformer of Benedictine monasticism—St. Bernard of Tiron—and had adopted him as our patron.   In short, we were making the mistake of attempting too many things at once which could not be combined—protesting that we were loyal members of the Church of England, yet at the same time modelling our manner of life as closely as possible on that of contemporary Roman Catholic monks.

On the afternoon of February 19th, twenty-seven of us signed a letter to Bishop Gore, stating that we were sure that " our Life as a Contemplative Community under the Benedictine Rule would be quite impossible " if we acceded to his demands, concluding with the words: " Your requirements are so decisive that we are forced to act upon what we believe to be God's Will for us ", *i.e.*, we had finally decided to make our submission to the Holy See. This was really the end. To cut a long story short, the Abbot then got in touch with the Bishop of Menevia and Dom Bede Camm, begging them to come to our help. A few days later the latter arrived at Caldey, and on the morning of February 28th, said the first Catholic Mass which had been celebrated on the island since the Reformation. Things began to move rapidly: first came the Abbot of Maredsous from Belgium, followed by the Abbots of Downside and Caermaria in company with the Bishop of Menevia, in whose diocese Caldey is situated. On the feast of St. Aelred, March 5th, twenty-two monks were reconciled to the Catholic and Roman Church, including myself. Two days afterwards thirty-four nuns at St. Bride's Abbey, Milford Haven, made their corporate submission to the same authority.

*   *   *

A rather faded photograph of a group of about two dozen monks with an impressive-looking bishop seated in their midst, is a vivid reminder of an event in my life which affected my subsequent career. Some of the monks are dressed in black and white habits; the others in black or white. Two of them have pectoral crosses, indicating that they are abbots. About half the men have shaven heads and wide tonsures. The group is posed in front of a doorway, above which is a statue of the Good Shepherd. It was taken on March 5th, 1913, and shows the Caldey community just after their reception into the Catholic Church. The tall prelate is Mgr. Mostyn, Bishop of Menevia. On his right is Dom Aelred Carlyle, and in the same row are the Abbots of Downside and Maredsous. You will find me right in the foreground!

So I came home at last—I had been waiting outside the gates so long, and how often had I wondered when I should find myself safe within! My own mind had been made up long before this correspondence with the Anglican bishops started and brought matters to a head. Just why I never acted upon those convictions before the community arrived at the point which I had reached as far back as two years before our corporate reception into the Catholic Church, I cannot be certain. I am rather inclined to think it was largely due to my affection for my brethren; that I was held back by sentiment rather than by logical reasons. In recent years more than one Anglican friend has told me that I could never have been a convinced member of the Church of England. I believe they are right. I have frequently been asked why I became a Catholic. I think it is true to say that almost as soon as I began to take any interest in religious matters about the age of sixteen I came to the conclusion that there was such an absence of authority and such a contradiction of faith and practice in the Church of England that it could not be regarded as *the* Catholic Church, and that it was highly improbable that it was even part of it. It struck me that *if* there existed a visible Catholic Church on earth, then the only body of Christians which commanded my respect was that world-wide body in communion with the Holy See. I felt—and still feel—that a good case can be made out for Protestantism, but once I had accepted the authority of the Catholic and Roman Church in matters of Faith and Morals, it was just as important to submit to this same authority in matters of discipline. This sums up as briefly as I can do so the reasons why I became a Catholic thirty years ago. For similar reasons I am still a member of the Catholic and Roman Church to-day.

CHAPTER IV

THE CATHOLIC COMMUNITY OF CALDEY

In front of me as I write this chapter are two photographs. One of them depicts a crowd of clerics in the midst of which is a row of vested clergy, including four prelates. They are wearing mitres, two of them holding croziers. There is an elderly abbot and three priests, vested in copes or dalmatics. The background is that same doorway already mentioned. This photograph is a record of the Blessing of Dom Aelred Carlyle as Abbot of Caldey on St. Luke's Day, October 18th, 1914. The other photograph, showing a group of white habited monks, kneeling before an altar in the presence of a seated abbot, is a souvenir of the Catholic profession ceremony of the convert monks which took place a day later. In the choir stalls of the church are a few monks, wearing black cowls or cassocks. One of these happens to be myself, for as I will explain further on, reasons of health prevented me from making my Simple Vows as a Catholic Benedictine monk on that October morning thirty-five years ago. So, I was merely a spectator.

" As new-born babes, desiring the sincere milk of the word: living stones to be built up a spiritual house ", these words of St. Peter might well form the text of this chapter if it were a sermon. They convey a very true idea of the outlook of the Caldey Benedictines after they had made their submission to the authority of Rome. A new phase in their life had begun. To understand the next few pages, it must not be forgotten that, in the spiritual state, the monks of Caldey were still children. As a Catholic community we were in the nursery of God's Church, so to say. We had not begun to put away childish things: we still spoke as children and understood as children. What is more, our future was uncertain, and we could only see through a glass darkly.

Within a month or so of the events recorded in the last chapter Abbot Aelred went to the abbey of Maredsous in Belgium for his year's canonical novitiate. The rest of the community remained on Caldey. Dom John Chapman, afterwards Abbot of Downside, became our Superior, while Dom Bede Camm acted as novice master. Very little changes were made in our outward observances. A visitor who had been familiar with our life before the submission of the community to the Holy See would have found it difficult to realise that any change had taken place in our ecclesiastical allegiance. Strictly speaking, we had no right to go on wearing the Benedictine habit. But the difficulty was overcome by Abbot Columba Marmion making us Oblates of Maredsous. We enjoyed this status for several months until we were allowed to begin our canonical novitiate with permission from Rome.

Had I myself fully realised that I was still only a child in the Catholic Church I rather doubt if the following incident would have occurred. Even before I joined the Anglican Benedictines of Caldey in 1910, I had been drawn to the solitary life as opposed to the ceno-bitic form of monasticism. I have already related how I visited St. Hugh's Charterhouse, and how it attracted me. No sooner had we come to our moorings in the Catholic and Roman Church than my Carthusian microbes became virulent. In less than three weeks after the water of conditional Baptism was dry on our foreheads, I wrote to him, for he had already left the island, that I could not begin my Catholic novitiate with the Benedictines until I had made sure of my Carthusian vocation. I must have forgotten what St. Benedict has to say about anchorites and hermits, i.e., " monks who, not in the first fervour of religious life, but after long probation in the monastery, have learned by the help and experience of many to fight against the devil, and going forth well armed from the ranks of their brethren to the single combat of the desert, are able without the support of others, to fight by the strength of their own arm, God helping them, against the vices of the flesh and their evil thoughts ". On the contrary, I felt it would be much easier—for me at least—to " go out into the desert " and that I did not want others fighting by my side!

" Of course, I surmised that directly the ' Roman Question ' was settled," my ex-Abbot replied, " you would begin on the ' Carthusian Problem '. Fortunately, this last one may be easier of solution than the first. I feel strongly that your first steps in the Catholic Faith should be made with your own brethren, *where you are*. Apart from other considerations, it would surely seem a little unbecoming for one so recently converted to wish to offer himself at once to so specialised a form of Catholic and religious life; and if I mistake not, the Prior of Parkminster, who is a cautious and wise priest, will him-self suggest a period of waiting as a preliminary test. Get on with

F

your studies, live your life at Caldey as strongly and truly as you can. Then when the question of your Benedictine profession comes up, and you feel of the same mind about the Carthusian life, I dare say it could be arranged for a community at Parkminster to give you a good preliminary trial."

This sound and practical advice failed to convince me. Carthusian Microbes had "got" me even more acutely than Roman Fever. With an ignorance and obstinacy quite characteristic of many another recent convert from Anglo-Catholicism I stuck to my own point of view. I refused to be clothed as a Benedictine novice until I had tried the Carthusian life. In despair, my Superior, Dom John Chapman, put the case before the Prior of Parkminster. The latter replied that he was willing to give me a month's trial. So I left Caldey and arrived at Partridge Green Station on the Vigil of St. John the Baptist, June 23rd, 1913. I well remember walking from the station to the Charterhouse on that hot summer afternoon. Recalling that the following day was a great feast with the Carthusians I was determined to be there in time for first Vespers. An hour or so later I was sitting in the tribune, looking down on the choir. The white habited monks entered one by one. The four great candles were lit on the sanctuary steps in honour of the feast. Then that slow, drawn-out *Deus in adjutorium* so different from the quick Benedictine manner of intoning—and the curious unaccompanied chanting of the psalms . . . it all seemed to belong to yet another world.

One of the thirty-six four-roomed little houses was allotted to me, and here I spent four happy and peaceful weeks. The life did not seem difficult. It was no great strain getting up in the middle of the night for the long offices of Matins and Lauds. I did not find the fasting until the middle of the morning—with no breakfast—very exhausting, though I admit I was always ready to do full justice to the more than ample meal left at my door by one of the lay brothers. The only feature of the life which I found rather hard was the sense of never having a moment's rest. The Carthusian novice has to observe a carefully mapped out time-table, one duty following on the other without any leisure—domestic duties, such as sweeping out the little house, gardening, etc., the Little Office of Our Lady and the Office for the Dead to be recited; spiritual reading, meditation, journeys to and from the church for Mattins, High Mass and Vespers, never sure just when the French novice master would pop in to see how one was getting on and not wasting time. True, one was living alone in a nice little house with its own garden, but one was being watched all the time—watched in a manner that was utterly different from anything I had been accustomed to in Benedictine life. It gave me the feeling that the novice master always suspected I would be up to mischief once he was out of the way, and so he never visited me at stated times, his appearances being always without warning.

Towards the end of those four weeks I began to realise that my Benedictine superiors might be right after all. It was not that I was unhappy or that the life proved to be beyond my capacity, merely that it dawned on me that it was a highly specialised form of spirituality as well as of monasticism. It struck me that I knew little or nothing about ordinary Catholic life and that it would be wrong for me to embark on the abnormal without an insight into the normal; in other words, I realised that one does not suddenly acquire a Catholic outlook merely by the formal act of being received into the Church. It was during those four weeks at Parkminster that I awoke to the fact that in renouncing communion with Canterbury for that of Rome, I had made a wider gap with the past than I had realised.

So, reluctantly, I left that great monastery whose spire dominates the Sussex Weald and returned to South Wales. Passing through London I listened to Mgr. Benson preaching at the Carmelite Church, Kensington, on the Feast of Our Lady of Mount Carmel. A week later I began my Catholic Benedictine novitiate. I still hoped that I should be able to resume the Carthusian life later on, and I confess that from now onwards Caldey ceased to appeal to me as in the past. I became restless—the first symptoms of that acute neurasthenia which no doctors—I forget how many specialists were consulted—were able to cure. It lasted with brief respites for more than ten years, and eventually led to my being obliged to give up the religious life and adopt a lay career.

This second novitiate only lasted six months, at least so far as my residence in the monastery. By the end of January, 1914, I was in such a restless and unsettled state that Fr. John Chapman decided that it would be better to send me away for a complete change of environment. I spent two months at Llanthony in the queer surroundings of what had formerly been the nuns' quarters in Fr. Ignatius's double monastery. At that date an oblate brother of Caldey was living there as caretaker and looking after the property. I rather liked this more or less solitary existence in the heart of the Black Mountains. There were opportunities for long walks. The

isolation from the outer world became even more complete when
we were snow-bound for about a week. I had my first experience of
life in a Catholic Benedictine community when I went off to spend
Holy Week at Belmont Abbey, near Hereford. The placid calm of
the black-habited monastery struck me as so different from Caldey.
Then I went on to Stanbrook Abbey for Easter, where for the first
time I enjoyed the hospitality of the Lady Abbess and listened to the
perfect Plaint Chant of the fifty or more nuns of that venerable
community founded over three centuries ago. Dom Gregory Ould,
a monk of Fort Augustus, was resident chaplain at that time, had a
monk of Quarr Abbey staying with him. Thus I met Père Bouvet,
later on Prior of Quarr, whose kindness to me in after years can
never be repaid. We used to go for walks together in that lovely
Worcestershire countryside; every garden gay with apple blossom
and daffodils in bloom. I was not yet able to re-face life at Caldey,
so the next few weeks were spent at St. Bride's Abbey, Milford
Haven, in company with the chaplain, Dom Paulinus Gorwood, an
artist-monk of Fort Augustus. In his youth he had been a pupil of
the famous art school at Beuron Abbey, and still retained a great
veneration for his master, Dom Desiderius Linz. He tried hard to
convert me to the Beuron Canons of art, based on those of ancient
Egypt. But I confess they struck me as much too rigid, and not
likely to help me to sketch boats and barges, such as tempted me
when moored in the creeks of Milford Haven. An even more drastic
change of environment was now recommended by the doctor: a
complete return to lay life for a time, resulting in my spending a
month or two with various relatives and with my own family, then
residing in Chatham Dockyard, of which my father was Admiral
Superintendent. I was extremely miserable, and felt like a fish out
of water. My imagination became filled with the idea that it would
do me good to go off to France on a solitary walking tour in
Normandy, inspired, no doubt, by the recollections of a similar tour
some years before. I got no further than Dieppe. Within twenty-four
hours I was back in England, more at a loose end than ever. Not
knowing what to do or where to go, I eventually drifted back to St.
Bride's Abbey, and here I remained until the beginning of July, when
I was allowed to return to Caldey after an absence of seven months.
    On a stormy afternoon of the last week in July, 1914, the com-
munity, clad in sou'westers and oilskins, embarked in *Firefly* to meet
Dom Aelred Carlyle at Tenby on his return from his year spent at

Maredsous. As the little steamer came in sight of the island the quarry-men saluted their former abbot with a deafening cannonade. We were told that the inhabitants of Tenby and other places on the mainland thought that war had been declared. They were, in fact, to get that news five days later. The sea was too rough for the steamer to come alongside the slip, so we disembarked in small boats, while the population of the island awaited us on the shore. The village was decorated with flags and triumphal arches. A Papal standard flew from the church tower. The bells pealed loudly. While rumours of imminent war filled the newspapers, the island festival of St. Samson was kept as usual on August 3rd. The first movie show ever held on Caldey took place that evening. As rockets, fireworks and flames of a giant bonfire lit up the sky later on, Germany invaded Belgium. Before the embers of that bonfire had cooled Britain was at war.

Nobody seemed to think that the war could last very long. It was all very remote from us on Caldey Island and we were much more occupied with preparations for the installation of Dom Aelred Carlyle as Abbot. This function took place on August 10th and was performed by Mgr. Mostyn, Bishop of Menevia. It was in a maritime sense that we first felt the effect of the war. The crew of our ketch, *Cornish Lass,* were all Naval Reservists and had been called up, so that she was unable to sail with her usual cargo of stone from the quarries. Not until a fortnight later was another crew found. One morning early in September came a telegram from the Abbot of Saint André, near Bruges, asking if we could receive his novices and some of the clerics. They had fled to Ostend and managed to reach London. It was only just in time, for otherwise they would have fallen into the hands of the German troops who took possession of the monastery. We did not quite know how to find room for this influx of Belgian monks, but somehow or other we managed to provide accommodation. What an odd looking crowd they were when they arrived, dressed in the weirdest of clothes! Belgian refugees were still welcomed as heroes and the Mayor of Tenby gave these monks a great reception.

There were busy days on Caldey during the autumn of 1914. After a series of incredible adventures the Irish Abbot of Maredsous, Dom Columba Marmion, had managed to escape from Belgium disguised as a Dutch professor, although he gave us to understand that he resembled what he called a jockey. This provoked one of the

Community to make a drawing of the abbot in this guise. When shown the caricature he explained that he did not mean a jockey—in the English sense of the word—but a typical Irish car driver. Abbot Marmion had already become a devoted friend to our Community and we regarded him as our spiritual father. Never shall I forget that fat old monk giving us conferences during a Retreat. It was an experience of the Benedictine spirit at its best. Without a note of any kind and relying solely on his memory he would make long quotations from the Bible, the Rule of St. Benedict or the Fathers of the Church, passing with ease from intense seriousness to breezy humour—like the clouds and sunshine of his native Ireland. He would pass from some explanation of a profound mystery of the Catholic Faith to a searching analysis of human character, then break off into a story to illustrate some point. Only those who were ever privileged to listen to Abbot Marmion will understand what he was like. His books may be inspiring to read, but they lack the intense vitality of the man himself.

The Blessing of Dom Aelred Carlyle as Abbot took place with much external pomp on St. Luke's day, October 18th. In spite of the war the Abbots of Downside and Farnborough managed to be present, and the ceremony was performed by the Bishop of Menevia. It had never occurred to me that I should not be allowed to make my monastic profession with the other twelve monks who had come through their Catholic novitiate, and I was greatly distressed when, a few days before the event was due, Abbot Aelred informed me that owing to the uncertain state of my health my profession would have to be postponed. So, on the morning of October 19th, I sat in choir and watched my brethren make their simple vows, wondering how long it would be before I could do likewise.

My health did not improve, and after dragging on at Caldey for about nine months after the date when I was due to make my monastic profession, I was advised to get right away from the island for another complete change of environment. This was the result of having been psycho-analysed by a doctor staying on Caldey. He came to the conclusion that I was suffering from some curious repressions, connected with the sea, ships and sailors. I can still remember him sitting over me and noting down that all my associations of ideas appeared to be linked up with the colour "blue", including blue seas or blue uniforms! So early in September, 1915, I found myself as the guest of Fr. Hamilton Macdonald at Portsmouth, where I could not complain of any lack of maritime atmosphere, or a lack of blue uniforms. But there were Benedictine complexes as well as maritime repressions upsetting my mental balance at this time: it was not long before I felt I must get back into a monastery! The Abbot of Caldey did not see his way to receive me again. Eventually I tried Farnborough Abbey, and was told by Abbot Cabrol that I could come there on trial.

I arrived at Farnborough shortly before Christmas and remained there three months. Here I found an observance and spirit that were utterly different from that at Caldey; a Community of learned and elderly monks engaged in literary work, a quiet and uneventful existence; centring round the celebration of the Divine Office in that ornate Flamboyant French Gothic church, erected by the Empress Eugénie in the eighties of the last century, to house the tombs of the Emperor Napoleon III and the Prince Imperial.

Adjacent to the church the Empress built a small monastery, at first occupied by Premonstratensian Canons. In 1895 they returned to France, and the Empress invited the Benedictines of Solesmes to make a foundation in England. The community became independent in 1900 and three years later Dom Cabrol was elected its first abbot. Under the leadership of Abbot Cabrol, the community of Farnborough had acquired a world-wide reputation for scholarship. Among its members were the famous *savants,* Dom Ferotin, Dom Leclercq, Dom Gougaud, and Dom Wilmart.

Compared with our restless existence at Caldey, where the absence of any definite traditions or stabilised routine resulted in constant changes in the daily time-table, and where the very fact of being on an island added to the uncertainty of life, Farnborough, secluded in dark pine woods, was placid and restful during the winter of 1915 and the early spring of 1916 when the abbey was my temporary home. My health improved rapidly and I was fairly happy. In a letter to Fr. Macdonald I summed up my impressions of Christmas: " The ceremonies were carried out with great dignity. Everybody knew what we had to do. There was no hurry, no rush. The Master of Ceremonies was infinitely polite and gracious. Matins began at 10.30 p.m. and Lauds ended soon after 2 a.m. Then followed the first series of Masses. I served one of the monks and got back to bed somewhere about 3.30. Everything was so quiet and orderly that I did not feel tired, as has invariably been the case in former years at Caldey."

I went on to tell my friend that I had a " kind ' *père zélateur* '—Dom Dumaine—who takes charge of me and superintends my work. My day is chiefly given up to study. As there are no novices I have to make up for the lack of conferences by my own reading. Generally I get in about five-and-a-half hours reading every day. In the morning I take the Holy Rule and the Solesmes Constitutions for an hour, and then devote the rest of the time to Holy Scripture; the Psalms (for which I use a German commentary by Thalofer), St. John's Gospel (with the Greek and Latin texts), and a French commentary by Père Calmes. After dinner I have an hour's recreation. Once a week there is a long walk in the country. On other afternoons I stay in the grounds and sweep leaves from the paths in the woods. This forms my ' manual work ', which is not exactly strenuous. From 1.30 till 3.15 it is more or less ' free time '. I amuse myself by copying examples of lettering and take notes on monastic history.

" After Vespers I study the Liturgy for the following day, and go through the Office and Mass, making notes on every detail. It seems that the novices are encouraged to take notes (' *fiches* ' they are called) on every possible subject and thus build up a series of card indices for future use. This is the method of making scholars! In the ordinary course of events the *zélateur* would give a conference on the Liturgy every evening, but, as there are no novices, I have to lecture myself! Then, about 5.30 I go to the Church for mental prayer. At 6.30, twice a week, we have a music practice. On other evenings I study Plaint Chant and ceremonial. We have supper at 7 p.m., with half an hour's recreation after. Then follows Compline, and when I get back to my room I am soon in bed, where I sleep soundly till the bell wakes me at 4 a.m."

It was an abnormally lonely existence. Never in my life have I done so much intensive reading as during those three months at Farnborough, and I am grateful for what I learnt about methods of study and taking notes of books read. They were to prove useful in later life, when I started to write books myself and found myself working in public libraries. Nearly everybody else in the monastery appeared to be engaged on some kind of literary work, and some of the monks often went to London to gather data in the British Museum Library. The manual work was done by a few brown-habited Lay Brothers. Most of the Community were French, and French was usually spoken. I recall those weekly walks through the pine woods or across heather commons, or as a change, through the monotonous roads of

19th century villas, or the dull streets of South Farnborough and Aldershot. The wind-swept cliffs of Caldey Island, and the wide views over the Atlantic seemed very remote, and I sometimes longed to be back there. This over-populated north-east corner of Hampshire was a poor substitute.

I see from another letter of later date than the former that the question of my receiving the habit of a novice had come up, and that I had long talks with Père Steuart (who was to become Prior of Prinknash many years afterwards). He thought that, despite my natural attraction for monastic life, I lacked that interior stability to enable me to settle down in *any* monastery, and that what I needed was a more external and objective form of life, to bring me into closer personal touch with people, and not merely books and ideas. Then on March 15th I wrote to Fr. Macdonald: " Yesterday evening I was summoned to the abbatial presence and told, kindly but firmly, that I have not got a vocation to the Benedictine life at Farnborough. Abbot Cabrol said that he had thought over the matter most carefully; that, much as he wished to keep me, he felt that I lacked the right type of ' character ', and that this was not my proper ' milieu '; that I should eventually ' deteriorate' because I did not possess the stability and steadiness essential for Benedictine life. But he hinted that perhaps I might succeed with another and more active religious Order, or in the secular priesthood."

However, the *père zélateur*—Dom Dumaine—did not agree with his Abbot! He wanted me to apply for admission at the abbey of Ousterhout in Holland, so it was difficult to know just what to do. My letter continues: " I want to be a priest. But I have not got the money to pay for my education or training. So I must either join another Religious Order, or get a Bishop to accept me as a ' Church Student '. But the only form of ' pastoral work ' for which I feel any attraction is that of a naval chaplain, and I wonder if it would be possible for me to be trained and ordained specially for work among seafarers? Maybe, as Cardinal Bourne is the ecclesiastical superior of naval chaplains, I ought to approach him first, to find out if he would be willing to adopt me, and eventually send me to minister to those of the Household of Faith whose business it is to ' go down to the sea in ships, doing business in the great waters '. I am feeling rather learned about chaplains at present, having just completed several pages of notes and bibliographies from the point of view of Church History and Canon Law! Père Dumaine is now telling me that my vocation may lie with the Dominicans, but I don't feel drawn that way."

However, I did not approach either Cardinal Bourne or the Dominicans, nor did I write to Ousterhout: I suddenly made up my mind I
would appeal to Abbot Aelred to let me return to Caldey! Had he
refused, as he well might have done, I wonder what my future would
have been? I cannot tell. Anyhow, he replied that I could come
back, but on condition that I became a postulant and went into the
novitiate; in other words that I was to make a fresh start. So, after
an absence of about five months, I returned to the island. My impressions of this new beginning are thus summed up in a letter, dated
Easter, 1916. " After the placid tranquillity of Farnborough, the intensive rush of the Caldey novitiate is a discipline, possibly good for the
soul, but not exactly pleasant! From cleaning the cloisters, one is
bustled off to cutting up cauliflowers, or to a conference on the Contemplative Life. Or it may be a practice in ceremonial—the right way
to hold a censer or a candlestick in a procession. Just a rush all day
long at high speed. There are twelve of us in the novitiate. They are
such good and simple-minded young men and they fill me with
shame. I say to myself: ' How edifying you are! but!' but I know
quite well that I could never become like them. One of the novices
is a Cockney from Islington. His ' speech doth discover him ' as the
maid said to St. Peter! There is a little Jewish lad, and another
novice of mixed Irish parentage and Welsh upbringing. His pronunciation when reading in the refectory is a curious combination of
' mixed Celt '. The others are all very good and devout, and they
are a happy crowd."

Then I go on to write. " Caldey is a perfect picture now. We
had a long recreation yesterday afternoon, and laden with baskets
and boxes containing our tea, we novices clambered down a steep
path to the shore of Drinkim Bay, where we amused ourselves in
sundry ways until nearly 6 o'clock. The cliffs at this time of the
year are carpeted with bluebells and primroses, mingled with the
vivid green of an undergrowth of ferns and shrubs. Beneath the cliff
and jutting out into the sea are broken rocks of red sandstone—the
sea on that afternoon pure cobalt as opposed to the ultramarine of
the bluebells. I wish I could reproduce all this loveliness on paper
and send it to tired and weary friends, such as yourself, whose lot
is cast in less favoured spots; in dusty, dirty towns, such as
' Pompey '."

I tell this friend that " on these spring mornings I try to get dressed as soon as possible, so as to have a few minutes out of doors before going into church for Mattins. . . . The sea and, indeed, the whole island, are so beautiful at this hour of the morning."

I must have always been visualising pictures if not painting them, for on June 29th I write. "To-day we are keeping Peter and Paul with all the glory of scarlet and gold and pontifical ceremonies. But far more beautiful than these ecclesiastical functions are the sapphire blue sea, decked with diamonds; a fresh south-easterly breeze veiling the mainland coast and distant mountains with a soft haze. There are some brown-sailed Brixham smacks racing along, just to remind me that this is the feast of the Fisherman Apostle."

Just before this letter there was another, proving that I was still suffering from Sea Fever if not maritime complexes. "The great naval battle (Jutland) is naturally the centre of my thoughts at the moment. The story of the battle was read aloud in the refectory. It is sad to think of the loss of old friends such as *Warrior, Defence* and *Black Prince*. For how many times have I not watched these ships steaming out of Portland Harbour through the narrow opening of the breakwater? *Queen Mary* was a 'great lady' of a later generation, with whom I was not so familiar. I had, so to say, only bowed to her from a distance, and the same applies to *Invincible* and *Indefatigable*. But I number many friends in both these ships, and suppose they have gone down."

My return to Caldey lasted only ten weeks. Abbot Aelred and the majority of his monks became convinced that my vocation did not lie with Benedictines, although my nervous symptoms were far less acute than the previous year, and my general health surprisingly good. These two factors prevented any confusion of the main issue. But the immediate cause of the Abbot's decision to send me away once more was a letter to Fr. Macdonald which clearly proved my state of mind: "I have been back here now more than nine weeks, and still feel that it is really impossible for me to settle down permanently at Caldey. Not that I think there is anything wrong with it, but that there is a great deal wrong with me, much too much Richard Anson, and almost naught of Brother Richard, the novice, who is the person who is wanted! Consequently R. F. A. lives his own rather selfish life and *looks on* with approval, interest, and with a certain critical amusement at everybody and everything in the monastery, from his Abbot down to the last Postulant. It amounts to this: I feel I *cannot* become a member of a family. In my effort to do so, I turn sour and cross, and more conscious of my isolation, and always on my guard against being natural."

Quite obvious that I was a square peg in a round hole! But the queer thing was that I would take so many years before I would finally be convinced of this error, and that I would go on trying again and again to fit myself into that round hole! There must be a strong streak of obstinacy in my character! So I packed up my belongings once more, feeling convinced at the moment that this was to be a final parting from Caldey for, as I expressed in a letter: "It is over now, and I have finished with St. Benedict. It was terribly hard saying good-bye to Caldey, and as I missed the boat that morning, the agony was prolonged for another twenty-four hours. Still, the Community were most kind. To force myself to realise that I have done with monastic life, I have discarded the Benedictine Breviary for the Roman. It may sound trivial, but it means a lot."

*   *   *

Portsmouth was again my city of refuge. For the next four months I stayed with my maternal grandmother at 39 South Parade, Southsea, a few yards from the house where I was born. Here I occupied myself with drawing and painting ships and, as I have already related in *Harbour Head,* spent much time with Fr. Macdonald, the Catholic chaplain, and was often in and out of the dockyard. But even now I could not keep away from monasteries! I went over to the Isle of Wight and visited Quarr Abbey more than once, and I still dreamed dreams of becoming a naval chaplain. I also toyed with the idea of joining Fr. Benedict Williamson's foundation of Bridgettine monks, but discovered that the Community now consisted of nobody else but the Founder himself. Then, towards the middle of September, feeling very uncertain about my future, I acted on the advice given me by Fr. Williamson and made a Retreat with the Jesuits at Manresa House, Roehampton. The Spiritual Exercises of St. Ignatius churned me up inside and had precisely the opposite effect to what I expected: in short, I became completely convinced that I must appeal to the Abbot of Caldey to have me back again!

Incredible as it may seem, my long suffering Superior, who had more than sufficient excuse to close the doors against me for ever, replied that he would let me return. So once more I made that familiar journey to South Wales; this time for a period of eight years—more or less—for I did not remain on Caldey continuously. Very wisely it was decided that I should become an *Oblate Brother* of the Community. An Oblate is not a monk, strictly speaking. He lives under a modified rule of life. The word " oblate " signifies an oblation or offering; the gift which a man makes of himself to the Community. In these days, oblates—they were usually children in early times—are men who lack the health to follow the normal observance, but they can be useful in many ways. At Caldey, the oblates wore the same white habit as the rest of the Community. They sat in choir and were treated as definite members of the monastic family. But they were not bound by vows, and could retain their personal property. Such then was my status from the autumn of 1916 until I finally ceased to wear the monastic habit in the summer of 1924. In my own case I did pretty much what I liked, though supposed to keep a modified Rule! I was employed in various jobs including working in the kitchen, refectory and gardens. I was librarian for the whole of this last period. I wrote numerous articles and book reviews for *Pax*—but even more numerous letters to naval chaplains and naval ratings. Then, as I have already related in the pages of *Harbour Head,* I found myself in charge of the Apostleship of Prayer " Work for Catholic Bluejackets ", handed over to me by Miss Mary Scott-Murray. From July, 1917, my mind and most of my time were devoted to directing the remailing of reading matter to seafarers, likewise the editing of the annual *List of Catholic Naval Officers.* Indeed, it might be said that it was during those last years on Caldey that I gradually evolved the vague outlines of a society that would devote itself to the welfare of Catholic seafarers as a whole. Lastly, I never ceased to carry on my drawing and painting, and during those years there was a steady output of maritime water colours as well as of other subjects.

References to marine paintings occur in a letter dated October, 1916, where I mention " such wonderful—almost terrible seas all this past month. I have never seen such waves in my life. And the wind! It whistles, howls and screams through every door, window and cranny in the monastery. One would not be surprised to find ' fiddles ' on the refectory tables some morning, or to feel the church rolling and pitching at High Mass. The telegraph cable has been broken, so we are cut off entirely from the mainland until it is calm enough for a boat to cross from Tenby. However, I have got some valuable notes of wave formation, and have done one or two fairly successful water colours of rough seas."

A year later I find other references to drawings of a different character: " plans, sections and elevations of the vast abbey, which

Fr. Abbot intends to have made into lantern slides, wherewith to stagger and amaze the rich Catholics of New York, Baltimore and Boston, etc., when he lectures to them on Caldey during his forth-coming American tour.   The whole scheme can only be described as grandiose.   The church and monastery are designed in a free Romanesque style. The former is 340 ft. long, with a nave 35 ft. wide. The main cloisters are 200 ft. square, *i.e.,* 20 ft. longer than those at Salisbury, which are the largest in England ".   Then I go on to describe " a large, high-coloured aerial perspective, intended to rouse American millionaires to contribute generously towards the erection of this monster abbey between the pine woods and Paul Jones Bay ". Abbot Aelred could hardly have chosen a worse moment for his begging tour of the United States, for Americans were mainly preoccupied with the war, and he did not find it so easy to interest them in the financial needs of a small Community of convert Bene-dictine monks on the other side of the Atlantic. Instead he went off to Jamaica for a badly needed rest. In January, 1918, we listened in the refectory to glamorous descriptions of this island given in his letters, which made me eager to record the colours on paper.   It seemed more than probable that we should be making a foundation in Jamaica, for the Jesuit Fathers were eager to welcome a Community of monks : " to teach nigger boys arts and crafts ".

But, like many other rumours of Foundations nearer home, the Jamaican Priory never materialised, and none of us were sent off to that delectable island in the West Indies.   Neither did my painted visions rouse American millionaires to sign cheques for thousands of dollars needed for the erection of an abbey which, if it had been built, would have surpassed even Monte Cassino or some of the great monasteries in Bavaria and Austria for sheer size and magnificence! It is more than a quarter of a century, and no buildings ever arose on that eastern corner of the island. The sea still beats against the lime-stone cliffs of Paul Jones Bay; gulls nest on the rocks; rabbits burrow beneath the bracken and gorse, and the shrubs and trees, intended to form part of the future monastic gardens, are the only feature of the scheme visible to-day. Few visitors to Caldey guess the reason of this plantation.

Life on the island was always in a state of crisis during those years, and we were never sure where money was to come from to keep the Community going. So many things appeared to be needed to make us self-supporting, and so many schemes were drawn up again and again, and launched with every chance of success, none of which functioned very long. I remember that among these financial projects was the St. Joseph's School for Boys, in which they would be taught farming, gardening and other arts and crafts. Then there was a seminary for late vocations to the priesthood, housed for a time in the Old Priory. There were several schemes for making increased profit from the stone quarries, gardens, and poultry farm, which involved the purchase of all sorts of up-to-date machinery—even a pedigree bull for the farm! During the last years of the war the growing of medicinal herbs was another form of profit-making. There were schemes of a Catholic village settlement, with bungalows and villas on every available plot. In fact, the financial situation became more and more serious. Despite constant appeals, all of which met with generous response from the already overburdened Catholics in England, there had never been raised a large enough sum to place the Community on a secure basis and to make it self-supporting*. In August, 1916, if I remember rightly, Pope Benedict XV agreed to contribute £100 annually for four years. Backed by the Pope's support, yet another attempt was made to create an endowment fund, but the results were far from satisfactory. Hence the begging tour in America made by Abbot Aelred during the winter of 1917 and the spring of 1918. After his return home working expenses on the island were cut down to a minimum. In Lent, 1919, so I related in a letter: " there are to be drastic changes in our mode of life. Financial and economic reasons have induced Fr. Abbot to reduce the outside labour, and the Community are to do practically all the work themselves. Our time-table is to be revised so as to give seven to eight hours daily for manual work, instead of three or four hours. I am told off to work on building jobs, such as masonry, plastering, painting, etc. I have already learnt how to repair dry stone walls, and find it quite interesting. Fr. Abbot tells me that, when needed, I can also work with the boats and go fishing, which will be far more congenial. We shall recite all the Office, except Vespers, and Matins will be said overnight, with Lauds in the morning. There will be no daily High Mass. It will be interesting to see how this experiment works out."

Two months later I wrote to this same correspondent: "We are

---

* Strange to say the Cistercian monks who have owned Caldey since 1928, admit that there has been no difficulty in making the island 'pay', even during the war years, with much reduced numbers in the community and no outside appeals for financial support.

getting used to sudden and drastic changes in the monastic time-table.
We have now returned to more or less our normal horarium, and
a daily High Mass, which is sung at 10, with dinner immediately
after. But we still have a very long afternoon spent in manual work,
and coffee is most welcome by 4.30."

This brief attempt to transform us into quasi-Cistercians, so far as
intensive manual work and the singing of the long, drawn-out
Cistercian *Salve Regina* at Compline could do it, proved a failure.
It was not long before we reverted to our former observance. This
well-meant experiment can be traced to a visit paid by Abbot Aelred
to the abbeys of Roscrea and Mount Melleray in Ireland, from which
he returned full of new ideas and visions for his own Community.
During those first years after our reception into the Catholic Church
our manner of life was always being shifted from one mode of Benedictines to another, according to what happened to be the ideal current
at the moment. In a comparatively brief period we passed through
successive phases of Beuron, Cistercian, Solesmes, and English-Con-
gregation influences, with Camaldoli and the Carthusians lurking in
the background, not forgetting our past Anglican traditions based on
the observances of Buckfast!

To add to the physical strain of the Community there was the
introduction of what Fr. Abbot was firmly convinced at that period
was the diet originally intended by Providence for human beings, *i.e.*,
uncooked food, mainly composed of salads, fruit and raw vegetables!
"We have a Brother in the kitchen who makes wonderful and
beautiful salads," so I wrote in a letter early in 1919, "which are an
inspiration in their colour schemes of reds and greens. Like the
æsthetic gentleman in one of Du Maurier's ancient jokes in *Punch,*
one can at least obtain artistic satisfaction from eating them, if not
animal repletion." A few weeks later I wrote that "my almost
exclusive diet of raw vegetables and fruit seems to agree with me. I
have quite lost any desire for cooked food now. Very shortly everybody in the Community will be able to adopt this diet if they wish
to do so, as enough salad and fruit will be placed on the tables at
meals. I notice that some of the monks already refuse the fish and
cooked vegetables that form the second course, as they are full up
with salads!" Both tea and coffee were frowned upon, though not
absolutely forbidden, and a special brand of coffee was used, guaran-
teed to be free from caffein. It was a poor sort of drink, with no
stimulating effects. I seem to remember that the apostle of this

PONTIFICAL HIGH MASS, CALDEY ABBEY.

austere form of diet was a Dr. Leonard Williams, in whom Abbot Aelred had great confidence, and who firmly believed that the sources of most evil in this world could be traced to poisons in the stomach. His treatment, not only included rigid diet but also the wearing of expensive and uncomfortable abdominal belts; his theory being that Man had originally walked on his arms as well as his legs, and consequently the abdominal muscles now tended to droop!

I wore one of these strange contraptions of steel and leather for a year or so, but doubt if my health was either better or worse for the penance! I have forgotten what happened to it eventually, but it was discarded. Then I remember the arrival of another apostle of the uncooked vegetable diet, whose headquarters was in a suburb of Brighton. With passionate conviction he lectured to the Community on the moral and physical effects of cooked food, trying to convince us that it was probably the greatest evil that ever happened to Man when he discovered how to light a fire and tasted roasted flesh for the first time: Adam's eating the apple in the Garden of Eden was a very mild offence compared with this first occasion when Primitive Man devoured his first pork chop or grilled roots! Bottles were produced, showing the horrible condition of the human stomach as the result of eating cooked foods and drinking tea and coffee. Most of the brethren were somewhat amused, and only a few were converted to this peculiar Gospel. For at least a year it was a Counsel of Perfection, if not actually binding by the Rule, to strive after this Back to Nature diet. Yet there were advantages as well as disadvantages in having an Abbot who had studied medicine in his youth! I am uncertain if it was before or after this period when his medical knowledge saved some of us from copper poisoning one evening in Lent, when the cook had omitted to clean the pan in which the soup had been cooked. What a night! The monastery resounded with the groans of those monks who had partaken of that soup, the effects of which started during Compline. Several of us only just escaped a sudden and painful death, and for nearly a week normal observance was upset. Abbot Aelred himself had not taken the soup, so he was not among the victims.

During these hectic years, the novitiate was always full. Men came and went and one lost count of them. A postulant was always arriving or departing. Caldey and its white-habited tonsured community exercised an irresistible appeal, not only to pious youths, but also to many a middle-aged layman. There were countless visitors, too, especially during the summer months. Writing in August, 1919, I informed a friend that "we are suffering from a terrific invasion of visitors of every sort, and I thank God I am not Guestmaster. He does not know where to put people. They turn up without previous warning, and seem to think that we shall be able to provide them with board and lodging. In the monastery there are three monks from Downside and numerous laymen of all types and ages, besides a host of women and children lodging in the Guest House and in the village. There is no room for them in the abbey church, so many have to kneel outside the door."

During the previous summer I had been allowed to spend a few weeks at Chipping Campden in Gloucestershire, to take lessons in architectural drawings from that famous topographical draughtsman and etcher, the late Frederick L. Griggs. I owe much to those lessons. My impressions are thus summed up in a letter: "Mr. Griggs is taking so much trouble over me, and giving advice and help without reserve. His chief object is to simplify my drawing, and to make it more accurate and careful, and to develop my powers of observation. He says that the ultimate value of my work will depend on pains-taking honesty rather than on superficial brilliance and cleverness. This past week I have done nothing but studies of buildings in the village, drawn very carefully with an H pencil. Mr. Griggs tells me that if I will work hard and do what he tells me I ought to become a really good illustrator at the end of two years. He is kind enough to say that my work has a definite 'personal quality', and that it is a pity not to improve it by sheer hard work. In fact he admits that this is all he can teach me: the value of honest and sincere draughtsman-ship." My teacher was right. I am certain, after more than twenty-seven years, that any success that I have achieved as a professional artist has been due entirely to the advice given me during that fort-night in July, 1918. It was a turning point in my artistic career.

My health remained precarious, and as I look back I am more or less convinced that this can be traced to an over-sensitiveness to the environment in which I was living, for it would be hard to maintain that Caldey Island between 1916 and 1924 was peaceful or soothing, very much the opposite in fact. Looking back, it is curious to recall how each doctor consulted diagnosed the case quite differently from the former and recommended a treatment that did not coincide in the least with what had been prescribed by the previous practitioner or specialist. When undergoing one form of treatment, I got so bored by being in London by myself, that I appealed to Mgr. Jackman, then acting as private secretary to Cardinal Bourne, to find me something to do. So it was arranged for me to go round to Archbishop's House every day to help Mgr. Jackman with the editing of the *Catholic Directory* and other jobs, for which I was paid. This regular occupation did me far more good, so I think, than the weekly talks with my doctor in Portland Place. I enjoyed being in close touch with Cardinal Bourne, for he was always in and out of the room where I used to be writing. His Eminence's friendship, which started in this manner, proved most valuable to me later on when I was helping to launch the Apostleship of the Sea.

Another time, I spent a month with Eric Gill at Ditchling Common in Sussex, about which I shall be writing further on. Yet, deep down in my mind, I had the conviction that the only permanent " cure " would be to get away to sea, or to be living among ships and sailors, and able to draw them and write about them. Letters written during those years show how this idea persisted, and it is a pity that I had to wait so long before I got the chance to test my convictions. Indeed it may well be said that it was Sea Fever that I suffered from. What I wonder at to-day is, why did the monks put up with my presence in their midst for so many years? There was no obligation on their part to keep me, yet never was it ever suggested that I had better sever my association with Caldey until the summer of 1924 when it was perfectly obvious that the moment had arrived to make such a step necessary, and then, rather for my own future welfare than for the benefit of the Community.

I have many memories of life at Caldey during those troubled years. For instance, there are mental pictures of those Christmas festivities which were such a regular feature when December came round. I must admit that I looked forward to Christmas at Caldey with mixed feelings, having a temperamental dislike to long hours spent in choir combined with even longer hours of recreation with my monastic brethren. December 17th ushered in the solemnities. The " Great Os "—the special antiphons which are sung before and after the *Magnificat* at Vespers—began that day. It was our custom to sing each antiphon between each verse, the big bell in the church tower being rung from the first intonation till the last repetition after the *Gloria*. Then, after supper, to quote from notes in *Pax* (February, 1920) from which I refresh my memory, " the Community meets in the calefactory for what used to be called ' the scholastical and

moderate congratulation . . . and thereof no superfluity or excess!'
As was ordered at Sarum, 'the place is properly lighted, and a fire
which does not smoke, if that is possible.' As at Abingdon and
Sarum, the three-handled loving cup is then passed round, and we
sing the first carol—' Shepherds in the fields abiding'—before going
on to the Nativity Play which is performed by the villagers for the
first time that night." How well I recall that walk down to the
village hall in the darkness, with the distant roar of the surf breaking
on the beach of Priory Bay!

It was now only seven days to Christmas and every department in
the monastery became more and more busy. There were special music
practices and the master of ceremonies put up notices bidding all concerned to rehearsals of the pontifical functions. Shall I ever forget
one Christmas when the monk who was in charge of the poultry farm,
put down to be sub-deacon at the midnight Mass, dashed into church
a bit late? Somewhat out of breath—for he was a victim to asthma—
he sat down on some eggs which he had hastily shoved into his
pockets—with disastrous results to his white habit. Our rehearsal
had to stop, for we collapsed with laughter.

It was our aim to keep Christmas in what is known as the " good
old-fashioned way ", with holly, yule-log, ghost stories and an
atmosphere suggestive of Dickens. About December 22nd a division
of labour was made; notices were pinned up in the cloisters informing
novices that they were to decorate the church; the boy-alumni the
cloisters, and the professed monks to take charge of the refectory
and calefactory. Some years the holly—which came from Llanthony
—did not arrive on the expected day, probably due to the steamer
being storm-bound at Tenby. The refectory would be hung with
bunting and heraldic shields, logs and pine cones being laid in the
great open fireplace beneath the statue of St. Michael, ready for
Christmas morning. In the Abbot's chapel two brothers were hard
at work erecting the crib, a baldachino-shaped structure with a
thatched roof beneath which lay the figure of the Holy Child.

I have since stayed in many other Benedictine abbeys for Christmas
and nowhere do I remember such long and intricate notices being
for the proper carrying out of the different functions. Year by year
these Christmas Notices seemed to grow longer and yet more
detailed. When I first joined the Community the typescript was
timidly decorated with roughly drawn holly leaves and berries in
black and red ink. Later on the decorations assumed the nature of

elaborate illuminations in gold and colour, involving many hours' labour for the artist-monk responsible for them.

Christmas Eve was a strenuous day. Mountains of parcels and bulging mail-bags accumulated in the cellarer's office until they were disposed of on Christmas morning. After supper everyone was supposed to go to bed until the bell rang at 9.30 p.m., although most of us were usually far too busy with final details that cropped up at the last moment to be able to take any rest. There would be monks in the Chapter House rehearsing the lessons which they had to sing at Matins, maybe a deacon or sub-deacon going through the epistle and gospel for the last time just to make sure they had mastered the chant. In the Sacristy a harassed master of ceremonies might be found giving final directions to new novices as to their duties as thurifer or acolyte, or showing them how to hand the crozier to the Abbot, or the right way to hold his mitres. A weary sacristan, who has been at work since dawn, would probably be trying to provide extra seats in the gallery and narthex for the secular congregation. The cook and his assistants could be found in the kitchen, still hard at work with turkeys, plum puddings, mince-pies and other festive fare. Lastly, a few monks who had been too busy during the day to get to Confession, would be waiting outside the Abbot's chapel.

Matins started at 10 o'clock and lasted two hours, for the whole of the long Office was sung. It was seldom that we got back to bed much before 3.30 a.m. for after Lauds followed Low Masses. Altogether it was an exhausting night, about five and a half hours being spent in church, more than enough to make even the most ardent liturgical enthusiast wish to become a Quaker! One of my monastic brethren—to-day a Canadian Army chaplain—had romantic ideas about yule-logs. He loved to hide one such log in a remote part of the spinney or elsewhere a few days before Christmas, and then make up a party to look for it! I recall that he used to tell us that it was our duty to dance round the yule-log before we carried it back to the monastery, where a crackling fire in the refectory was in readiness. On Christmas Day and Boxing Day talking was allowed at meals, a contrast from other times when silence was never broken in the refectory save by the voice of the reader. Instead of sitting in our usual order of seniority we were allotted special places, indicated on slips of paper. This same monk, now far away in Canada, used to choose some suitable passage for each monk, generally taken from Chaucer's *Canterbury Tales,* the *Ingoldsby Legends* or other book—always a cause for merriment and jokes. Dinner was a long and elaborate repast. It seldom lasted less than two hours, and then we retired to our beds for a badly needed rest. The more energetic monks took a sharp walk round the island later on to work off the effects of their gargantuan meal, and to give them an appetite for tea—really a superfluous item on the programme. There would be carols after Vespers, and later on an informal concert in the cale-factory. At last, very tired and weary, we got to our cells, having passed nearly twelve hours in church since the night before. Those Caldey Christmases have given me an intense distaste for similar festivities ever since and in recent years I have been quite glad to spend the festival season in solitude, so great has been the reaction!

Other memories that may be worth recalling are connected with the first of several Passion Plays performed by the monks. To quote from a letter which I wrote to a friend in the Lent of 1919: "Every-one is full of the Passion Play and we have rehearsals daily. Yester-day there was a notice put up in the cloisters 'Rehearsal for Last Supper at 2 o'clock. Please bring straw pillows.' The twelve Apostles tell me they are getting quite accustomed now to leaning on their elbows! You hear music being practised in the chapter house all day long. The villagers are making the costumes. I have been cast to play the part of Mary Magdalene."

Not only did I play Mary Magdalene in a golden wig, but it was my lot to design the scenery and arrange the lighting effects. I went out all modern and dispensed with footlights. For I had been studying the latest developments of stage production in Germany, Russia and America, having got hold of all the back numbers of the *Theatre Arts Magazine*. I was also in correspondence with the director of the then newly-opened Everyman Theatre at Hampstead and Miss de Reyes of the Citizen House Theatre at Bath. My Abbot had given me per-mission—for I was not, strictly speaking, a cleric—to see the Russian Ballet at the Coliseum and the Alhambra. My imagination was filled with memories of the *décor* of *Carnival, Children's Tales, Petrouchka,* the *Three Cornered Hat* and the *Good-Humoured Ladies*. But the stage manager responsible for the success of the production was Dom Wilfrid Upson—now Abbot of Prinknash—who might have earned his fortune in this line of business had he not found his voca-tion as a Benedictine!

We decided to put the audience on the stage of the Village Hall

and to use the main part of the building for the action. This innovation was most successful. The scenic effects were built up by a
rearrangement of the original elements, consisting of four pylons,
three sets of steps, three low platforms, an arch and a few canvas
flats—all painted a dull cream colour, and heavy blue curtains draped
at the back and sides of the hall.

" Not since Gordon Craig's *Masque of Love,*" wrote Miss Chris-
topher St. John in *Time and Tide,* " have I seen such harmonious
grouping and movement . . . the great achievement of the Caldey
Passion is that visions are created instead of illusions. Visions of the
institution of the Eucharist, of the journey to Golgotha, of the
Crucifixion, of the entombment and resurrection, of the walk to
Emmaus."

On Good Friday afternoon I wrote in a letter: " The Passion Play
has been occupying nearly all my time the past fortnight. It has been
interesting but absorbing work, what with rehearsals, scene-shifting,
stencilling fabrics, and making drawings and plans of different scenes.
We give our last performance at 3 o'clock this afternoon. It will be
over about 6. Then we change, and having removed our ' make-up '
(I fear that Mary Magdalene is far too much addicted to powder,
lipstick and rouge!) come back from the Village Hall to sing
Tenebrae. Rather a hustle, isn't it?"

There can be no doubt that this first Caldey Passion Play was
something unique in religious drama, and it created much interest,
not to say enthusiasm, among the visitors who came to the island to
see it. The play was repeated for several years. But ' make-up ' and
special costumes were latterly dispensed with; the monks appearing in
their ordinary white habits and cowls, which really improved the
play from all points of view, giving the production the right note of
austerity and simplicity.

*   *   *

Another picture comes to mind—an autumn morning of 1919 when
part of the relics of St. Samson, the 6th-century Abbot of Caldey,
who afterwards became Bishop of Dol in Brittany, was brought back
to the island. I can still see our motor boat, *Stella Maris,* towing a
strange and almost medieval looking craft, whose original use as a
naval cutter might not be guessed from the array of heraldic shields
displaying the arms of the chief Benedictine abbeys of Europe. Ivy
is entwined about her gunwales and an image of the Holy Child

stands at her bows. She is cast astern and a crew of white-habited monks man the oars and row her to the shore. Amidships is a shrine over which four priests support a silk canopy. So, after more than fourteen hundred years, the fragment of bone which had been part of the living temple of St. Samson found rest again on Caldey Island. It was placed in a small casket and stood above the High Altar in the Abbey church. To-day it is honoured by the Cistercians who succeeded.

* * *

It would be quite wrong to form the impression, from what I have written, that life at Caldey was nothing more than a picturesque pageant. Beneath all this externalism lay hidden a very deep spirituality, which found expression in three or four of the monks being allowed to follow a somewhat stricter observance of the Rule than the majority of the community. They were known as Solitaries. They kept more or less perpetual silence, in so far as they only took part in our recreations at Christmas and other great feasts. They were given more time for private prayer and recited the Little Office of Our Lady (according to the Carthusian rite) in addition to joining in the Divine Office in choir. Their daily work was arranged so that normally there was no occasion even for legitimate conversation. In other words, these Solitaries would be better compared to monks who never ceased making a Retreat. The term Solitaries was somewhat inaccurate, for their lives, in the material sense, were not in the least solitary, since they were always in the midst of their brethren. They were definitely not Hermits.

But it was possible, not only for the Solitaries, but also for the rest of the Community to live an eremitical life for brief periods. For— as I have related in *Harbour Head*—a little hermitage was built on the cliffs of Paul Jones Bay in 1915, and practically all the year round it was occupied by one of the monks, who lived there in complete solitude. If he happened to be a priest, another monk would turn up each morning to serve his Mass in the tiny oratory; or a priest would say Mass here should the temporary hermit happen to be a choir or lay-brother.

We had another abbot living in our community from 1918 to 1920—the Rt. Rev. Sir David Oswald Hunter-Blair, Bt.—who, on resigning his office as Abbot of Fort Augustus, took up his residence at Caldey. He was then in his sixty-sixth year, and full of life and energy. He acted as our librarian and in every way took a keen interest in the convert community, of whose " constant and unfailing kindness " he wrote so appreciatively in his first *Medley of Memories,* published in 1920. He asked me to make some drawings of Benedictine abbeys for this book. They were my first attempt at decorative illustrations.

Abbot Hunter-Blair had had an eventful, not to say an exciting career. He was the eldest son of Sir Edward Hunter-Blair, Bt., of Dunskey in Galloway, and on both sides he was descended from a long line of distinguished ancestors who had taken a prominent place in Scottish affairs. While still an undergraduate at Oxford he was drawn towards Catholicism, and was received into the Church at the age of twenty-two. Having obtained his degree, he found himself a very rich young Catholic layman, and it was taken for granted that he would make a brilliant marriage—for he was much sought after by the mothers of débutantes as a highly eligible son-in-law. But in the end he disappointed all of them. He announced that he was going to join the then newly-founded Benedictine community at Fort Augustus, and the future Sir David discarded the uniform of a Papal Chamberlain, and of a captain in the Ayr and Wigtown Militia when he put on the Benedictine habit and became Brother Oswald. Had he ever imagined that the rest of his life would be spent in the seclusion of his Highland abbey he was mistaken. Few monks have ever lived such a roving life. Even when he was headmaster of the abbey school he was constantly on the move during the holidays, acting as chaplain to one or other of the many Catholic families with whom he was a *persona grata,* or preaching up and down Britain. Yet he also found time to translate from the German the four big volumes of Bellesheim's *History of the Catholic Church in Scotland.* In 1896 he went off to Brazil, to assist in an attempt to revive the almost defunct Benedictine abbeys in that country. After two years in South America he returned home and was placed in charge of the first Catholic House of Studies established in Oxford since the Reformation. As Master of Hunter-Blair's Hall he became a well-known and popular figure in Oxford. The long vacations gave him unlimited opportunities for travel, and, as can be proved by reference to his three volumes of reminiscences, he kept in close touch with a vast circle of friends. In fact, there was scarcely a country mansion in Great Britain where Father Oswald was not made welcome, or where he could not invite himself if in need of a temporary *pied-à-terre*!

He was elected Abbot of Fort Augustus in 1913, and immediately threw himself into the task of building the choir of the abbey church, nothing having been done to complete this building since the foundations had been laid some twenty years previously. In spite of endless difficulties, due to the last war, the choir and Blessed Sacrament chapel were opened in 1916. Nothing more has since been done in the subsequent twenty-seven years to complete what would be such a magnificent church.

Abbot Oswald's stay on Caldey came to an end in 1920, when he returned to Brazil for some years. Then he came back to England, and found it hard to settle down anywhere—it must be admitted that in his later years he was not the easiest of men for any household to put up with. His mind was so restless and his energy of body quite remarkable for his age. Finally he established himself at the New Club, Edinburgh—a somewhat unusual retreat for a retired Benedictine abbot! Here he spent the greater part of his latter years. His literary output was amazing, for in addition to nearly always having a book on hand, he turned out regular articles for Catholic papers and magazines, not to mention the long letters he contributed to the secular Press, dealing with every conceivable subject. He was a first-class journalist with a ready pen and a keen sense of humour. He was always on the move, for there was never an important function at which he failed to put in an appearance. Centenaries, jubilees, weddings, no matter what might be the event, Abbot Hunter-Blair was almost sure to be there, and always the life and soul of the celebrations. But he seldom attended funerals, in fact he avoided them, if possible. Nobody could tell a story better than " Sir David " (strangers were never quite sure how to address this baronet-Benedictine!), and his fund of reminiscences was unending. The most boring function would be enlivened by his genial presence.

Finally, old age began to tell on him. Attacks of gout and partial blindness, not to mention other minor ailments incidental to advancing years, could make him extremely irritable. Yet there was something so lovable about the venerable old monk, with keen blue eyes, rosy cheeks, and white hair. One forgot those sudden outbursts of temper. His was a child-like simplicity; a child-like piety, and beneath it a real humility that few persons discovered beneath the frequent pomposity of manner. He never forgot that he was a baronet as well as a Benedictine, and he expected other people to remember it. Only a man who had retained that precious spirit of childlikeness would have been able to amuse himself with the harmless pleasure of " dressing up "—if one may use the expression? Abbot Oswald loved to pontificate, even when his gout, rheumatism and partial blindness must have made the ordeal extremely painful. He usually travelled about with several pectoral crosses and rings, and never forgot his baronet's insignia in case he should find an occasion to deck himself out in it. His luggage generally contained a couple of mitres, for his head was so large that no ordinary size of headgear would fit him. Criticisms of Abbot Oswald were sometimes made by those who did not know him intimately, or who had narrow ideas of the spirit and traditions of Benedictine monasticism. Now the *Rule of St. Benedict* makes no attempt to turn out monks according to a standardised pattern. It allows the widest latitude for individual characteristics, even for eccentricities. It orders no particular kind of work to be done. If one knows even a little Benedictine history, one sees how remarkably true to a certain traditional type of Benedictine was Abbot Oswald.

He loved his Order and his own monastery more than anything in the world. Never would he allow the least criticism to be made of his Community in his presence—as I know from my own experience when I said something about individual monks which he felt deflected from the honour of the Community to which he belonged. The surprising thing was to discover how a man who never stopped pouring out social gossip was so utterly discreet when it came to the private affairs of his monastic brethren; what is more, so charitable. Then there was his love for Scotland and her ancient Church. He longed to see Scotland Catholic again, and he never grudged any labour towards her re-conversion. " Sir David " was unique—there could never be anyone the least like him. He belonged to an age which is past, and that perhaps explains why he was so little appreciated by some of the younger generation.

*   *   *

In December, 1919, having been ill on and off for most of the autumn, Abbot Aelred was quite relieved, so I imagine, when I asked his permission to depart for Scotland; my conversations with Abbot Hunter-Blair having filled me with a violent desire to visit my mother's native country, of which she used to talk so much when I was a boy. So, on a dark winter morning, with snow all the way from Glasgow, I found myself at Fort Augustus Abbey. My first impressions of this monastery, which was to become a more or less permanent home for the next two years, can be found in *Harbour Head*. By the shores of Loch Ness the dreams and visions of a world-wide Catholic Sea Apostolate began to shape themselves into definite form.

Nine months were to elapse before I returned to Caldey, and then only for a brief visit. During most of this period I was travelling around England, Scotland, Ireland, Belgium, France and ended up in Rome. The Apostleship of the Sea Society had been launched and I was acting as Honorary Organising Secretary. In the spring of 1922, shortly after that memorial visit to Port-en-Bessin, recorded in the pages of *Harbour Head,* I took the opportunity to make a short retreat at the monastery of La Grande Trappe, which lies in a remote district to the south of Normandy. It took me all day to get there from Fécamp, and when I arrived at the wayside station of Soligny-la-Trappe late on a dark February evening with snow falling, I found that there was nothing to do but to walk the four kilometres from the station to the abbey, as no sort of conveyance could be got. So I set out along that dark road, and if it had not been for the welcome sound of the abbey bell ringing I doubt if I should ever have reached my destination, for no sign of human habitation appeared in sight. At last I arrived at the entrance to the monastery, and rang the great bell by the door several times without anyone coming to answer it. Then a harsh voice inquired from within " *Qui est là?*" I did my best to explain who I was and what I was doing, and then the voice said that he would go and fetch the guest-master. There was another long wait—the guest-master had to be dragged out of choir, for the monks were now at Compline. The snow had turned to a drizzling rain, and I thought that even the " *Abbé tempête*" De Rancé himself could not have planned a more penitential welcome to the monastery he had made famous. When the guest-master did arrive he was not in the best of tempers. "Why had I not written to announce my arrival?" he asked. I explained that I *had* done so. The letter had not arrived (it turned up two days later). I introduced myself and explained the reason of my visit. Then another and quite unexpected query—had I also followed the example of the rest of the Caldey Benedictines and

returned to the Church of England? If so, what was I doing here?
I assured the good father that the Caldey Benedictines had not relapsed
into Anglicanism, and that the strange rumour which had reached
La Trappe was entirely false. Had I anything to prove my identity?
It was extremely fatiguing on a cold winter night after a more than
twelve hour journey to be put through the third degree like this by a
sceptical monk, when all I wanted was supper. Fortunately I had
with me a letter of commendation from the Bishop of Bayeux, and
another written in French in his own hand by Cardinal Bourne, with
the archiepiscopal arms of Westminster blazoned at the top. The
guest-master scrutinised both very carefully, holding them up to the
light as if they were forged bank notes. Apparently they satisfied him
that I was worthy of hospitality, and he took me across an open courtyard to the guesthouse, gave me a room, and soon after brought
supper. In spite of this forbidding welcome I spent a whole week at
La Trappe, and had a very happy time there. My host of the previous
night apologised for his brusque behaviour, and explained how
relieved he was to hear that the rumour about the apostasy of
the Caldey Community was untrue. I have stayed in many
monasteries, but La Trappe is certainly the most grim and forbidding
of any I know, largely owing, I think, to the cold, machine-like
character and appearance of the modern Gothic buildings which have
replaced the original abbey. The weather too was cold and wet. It
rained nearly every day, but in spite of it I took long solitary walks
through apparently endless forests, where one met nobody save an
occasional woodman or charcoalburner.

After six months spent on the Continent of Europe, and a further
long sojourn at Fort Augustus, I was off again on my travels in
Belgium, France and Italy; this time with the intention of studying
for the secular priesthood with the Benedictine monks at Saint-
André, near Bruges. But I did not remain there more than three
months. Once again Caldey became my anchorage between
voyages, as is related in *Harbour Head*. Then in September, 1923,
I found new moorings at Quarr Abbey, Isle of Wight. This was
my final phase of Benedictine life, at least as a member of any Community. In June the following year, Dom Wilfrid Upson, who
became Prior of Caldey after the resignation of Abbot Aelred Carlyle,
decided that the moment had come at last to cast off the monastic
habit, which I had worn on and off for the past fourteen years. So
ended a long phase of my career as a *Roving Recluse*.

CHAPTER V

FRANCISCAN ITALY

Yet more pictures on the walls of Harbour Head record the next phase of my life. Facing me is a lithograph of St. Francis of Assisi by the 17th century Bolognese artist, Giovanni Barbieri, called from his squinting *Il Guercino*. Then, fitted into spaces between over-crowded bookshelves are four frames, each with two photographs of places in or near Assisi—the exterior and interior of the Franciscan friaries of S. Damiano and the Carceri. If I turn round St. Francis blesses me from another corner of the room. There are three large water-colours given me many years ago by Dom Pedro Subercaseaux, the Benedictine artist-monk of Quarr Abbey. They were among the originals of a *Life of St. Francis* published in the United States. There is a shelf entirely filled with books on Franciscan history and spirituality. Another shelf is taken up with books dealing with Italian topography, among which is a small brown-covered volume, by P. F. Anson, entitled *The Pilgrim's Guide to Franciscan Italy*. Lastly a rosary of seven decades—much too big to carry about—which hangs on a nail, is a souvenir of the months when it formed part of my uniform as a Franciscan novice in Italy.

A few days after I had severed my official relations with the Benedictines of Caldey, I received an invitation from an old friend, Tommy Croft-Fraser—in later years Choir Sacristan and Chief Master of Ceremonies at St. Peter's and a purple-robed Monsignore—to join him and his mother at the village of Gavinana, high up in the Tuscan Apennines, about half-way between Florence and Bologna. They were spending the summer at Gavinana, and suggested that it would be an ideal spot for me to make drawings and paintings. For I now realised that I should have to try to earn my own living as an artist. I had already begun to make a name for myself as a painter of maritime subjects and had had my first one-man show in London. Still it was not easy to make a start in a new career at the age of thirty-five.

With the feeling of setting out on a voyage of discovery to an unknown land I left London on the morning of July 3rd, 1924. For it was quite a different thing going to Italy as a layman and an

artist to going there as a Benedictine oblate in connection with the
Catholic Sea Apostolate. How vividly I recall that long motor drive
from Pracchia station to Gavinana; the sky ablaze with stars, and
myriads of fire-flies dancing against the jagged black silhouettes of
the mountains. The reckless extravagance of electric light in the
numerous villages scattered far below in the valleys and far up on
the peaks. The car whirled round hair-pin bends; climbed up and
up, mile after mile, until at last it stopped in the now deserted *piazza*
before the Albergo Ferrucio. This was to be my home until the
middle of September.

On starting to explore Gavinana after coffee and rolls the following morning, it revealed itself as a village of grey stone houses, most
of them with roofs of big, grey stone slabs, perched on the northern
slopes of a steep valley so that it got the full benefit of the sun; an
advantage in mid-winter, when the district is often snowbound,
being situated between three and four thousand feet above sea-level.
The life of the village centred in the little stone-flagged piazza, where
on Sunday nights a band played; the young men and maidens dancing,
with crowds of onlookers sitting at the tables in front of the cafés.
On one side of this piazza was the church: a venerable and much-
rebuilt edifice, full of faded and tarnished baroque altar pieces and
carving. I have tender memories of this church, for here I learnt
to understand and appreciate the everyday religious life of a fairly
typical Tuscan village. How different it was from Catholicism in
England, in its outward manifestations, yet in no way different as
to the essential truths.

Nearly every morning I started off with my sketching materials
immediately after Mass and a quick breakfast, making my way to
some shady spot where the view attracted me, and it was not difficult
to find them on those hillsides, generally with one or other of those
musically named villages—Mammiano, Campiglio, Maresca, Pom-
piglio—or else a picturesque group of farm buildings to help the
composition. I might climb up and up the winding paths on the
mountains above Gavinana, with lizards basking in the hot sun, until
I reached the summit where I could look down into another valley
over miles and miles of vivid green chestnut forests, with the red
roofs of Spignana, Lizzano and Cutigliano, in the middle distance,
and far away to the north the peak of Monte Cimone shimmering in
the dim blue haze. If I felt lazy and disinclined for a long walk
there was always plenty to draw in Gavinana itself. During those

three months I discovered what appeared to be my own individual method of drawing and painting. In these Tuscan Apennines I produced what I always feel to be the best work of my life. Something inspired me that summer.

I soon became friendly with the village folk, thanks to my friend "Don Tommaso"—as they called Tommy Croft-Fraser—who, having already lived two years in Italy, could speak Italian fluently. Although I myself was as yet unable to converse much with the people, I used to go about with Tommy, visiting the *contadini* in their homes. Sometimes after dinner the two of us would go round and call on Don Antonio—the parish priest. We sat in his little study with its rough brick floor and hard, straw-bottomed chairs. A big *fiasco* of wines and glasses would be produced by his housekeeper, and thus we would spend an hour or two, Don Tommaso doing the talking while I sat and listened, trying to follow the gist of the conversation. The sun had set behind the mountains to the west, and through the open window one got a glimpse of the sky, like blue-black velvet embroidered with millions of diamonds. More often than not other men would wander in—maybe the old sacristan or his nephew—tall, good-looking Nando Tognelli—or a young seminarist, Gino Iori, who was home for the summer vacation. When I was sketching in or near the village I was certain to be joined by a crowd of bright-eyed, eager and interested youngsters, who would ply me with questions or criticise my drawing. So I began to speak Italian, the beautiful, highly idiomatic Tuscan spoken by Saule Vignozzi and other boys! It was difficult to follow because of the numerous aspirates which changed every "c" into a "h". When trying to learn a new language there is no better practice than to talk to children. If they cannot make themselves understood by words, they will resort to signs. Days and weeks sped by almost unrealised. England and everything connected with it seemed strangely remote. I began to feel as if I had lived all my life in this remote corner of Tuscany.

*　　　*　　　*

It was eleven years since I had been received into the Catholic and Roman Church, during which period I had knocked about a good deal and experienced Catholicism in various aspects, both in Great Britain, Ireland, France and Belgium. In England I was always *conscious* of being a Catholic; in France and Belgium much less so,

H

but I used to get tired of being reminded so often of my conversion and questions asked about it. In Ireland I found a fervent but individualistic type of Catholicism which I admired, yet I could never quite enter into it. But when I had spent a few weeks in Italy I felt that here at last was just the kind of religious atmosphere that suited me completely. Any remaining Protestant inhibitions fell away; religion became as natural as breathing and sleeping—part and parcel of everyday life and not kept bottled up in water-tight compartments. Prayer became, not only an *"ascensio mentis in Dominum"*, but there was also an easy unresisting *"ascensio corporis in Dominum"*, by which I mean that one's whole personality became fused, and one saw that every action, bodily as well as spiritual, could be made to contribute towards the end of life. The doors of that church at Gavinana were open all day long; the cheerful noises of the *piazza;* the singing and shouting and laughter, mingled with the mutter of the Mass and the chink of rosaries. People wandered in and out, their church was their home as well as the House of God. I realised for the first time how Catholic moral teaching could control otherwise wayward temperaments—the men and boys of Gavinana had their vices as well as their virtues as I soon discovered. But they knew how to put themselves right with God, and did so in the most natural way possible. Sin was sin—no doubt about that—but there was always the Sacrament of Penance of which they could avail themselves at any moment. Then, although I was a foreigner and could then only speak very little Italian, I never felt I was an alien in church—here I was one of a great family, having a right to share in all that was provided by way of spiritual nourishment and the worship of God.

From time to time there would be a *Festa,* with processions that started from the *Piazza* on a Sunday afternoon amid the clanging of bells, the blaring of a brass band and the chatter of on-lookers. Most of them would join in and follow the procession as it wended its way through the narrow, tortuous streets of the village. The more devout men-folk would be vested in an abbreviated alb, reaching to their knees and open down the front. Another year when I went back to Gavinana I took part in the Rogation processions which were unlike any which I have ever come across. We started out soon after dawn, and how bitterly cold it was at this high altitude on those mornings of the second week in May! Snow was still lying on the more lofty peaks of the Apennines, as one realised from the nip in the wind. Practically everybody in the village accompanied the priest and his acolytes, even old men and women, and we must have covered three or four miles climbing up and down steep paths on the mountain-side before we finally arrived back at the church for Mass. As we struggled on through the still leafless chestnut woods, we bawled (chanted would be the wrong verb to use!) the Litany of the Saints.

A pilgrimage to the famous shrine of Our Lady at Loreto was a break in this summer at Gavinana. It was a long and tiring journey, but well worth while. I celebrated my thirty-fifth birthday at Loreto, and no other shrine—and I have since visited a good many—ever made quite the same impression on me as the *Santa Casa*—the Holy House of Nazareth which, according to the venerable legend, was transported to the shores of the Adriatic from Palestine. Maybe it was liturgical worship which attracted me just as much as anything else. Every morning there was a perfectly rendered Sung Mass with plain chant, while in the afternoon one could assist at Vespers. I stopped at Bologna both going and coming, a city which has always appealed to me, especially its churches, above all S. Domenico, with the tomb of the Founder of the Order of Friar Preachers, and La Santa where is exposed the incorrupt body of the 14th-century Poor Clare nun, St. Catherine of Bologna.

*　　　*　　　*

So far as I can remember, my interest in St. Francis and his Order was first awakened by a visit to the little red brick friary among the pine woods at Ascot one summer afternoon in 1906, when I cycled over from Windsor. It is nearly forty years ago, but I can still recall the details of that afternoon. There must have been something about the place which attracted me quite apart from the architecture or decorations of the church, best described as a typical example of that uninspired architect, the late Canon Scoles—all of whose churches seem to have the same Early English windows, red brick exterior walls, and red tile roofs.

I recall putting up a votive candle before the statue of St. Francis, kneeling down and saying a prayer. It was the first occasion that I spoke to him whom in later years I came to regard as my Seraphic Father and towards whom I was to develop such a special affection. Behind the High Altar the friars were reciting Office. I sat down in a bench and listened to the rapid and confused murmur, trying to

follow what they were saying, but with no success. I waited until
they had finished. I wanted to see what they looked like, and my
patience was rewarded. What I now realise must have been Vespers
and Compline were ended, the friars passed out through the doors
on either side of the altar and made their way into the sacristy. I
gazed at their brown habits and sandals with youthful curiosity. Little
did I guess that one of these priests would receive me into the
Franciscan family seventeen years later!

                    *   *   *

During the summer of 1910, when I had practically made up my
mind to try my vocation in the then Anglican Benedictine community
on Caldey Island, I thought it might save possible doubts later on if I
were to visit the Franciscan brotherhood, known as the Society of
Divine Compassion, whose novitiate was at Stanford-le-Hope in
Essex. This Church of England community had been founded in
the nineties of the last century, its main work being among the poor of
East London. The Fathers had charge of the parish of St. Philip's,
Plaistow. So one Saturday afternoon I found myself in a train at
Fenchurch Street station bound for Stanford-le-Hope. On arriving at
the friary I immediately felt an indefinable kinship with the Brothers.
They wore the black habit of the Conventual Franciscans, but their
ethos was rather that of the medieval Spiritual party, and far
removed from that of Br. Elias. They welcomed me with simple
and unaffected kindness. I lost my heart to that friary, originally a
half-timbered farm house. The stable had been transformed into a
chapel, and its open roof revealed rough hewn beams. There was a
quiet and secluded garden, green lawns and colourful flower beds; a
stream crossed by a rustic bridge, and a Calvary standing against a
background of elm trees. Far away beyond the flat fields and marshes
there were glimpses of the Thames, with brown-sailed barges drifting
past on their way to and from the open sea. I returned to London
that same evening, wondering if after all I might have a vocation for
the Franciscan instead of the Benedictine life.

                    *   *   *

Time rolled on, and with my joining the Caldey Benedictines, I
ceased to think much of St. Francis. As I have already related in
the previous chapter, I returned to the world. It was in the
summer of 1924, spent in the Tuscan Apennines, that my long dor-

mant interest in Franciscanism suddenly revived. I decided to make a pilgrimage to Assisi.

Early one autumn morning I started from Florence on what my friend, Edward Hutton, so happily described in one of his books as "the noblest day's journey in the world". Up the valley of the Arno, with a glimpse of Vallombrosa half-hidden on dark pine-clad mountains; the far off peak of La Verna (if you know where to look for it on the left just before the train slows down into Arezzo); Cortona, surveying the wide expanse of the once swampy Val-di-Chiana from its lofty eerie, crowned by the shrine of the great Tertiary penitent, St. Margaret. Then at Terontola you leave the Rome express to hurry onwards, and by slow and painful joltings are ushered into that exquisite land of blue and silver distances, pale grey-green foregrounds over which broods a light, so Edward Hutton maintains, " that never was in any Tuscan vale ". There is nothing spectacular about Umbria. It is a country which, like its normally silent and moody people, has to be wooed patiently before one is allowed to fall a victim to its strange and indefinable charm. But once you have taken *Umbria mystica* to your heart—or she has taken your heart to herself—there will come moments in after years when you are seized with a mad longing to be back again among the olives; to see once more those age-old cities crowning the hills and nestling in the valleys—Spoleto, Trevi, Montefalco, Foligno, and Assisi; to recapture the impression of Todi on its mound beside the yellow Tiber; to wander amid the barren mountains or silent, deserted streets of Gubbio; or to climb as it were to the very roof of Italy among the inaccessible gorges of the Apennines between Fossato and Fabriano.

I made that oft repeated journey from Tuscany into Umbria for the first time on the morning of September 24th, 1924, when the white and purple grapes were hanging thick on the vines, all ready for the vintage. And so I came to Assisi.

The first few days passed rapidly. I explored every nook and cranny of the city, beginning with a visit to La Rocca, the medieval fortress. I studied the frescoes in the Upper and Lower Churches of S. Francesco; I walked down the long dusty road to Santa Maria degli Angeli, beneath whose great dome stands the original chapel of the Portiuncula. More than once I climbed the steep path up Monte Subasio to the hermitage of the Carceri, where I made friends with the two *frati* who formed the Community. On Michaelmas Day they invited me to dinner in their tiny refectory, hewn out of the mountain rock.

Again and again I wandered through the olive groves to the convent of San Damiano, situated outside the Porta Nuova.

During the long waits between courses at dinner and lunch at the Albergo Giotto, I devoured Jorgensen's *Life of St. Francis,* a copy of which I bought the day I arrived.

Finally I made up my mind that I must become a Franciscan Tertiary. St. Francis was now calling me too strongly to be resisted. Such a step meant a final burning of my Benedictine boats, for I was still an extern oblate of Caldey, and I hesitated before making a complete break with the associations of more than fourteen years. It was not that I was merely slightly intoxicated with the romance of the *città serafica*—and never is it so romantic as during the early autumn. Now that I look back in a more critical state of mind, I honestly believe that I felt that it was the right thing for me to become a member of a world-wide fraternity in which, figuratively speaking, instability is a virtue to be aimed at, and not a vice to be uprooted. For in the past my superiors had often told me that what was mostly lacking to my Benedictine vocation was stability—that I had no sense of the family spirit which is so peculiar to Bene-dictines. I realised my own instability and I wanted to be attached to some other kind of link, more in keeping with my temperament. And the more I studied the Third Order of St. Francis, the more certain I was that here was what I needed.

So I walked out of the hotel on the morning of October 1st and made my way to Our Lady of the Angels, where I had a talk to Padre Bernardino (one of the friars whom I had seen in the Fran-ciscan Church at Ascot seventeen years before), asking him if I might be received into the Third Order. He raised no objections, and bade me return the next day. It was the feast of the Guardian Angels, and after assisting at the Sung Mass, I waited the Padre. He took me into the chapel of the Portiuncula, the veritable heart of the Franciscan Order, where, kneeling before the altar, I turned over the pages in the Tertiary Manual for the ceremony of being clothed with the habit.

"*Quid postulas?*" "What dost thou ask?" the old white-haired friar demanded, and I replied in Latin that I sought the "habit of the Third Order of Penance that I might the more easily obtain eternal salvation." Then, various prayers having been recited, Padre Bernardino placed the brown scapular of the Little Poor Man over my head and shoulders and girded me with the knotted cord. Kneeling behind me at the back of the tiny chapel were three peasant women, rattling their rosary beads and murmuring *Paters* and *Aves* all the while. A group of nuns fluttered round the chapel, in and out of the two doors, intent on gaining Plenary Indulgences. Before the brief ceremony was ended in walked four young Benedictines from the Abbey of S. Pietro, Assisi, to assist as it were at the apostasy of one of their former brethren, who, at the age of thirty-five, was exchanging a white habit for a brown one. My name was entered in the register, and I decided to take as my patron St. Peter, the fisherman-apostle. From now onwards I adopted the name of Peter for all professional purposes, and few people except my relations know that it is not my baptismal name. Thus started my *vita nuova* as a Brother of the Third Order of Penance. It pleased me to recall that through my Vernon ancestors I could claim descent with at least two Franciscan Tertiary saints—St. Louis of France and St. Elizabeth of Portugal. I asked them both to pray for me and to help me in my new life.

The greater part of the feast of St. Francis—October 4th—was passed at the hermitage of the Carceri. I climbed up the mountain-side before the sun had risen above the top of Monte Subasio and the air was still chilly. I served a Low Mass, breakfasted off black coffee and dry bread, and remained on for dinner—a frugal yet thoroughly festive meal, where at any rate there was no lack of wine, even if the food was rough and badly cooked. Altogether it was a wonderful experience for me, and these two kindly friars, with whom I was not then able to converse with any fluency in Italian, made me feel completely at home, treating me as if I was indeed one of their own brethren and of the same family.

A month later I was back again in England, but early the following spring I returned to Italy, Holy Week and Easter being spent in Assisi as guest of the friars at San Damiano. This was the first of many experiences of life in an Italian Franciscan friary, repeated again and again during the following eight years. San Damiano consists of a group of low buildings, which, except for a small campanile and a cross on the roof, might be mistaken for a farm. It is approached by a steep lane that turns sharp right after leaving Assisi by the Porta Nuova. On either side are olive trees, many of them very old, standing in little patches of land where corn is growing; then a group of farm buildings on the right, and suddenly, just as the road begins to get steeper, a shrine of the Madonna set into a high wall. A few

yards further on, one arrives at an open red-paved courtyard, to the
right of which is a bronze statue of St. Clare. At the time when St.
Francis left his father's home and adopted the life of a beggar, San
Damiano was a half-ruined chapel in the fields.   One day he
heard a voice saying: "Francis, rebuild My house!" and he obeyed
literally, collecting stones, dressing them, and repairing the chapel.
St. Clare and her first companions were brought here by St. Francis
and made their home in the adjoining buildings.   St. Francis himself came back to San Damiano when he was old and blind.   In
its garden he was inspired to compose the famous Canticle of the
Sun, one of the most perfect things in medieval literature.   And here
his body was brought back after death, so that St. Clare and her nuns
might look on his face for the last time and touch the marks of the
stigmata on his hands and feet.   Some years after the death of St.
Clare, her Community moved to a larger convent within the city
walls.   For over six centuries San Damiano has been occupied by
friars.   The buildings have been enlarged and rebuilt again and again,
but the place retains a primitive simplicity and charm.

*   *   *

In these surroundings, hallowed by such memories of St. Francis
and St. Clare, I spent Holy Week and Easter of 1925.   I occupied a
small white-washed cell that looked out over the garden, olive groves
and more distant mountains.   Then I got to know Padre Leone
Bracaloni, artist-friar and writer of many books and articles of
Franciscan art and history.   He was the " Padre Guardiano " of the
San Damiano Community, and he soon became both a father and
friend to me, for we had so many common interests.   Every afternoon
I joined the young clerics at recreation, and wandered about with
them, usually in the garden, or in the cloisters if it happened to be
wet.   It was not long before I got to know them intimately.   I still
cherish the *ricordo* which they gave me as a souvenir of that first
fortnight in their midst: a few dried roses from St. Francis' garden
at Our Lady of the Angels pasted on to a card.   Written on the
back are the words: *" Al buono e cortese fra Pietro Anson,
ringraziando per il gentile pensiero ricambiano auguri, saluti ed
unioni di preghieri, i chierici Francescani."*   When I re-read their
signatures—Basilio, Antonio, Pietro, Agostino, Serafino, Tommaso,
Alfonso, Domenico and Innocenzo—I can visualise each of them in
turn.   I recall those recreations in the garden or the cloisters, or other

evenings when they dragged me to the library and sat me down at that prehistoric piano from which two or three notes were missing, and made me perform for their entertainment. I used to buy chocolates and sweets for them, which were much appreciated, and maybe this is what they meant when they referred to my *gentile pensiero*.

The rosary made by Fra Innocenzo, and given me with the request that it should be my constant companion and a link between us, is still treasured. Nor do I forget the oft-repeated invitation given me by this vivacious young friar to spend a holiday with his family in a remote *paese* on the shores of Lake Bolsena. I never managed to arrange this visit, so I have not yet sampled that golden *vino spumante* which Fra Innocenzo loved to describe and which was made from the grapes which grew on the brown tufa hills around Montefiascone. But I am wrong—what about the bottle of this famous wine presented me one day some years later when Fra Innocenzo was a student in Rome? Did I not carry it under my arm all the way from S. Antonio in the Via Merulana as far as the Piazza Barberini? Yes! And I consumed the contents in the privacy of my bedroom and remember how good it was. Perhaps we may still meet again, who knows? If so I may yet have the chance to row and bathe on the Lago di Bolsena, and I will sketch all those places which he described to me . . . Grotte di Castro, Bagnorea, and the Monte Volsini.

*   *   *

I had already started work on the illustrations for *The Pilgrim's Guide to Franciscan Italy,* which was published two years later. The collection of data for this book involved much research and long journeys all over Tuscany and Umbria, for I was determined to make all the drawings on the spot and not to use photographs. I had armed myself with letters of commendation from Cardinal Bourne, and the Ministers Provincial of the Friars Minor and Capuchins in England, also from the Provincial of the S. Chiara province in Umbria. So I did not lack introductions when I turned up at friaries. I look back on those journeys during the summer of 1925 with the happiest memories, recalling the welcome given me by priests, innkeepers, peasants, and even beggars by the roadside, as well as by friars. I realised that the spirit of St. Francis is not dead in Italy. I shared the simple fare of I forget just how many friaries in Umbria, Tuscany and the Marches of Ancona. In addition to the Communities of San

Damiano, the Carceri, Sta. Maria degli Angeli at Assisi, I visited others at much more remote spots such as Greccio, La Foresta, and Fonte Colombo in the Valley of Rieti, where I could recapture the atmosphere of primitive Franciscan life better than in the friaries situated in or near towns. I spent four days on the little island of S. Francesco del Deserto in the Venetian lagoons—a picturesque cypress-girted convent on the edge of the water. I wandered round Lake Trasimeno more than once, and climbed the steep rock on which Cortona is perched, where I stopped a few days with the friars at S. Margherita, and from there visited the very primitive Capuchin friary of Le Celle. I paid two or three visits to the great monastery of the Osservanza outside Siena, not forgetting places of Franciscan interest in and around Arezzo (how friendly was that big Community at Sargiano!). Bologna, Florence, Chiusi and Poggibonsi—all these towns had to be included in my pilgrimage, for in all of them were churches or friaries associated with St. Francis. I followed the Little Poor Man through the streets of Rome, and traced his journeys through the upper valley of the Tiber. I made the ascent of Monte Alverna, that isolated limestone rock, over 4,000 feet above the sea, and spent a fortnight in the friary which now crowns its summit. Here it was that St. Francis received on his body the marks of Christ's crucifixion on the night of September 14th, 1224. The Community of La Verna has always been famous for hospitality, and pilgrims are given three days' board and lodging free of charge. Men stay in the great barrack-like dormitories in the monastery, while women are accommodated in a hostel situated in the village on the slopes of the mountain. I cannot pretend that there was much comfort at La Verna, and the food, though plentiful, was rough and not too well cooked. In that bracing air I used to get desperately hungry between the midday dinner and a very late supper. It was often bitterly cold at night, even though my visit took place at the end of June. I can still recall the thrill of getting out of bed shortly before midnight and groping my way down long corridors and dark stairs to the dimly lit church to assist at Matins, recited by the friars in their choir behind the high altar. Then I would follow them in procession to the chapel of the Stigmata, some distance from the church. This midnight procession was a never-to-be-forgotten experience. In winter time, before the building of the loggia, the friars often had to make their way through driving snow or torrential rains. There is a tradition that once, on the night of an exceptionally fierce storm, the friars decided to remain in church. The following morning a path to the chapel was marked on the snow by the footprints and claws of numberless beasts and birds, who had made up for the customary visit of the friars to the site of the Stigmata. After this silent reproof the Community was never known to omit the procession, no matter how bitter the cold or how deep the snow.

I was at La Verna for the feast of SS. Peter and Paul, and it was wonderful to watch the crowds of peasants from the neighbouring villages who climbed the mountain. Most of them came on foot, and so numerous were they, that it was with difficulty that they could be squeezed into the church for High Mass and Vespers. The music at La Verna has long been famous, and it was a delight to listen to the singing at the daily conventual Mass and Vespers. Nowhere in Italy did I hear better rendered Plain Chant. I made friends with many of the Community during that fortnight. After supper, when the weather was fine and warm enough, we used to sit on the terrace outside the church, watching the sun set over the mountains of the Casentino. I remember how quickly the time passed when chatting with Padre Pietro, Padre Geremia and others whose names I cannot now recall.

*   *   *

During that summer Padre Leone Bracaloni suggested to me one evening when we were together in the garden at San Damiano that it might be worth my while to consider the possibility of becoming a *Regular* Tertiary of this Community of which I had become so fond. He explained that I could make San Damiano my permanent home, share in the daily life of the friars, and that I would be useful as guide to the tourists and pilgrims of almost every nation who visited Assisi. Only a few weeks before the *Padre Guardiano* at La Verna had given me a similar invitation, but I was not attracted at the idea of residing all the year round on that lofty mountain, in winter time often shrouded in mists or covered with snow. Padre Leone, who seemed to take a great interest in my future prospects, made another proposal—that I should work in the library of Franciscan literature at the Chiesa Nuova in Assisi. He appeared to have made up his mind to keep me in Italy as a Regular Tertiary! I did not want to make any final decision in a hurry, so I went back to England for a few months, laden with a portfolio of drawings of all the Franciscan shrines I had visited. I felt somewhat homeless, and

S. DAMIANO, ASSISI.

having stayed with various friends both in England and Scotland, on the morning of September 17th, the feast of the Stigmata of St. Francis, when I had heard Mass in the Franciscan church of Our Lady of the Angels in Liverpool, I sat down and wrote to Padre Leone that I would accept his offer and that he might expect me back in Assisi within the next fortnight.

On Michaelmas Day I left England once more, took the now familiar route to Italy through Switzerland, and on the eve of the *festa di S. Francesco* found myself in my old room at S. Damiano. The vintage had started, and from my window I could watch the grapes being plucked from the vines and borne away in great open baskets by the *contadini*—a joyful scene, enlivened with much singing and laughter. The next few days were spent in Retreat as a preparation for my profession as a Tertiary. This ceremony took place on the evening of October 10th in the Choir of St. Clare, the Community kneeling in those rough wooden stalls used by St. Clare and her nuns 700 years ago. Dressed in the brown habit and girt with the white knotted cord, kneeling before Padre Leone, I promised to " observe during my whole life the Commandments of God, and the rule of the Third Order instituted by the Blessed Francis, according to the form confirmed by Popes Nicholas VI and Leo XIII ". Then Padre Leone replied: " And I, on the part of God, promise thee life everlasting if thou observest these things. In the name of the Father, and of the Son, and of the Holy Ghost, Amen."

The *Te Deum* was sung by the friars, and each of them came up to the altar step, saluting me with the kiss of peace. When this function was ended, they accompanied me to the dimly-lit refectory for supper. A vase of pink roses had been set before my place, and in honour of the event the customary silence was dispensed, my health being drunk with many a " *Prosit, auguri e saluti!* " It was good to be welcomed into the Franciscan family in this human way. I felt I had come home, or at least had found a very real spiritual home. Whether or no San Damiano, or any other Franciscan friary in Italy was to be my material home, had yet to be proved. That night as I got into bed I was almost certain that I could remain in these surroundings for ever.

I was under the impression that all had been arranged for me to take up my quarters at the Chiesa Nuova, and that I should find work to do in the library of Franciscan literature which had been collected there by Padre Bonaventura Marrani. But, apparently,

unsuspected obstacles had arisen, and so I remained on at San
Damiano, wearing the habit and sandals of the other friars, and
so far as externals undistinguishable from them. One morning,
about ten days after my profession, the Father Provincial said he
would like to have a talk with me. I wondered what was the reason.
I sat down in his room and he proceeded to explain that both he
and most of the Community were convinced that I had a vocation
to the priesthood, and that he wished me to enter the novitiate of
the Santa Chiara province. I was completely taken aback, never having
contemplated such a step for an instant. I was almost sure in my
own mind that my health would not stand the rigours of an Italian
novitiate, even less the six or seven years' intensive study of philosophy
and theology previous to ordination. But I had no wish to revert
to lay life again after this brief experience of living in Community
as a friar, so in the end I came to the conclusion that there was
nothing else to do but abide by the Provincial's conviction.

Accompanied by Padre Leone, I left San Damiano one bright,
autumn afternoon, our destination being the novitiate-house of the
province of Santa Chiara, which at that time was situated near Todi
in an old friary high above the valley of the Tiber. The *convento*
of La Spineta dates from the fourteenth century. It is a long low,
ramshackle two-storied group of buildings, erected with an eye to
economy rather than for architectural effect. Like so many Franciscan friaries in Italy it might be mistaken for a large farm if it
were not for the simple campanile. But the grey pantile roofs,
covered with yellow lichen, and the tiny cloister garth within, possess
real charm. From the large garden there is an immense panorama
across the valley of the Tiber, ending with the far distant range of the
Apennines, towering above the nearer slopes of Monte Martano that
hide Assisi and Foligno. Sometimes, on a very clear day, the jagged
peaks of the Gran Sasso d'Italia in the Abruzzi, some eighty miles or
so to the south-east, are visible, as well as sugar-loafed Monte Cuco,
near Urbino, fifty miles to the north. The tumbled surface of the
hillside below La Spineta is dotted with woods, where the oak trees
retain their golden-brown leaves throughout the winter. Little
villages, each with its campanile, break up this landscape of hills and
valleys. On those windless afternoons of early autumn during the
first weeks I was at La Spineta I used to listen to the voices of the
peasants working in the fields, the singing of a shepherd boy, or the
shriller cries of a small girl, evidently doing her best to prevent her

pigs from straying beyond the roadside where they were grazing . . . all these and other sounds were borne upon the clear dry air. A peaceful picture of pastoral beauty, typical of Umbria.

When I arrived at the friary about supper time on the evening of October 16th, 1925, and having gone up to the novitiate Common Room, I was confronted by six lads, whose ages ranged from fifteen to seventeen, all dressed in the brown habit, white cord, and sandals of St. Francis. With their tonsured heads, surrounded by haloes of black or brown hair, they were certainly a picturesque group. They studied me with an even greater curiosity, though without apparent shyness. All had been educated at the Serafic College at Todi under the Friars Minor, so were already familiar with Franciscan life. They were the sons of Umbrian peasants, and, as I discovered later on, had an ingenuous simplicity of character. I was old enough to be their father or uncle, but I felt rather like a new boy being plunged into school life for the first time.

It was quite a relief when the door opened and in walked another novice more of my own age—Fra. Bernardino—who had been a clerk in a Government office at Urbino, and who, socially and intellectually, was of a very different type to the six other novices. He could speak good French, and had a smattering of English. The novice master—Padre Gregorio—was, so I found out during the following weeks, a man of much sympathy and understanding. He did all in his power to make things easy for a thirty-six-year-old *inglese,* realising that I must find it hard in more ways than one to be confined to such a narrow and monotonous routine, petty rules and regulations, after the sort of life I had lived for so long.

The novitiate was housed in its own wing of the *convento,* quite apart from the rest of the Community, which consisted of four priests and two lay brothers. Each of us had a small whitewashed, brick-paved cell, looking out on to the cloister garth. It contained a bed, chair, table and washstand—nothing more. When the mild autumn days gave place to winter rains, and later on when La Spineta on its hill-top was exposed to the full blast of an icy *tramontana* from the snow-covered Apennines, these draughty cells could be painfully cold. Never in my life have I felt so miserable with cold as when sitting in that little cell on a December afternoon, trying to read or write. I used to wrap a blanket round my legs and over my stockingless feet—in the hope of keeping moderately warm. There was a stove in the common room where we had our conferences and met for recreations, but it was not always lit. Sometimes after supper, during the last weeks I was at La Spineta, Padre Gregorio used to order us off to bed and cancel recreation, saying that it would be better for us to get warm. When I recall those months in the novitiate, my mind always dwells on the intense cold and general sense of numbness, mental and physical. People who imagine that it is always warm and sunny in Italy in winter would get a nasty shock if they had to spend a few weeks on an exposed hillside in Umbria, and in many another province of the country. So far as comfort is concerned, they are far better off in Britain! For I also remember another winter when I was staying in Assisi, when almost every night during a bitter week in January I used to get into bed with all my clothes on.

This was our normal routine. We rose shortly before midnight for the offices of Matins and Lauds, recited in the choir behind the high altar. The office was said fairly quickly and we returned to bed about half an hour later. We got plenty of sleep, for we went to bed never later than 8.30, and after this break of half an hour in the middle of the night had another five and a half hours' sleep before rising at 6 o'clock for Prime and Meditation. Moreover, there was an hour's siesta every afternoon if one chose to sleep. After Terce and Mass we had breakfast, if a small cup of coffee (so called) and a piece of dry bread can be described by this name. The rest of the morning was spent in manual work or study, the former consisting of sweeping and dusting the church and cloisters—not very strenuous. I used to give lessons in music and drawing to the young novices, and found them keen pupils. I also played the harmonium at Sunday Mass and Vespers. The chief difficulty was to prevent the boys singing anything but *fortissimo*! They had no idea of modulating their shrill, harsh voices. Dinner, preceded by Sext and None, was at midday. The food was roughly cooked but plentiful, very much what would be found in any fairly well-to-do peasant family. Dinner usually consisted of a brimful plate of thick soup in which floated rice, vegetables or *pasta*. On Sundays and feast-days we were given *past asciutta,* i.e., macaroni with tomato or other rich sauce. This was followed by a second course of meat or fish, the latter generally dried cod or tunny fish in oil, occasionally salt herring; the meal ending with cheese or fruit. A small flask of much watered-down red wine was set before each place. So it will be seen that we did not starve, whatever may have been the other privations and hardships.

The community, like most other Franciscan friaries in Italy, lived entirely on alms, in money or in kind, supplied by benefactors and friends. Two or three times a year the Guardian or one of the lay-brothers went forth to quest for alms and food supplies. He might call at some neighbouring farm and find out how much corn or oil or wine they would be willing to contribute the next quarter towards the maintenance of the Community. Then visits would be paid to the grocers and butchers in the villages, so that in the end the friary was fairly well provided with necessities. Our own vineyard supplied most of the wine; and vegetables came from the garden.

After dinner followed an hour's recreation, when once or twice a week we went for a walk along the roads or across the paths through the fields and woods, maybe to some neighbouring village, where sometimes we would be entertained by the parish priest to wine and biscuits. Recreation being over, we retired to our cells for a siesta. Vespers were recited at 3 o'clock, the rest of the afternoon being spent in reading and study. Our evening meal consisted of soup, meat or eggs. Sometimes we got a salad. There was always more than enough wine to drink. Night prayers in church followed supper, and then came a short recreation before going to bed. It was not a strenuous existence; in fact, the main idea seemed to be that the novices must be kept out of mischief and given the minimum amount of occupation in conformity with the rules laid down by Canon Law. These forbid any studies in philosophy or theology being done during the twelve months' novitiate, which is regarded mainly as a time for absorbing the spirit and rules of the particular religious Order.

After the middle of November the weather broke up. For several weeks we had incessant rains, followed by snow. My health began to rebel, and it became difficult and then impossible for me to live the ordinary life of the Community. Eventually Padre Gregorio wrote to the Provincial and told him that he felt it would be better for me to depart. I bade farewell to La Spineta a few days before Christmas. Only those who know something of the hidden depths of the Umbrian temperament will understand the emotional, not to say embarrassing scenes that took place when I had to say good-bye to my fellow-novices. These lads had always been friendly and good-natured enough, but it never dawned on me how devoted they had become. The day before I left, nothing would keep these young *frati* out of my cell; each wanted to give me something by which

J

to remember him. And all they could give me, having nothing else they could call their own, were pious cards, on which they wrote their names, with some affectionate message.   I still cherish these crudely coloured pictures of saints—a " Sant' Antonio " scrawled on by Fra. Lorenzo; a " San Luigi " left me with many tears and embraces by Fra. Egidio; and other simple "*ricordi*" of those peasant lads in Umbria who were my companions that autumn and winter. Some of them returned to their homes, having discovered that they had no vocation for the religious life; others have long since been ordained priests, and they did not forget to send me their ordination cards.   A few used to write me an occasional post card until the out-break of war in 1939 put an end to our correspondence.

This Franciscan experiment failed as I rather expected would happen. But I am grateful to the Provincial for the opportunity he gave me to learn something of the inner life of a Franciscan Community in Italy. It taught me that the spirit of St. Francis is still very much alive, and that in his own Umbria he would still find his friars living in poverty and simplicity, just as he wished them to do. Those months at La Spineta might have killed all my love for every-thing Franciscan, but actually it was just the opposite. They taught me lessons which I hope I shall never forget.

*   *   *

It is now nearly twenty years since this incident in my roving career took place. During this period my knowledge of the Fran-ciscan Order has increased, and my circle of friends among the various branches of the Franciscan family has widened.   Among those many friends whom I have made since 1925, I must mention the late Fr. Cuthbert of Brighton. My friendship with him started quite casually, due to my having written to him for a letter of intro-duction to the Capuchin friaries I might have occasion to visit while collecting material for my *Pilgrim's Guide to Franciscan Italy*. This was early in the summer of 1925. The letter lies before me at this moment—a brief Latin document, quite in keeping with the Fran-ciscan spirit of poverty, for the paper on which it is written must have been torn off the cheapest of cheap blocks, probably bought at the nearest Woolworths. Not the sort of paper one might expect the Minister Provincial of the Friar Minor Capuchins of the English Province, and a Master of Arts in the University of Oxford *honoris causa* to use.

This scrap of paper was treated with great respect, so I soon discovered when I presented it at Capuchin friaries in Umbria and Tuscany. Every Father Guardian seemed to know of Padre Cuthberto—many of them had read his Life of St. Francis in the Italian translation. I spent some happy days in lonely friaries among the Apennines, thanks to this letter of introduction. I enjoyed the simple and often primitive hospitality of the communities of bearded *frati*, whose manner of life was not far removed from those of the first years of the Capuchin Reform in the 16th century.

When the *Pilgrim's Guide to Franciscan Italy* was completed I asked Fr. Cuthbert if he could find time to read the typescript. He agreed to do so, and returned it with valuable suggestions and criticisms. A few months after the publication of this my first book, he invited me to come to Oxford to take part in a Summer School of Franciscan Studies. So one afternoon in August, 1928, I journeyed to Oxford, just a little nervous of meeting this learned Capuchin and wondering how we should get on together. For I had heard that he was shy and reserved, what is more, that he could be positively rude to strangers. But my fears were needless: from the moment Fr. Cuthbert greeted me on the doorstep of Grosseteste House I knew I had found a friend, and a friend he remained until his death twelve years later.

That Summer School of Franciscan Studies was typical of its originator—one might say characteristically Cuthbertian! For was there any other English friar at that date who would have been so bold as to gather together some fifty or more men and women, only ten of whom were Catholics, to discuss Franciscan history and spirituality? Thanks to Fr. Cuthbert's rare gift for dealing with non-Catholics, and above all his sympathy, the school was a great success. We forgot we were in 20th century Oxford, and the differences which separated us in so many ways, for our minds were concentrated on the message of St. Francis to humanity. Perhaps never before did it dawn on us just how much this message could and ought to mean to ourselves and to our neighbours.

This was the first of many subsequent visits to Grosseteste House —a typical mid-Victorian neo-Gothic Revival red brick house in a terrace on the Iffley Road. For several years I always arranged to spend the feast of St. Francis in that friary, utterly Franciscan if only because of its entire lack of comfort or convenience. One day Fr. Cuthbert told me to look out of the window, remarking: " That's

where the new Greyfriars is to be built!" He went on to explain
that the church of SS. Edmund and Frideswide, which had been
erected by the Jesuits, was to be handed over to the Capuchins, and
that a new friary and House of Studies would be added to it, so
as to form a large group of buildings. He was delighted that the
project which had been in his mind for so many years, and of which
he had dreamed since he first came to live in Oxford in 1911, was
to be realised at last. We had long discussions about the planning
and style of architecture. The latter seemed fairly obvious, for it
would have been foolish not to have followed the lines of Fr.
Benedict Williamson's Romanesque church, with its red roof and
flint walls. Fr. Cuthbert held very definite views on the architecture
of Franciscan churches and friaries. He used to maintain that there
was only one *real* Capuchin Franciscan friary in England—Crawley
—and that all the rest were no more than makeshifts; none of them
expressing the spirit and ideals of the Order. Of one such Capuchin
church—I refrain from mentioning its name—he once remarked to
me: " It's so un-Franciscan in every respect that they've had to cast
' S.F.' in large capital letters on every drainpipe to remind one that
it was erected in commemoration of the seventh centenary of St.
Francis!" Fr. Cuthbert had a caustic tongue, and could make the
most withering statements at times.

One thing Fr. Cuthbert was determined to ensure in the new
friary at Oxford was the traditional, though rather inconvenient,
Capuchin arrangement of a choir behind the high altar. Some of
his brethren objected to this plan, maintaining that there was no
logical reason to adhere to what was no more than a post-Tridentine
or southern European position for the choir. They reminded him
that in the earlier days Franciscan choirs were invariably placed in
front of the high altar; that the new Greyfriars was to symbolise
the return of the medieval Franciscans to Oxford rather than the
arrival of the Capuchin branch of the Franciscan family. However,
Fr. Cuthbert got his own way, and it was merely a proof of his
almost passionate loyalty and love for the traditions of that reformed
branch of the Order to which he belonged.

It was my privilege to have helped Fr. Cuthbert to correct the proofs
and to check references to quotations in his monumental work
*The Capuchins—a contribution to the History of the Counter
Reformation.* This involved many visits to the Bodleian Library, not
to mention long hours spent in discussing each chapter. There can

be no doubt that this is his outstanding literary effort, and it is also the expression of his inmost feelings on the ideals of Franciscan life. He gloried in the fact that the first Capuchins had broken away from the older groups of Friars Minor. He used to tell me that if he were younger, he would like to start yet another reform movement within the Order, arguing that the essential spirit of Franciscanism lies in its capacity to strike off cuttings from the parent tree. Fr. Cuthbert was always just a little heterodox in his views on many subjects. There were many of his brethren who felt that he was inclined to be unduly optimistic about the chances of leading those outside the Church into the True Fold. This zeal for the welfare of the other sheep induced him to give lectures to a Franciscan Study Circle which met at the Guildhouse in London where services of an undenominational character were then carried on by Dr. Percy Dearmer and Miss Maude Royden.

Of his own Order he could write: " Br. Elias' greatest mistake was that he sought to develop the Franciscan fraternity in emulation of that most perfect piece of medieval organisations . . . the Order of St. Dominic." He maintained that the later Franciscan reformers too were " lured by the Dominican organisation ". They forgot the simple fact so emphasised by St. Francis, that the " fundamental purpose of the Franciscan vocation was to revive primarily in its own members a perfect Christ life as portrayed in the Gospels: to *be* rather than to *do* ". He was prepared to defend the possibly dangerous principle that " the Rule is above the Order and that the Order exists only to effect the full observance of the Rule ".

But it must not be imagined for one instant that Fr. Cuthbert lacked the spirit of true obedience to authority—it was very much the opposite. He showed this when the order came one day for him to leave his beloved Oxford, which had been his home for nearly twenty years, and to start for Italy. His superiors had selected this elderly English friar for the important post of President of the recently established Capuchin Commission for Franciscan Research Studies. So he packed up his few worldly goods and went off to Italy. It was not easy for this typical John Bull, aged sixty-four, to take root in Umbria. Poor Fr. Cuthbert suffered a good deal during the first few years as superior of a cosmopolitan Community of research students in a foreign land, where the climate, language, and food were unfamiliar and uncongenial. The vast *palazzo* in the via San Francesco—so utterly different from his own ideals of a

Franciscan friary—was still in the hands of carpenters, painters and decorators when I visited him during the winter of 1931. There was no central heating, and he seemed numb with the cold. But on my return a year later the situation had improved. He had discovered new interests, and talked much of the work he was doing among the poor of Assisi, especially the children—the last thing in the world one might have suspected from this old man who had been sent to Italy to direct students in historical research.

Among the different branches of the Franciscan family who dwelt in Assisi there existed—so it must be admitted—something of that aloofness one finds even in the best regulated families. It was but natural that each branch should feel perhaps a certain jealousy of the other; an unwillingness to make contacts. Fr. Cuthbert was much distressed at this state of affairs, and did his best to mingle with every branch of the Order, rather to their surprise, for this was something quite novel and a breaking down of centuries-old traditions. In his eyes they were all his brothers in St. Francis, no matter what colour their habits, or if they were shaven or unshaven!

Our last meeting was at Crawley in the summer of 1936. He had a lot to tell me about what he had endured during the war between Italy and Abyssinia. I never realised how intensely British he was in his political opinions. He said that it had been painful to him to obey orders and hoist the Italian flag on the college roof on the occasion of any victory for the troops of the country in which he was domiciled, for he was a firm believer in the policy of " sanctions ", apparently quite unable to appreciate the Italian point of view. He confessed that he felt very much out of touch with life and remarked that he would like nothing better than to be sent back to England to end his days working among the poor at Peckham or in the Kentish hop-fields. " It's all wrong to be living perpetually in the past centuries ", were his words. This erudite author of international fame remained the simple friar at heart. He firmly believed that his true vocation was to win souls to God by preaching the Gospel, following the footsteps of his Father St. Francis rather than to spend his time poring over manuscripts. He loved his native land perhaps more than most Englishmen, but I think he would not mind that his body was laid to rest on the hillside overlooking the tomb of the Little Poor Man of Assisi, of whom there was no more devoted disciple. It was good to read that not only such famous men and Franciscan scholars as Arnoldo Fortini, Mayor of Assisi, and Johannes

Jorgensen, the Danish convert writer, were present at his funeral, but likewise vast crowds of the poor folk of the city. May he rest in peace.

Fr. Paschal Robinson, now Apostolic Nuncio in Dublin and titular Archbishop of Tyana, is another famous Franciscan whose acquaintance I made in Rome many years ago. I called on him when he was living with the Irish Friars Minor at their college adjoining the Church of St. Isidoro, during the intervals between his journeys in Palestine, Transjordania and Cyprus as Apostolic Visitor for the Latin Patriarchate in Jerusalem and the Uniate Churches. He had many thrilling stories to tell of his experiences in the Near East, and later on of other adventures in Greece, Syria and Egypt. Then this busy friar managed to find time to read through the manuscript of my *Pilgrim's Guide to Franciscan Italy,* and his suggestions and corrections were well worth accepting, for Fr. Paschal, as he then was, had a world-wide fame as an authority on medieval history, and in particular of his own Order.

Padre Livario Oliger, O.F.M., is a Franciscan historical writer of almost equal fame with whom I was also in touch during the years I lived in Italy. He, too, revised the manuscript of my first book, and it was always a pleasure to call on him at the International Franciscan College of St. Antonio in the via Merulana—that great barrack of a place where young friars from almost every nation in the world make up the big cosmopolitan Community. I can only claim a passing acquaintance with Padre Agostino Gemelli, Rector of the Catholic University at Milan, and I doubt if that other famous Italian Friar Minor, Padre Vittorino Facchinetti, would recall meeting me one day in Assisi, though I have not forgotten the occasion.

Nearer home there have been friendships of a much closer nature with Fathers Stanislaus, Alfred, Paul, Dunstan, and many other Capuchins, some gone to their eternal reward, others still working for souls up and down England. Not only priests of the Order can I count among my friends; there are innumerable lay-brothers, especially Bro. Paschal of Preston, who was the first visitor who came to stay with me after I had made my home in the north-east of Scotland.

My knowledge of every branch of the Franciscan family has gone on increasing, not to speak of my affection, admiration and respect for individual Friars and Tertiaries. I have stayed with the Franciscans in Egypt and Palestine, and could write a whole chapter dealing with life in the various hospices for pilgrims where I was their guest. I have also stayed with the Capuchin Fathers in France and in Holland. I have happy memories of several weeks with the Capuchins in Rotterdam at their little friary hidden away among the docks, and of the Seamen's Institute of which they were in charge. I hope that neither Pater Quirinus nor Pater Adrianus, wherever they may now be, think I have forgotten all about them or the times they entertained me at Amsterdam and Ymuiden. It would be impossible to forget that original and kind-hearted French Capuchin, Père Colomban Lefebvre, who after many years as a naval officer found a late vocation in the Franciscan Order. He had a way of turning up in the most unexpected places during the years that I was often in France. I was sure to run into him at maritime congresses, and on another occasion he appeared on the remote Isle of Ushant; then I collided with his tall bearded figure in the vast crowds of a French National Pilgrimage at Lourdes. If I went to any dockyard town, such as Brest or Toulon, Père Colomban followed me, or was there to greet me on my arrival—always with a more than fraternal embrace and kiss on both cheeks and an outburst of nautical language. Nor must I forget Ireland, where the Capuchins in Dublin have long been good friends, especially Fr. Senan, Editor of the *Capuchin Annual* and *Father Mathew Record,* who invariably manages to find space for articles I inflict on him, and unlike the editors of many other religious periodicals, pays for them generously.

Nearer home I have been the guest of both Friars Minor and Capuchins in many parts of Great Britain—Panton Hall, Over Wyresdale, Pantasaph, Olton, Crawley, Peckham, Forest Gate, Gorton, Glasgow, Chilworth, Walsingham—all these place names recall enjoyable times spent with Franciscans during the past twenty years. Had it not been for apparently impossible obstacles to my getting into the United States at one time I might still be teaching drawing in the Franciscan Colleges at San Luis Rey or Santa Barbara in California, or among the Indians in New Mexico. The friars wanted me to come, but the door was closed—still there is no knowing if it may not open in the future!

CHAPTER VI

MORE MEMORIES OF ITALY

I must now go back a few years: I have allowed myself to look ahead and to recall events out of their strictly chronological sequence, just to show how my life was developing on new lines. Back then I return to the spring of 1925 when I again found myself in Italy. One of my father's brothers, Arthur Anson, who had been a tea-planter in Ceylon for the greater part of his life, decided to retire and to end his days in Italy. One day I received a letter from him, asking if I would care to meet him on his arrival at Venice, with a view to helping him to settle in at the villa he had rented at Asciano in Southern Tuscany. He felt that my knowledge of Italian would be useful and that I could act as interpreter. Such an invitation needed no consideration. I was at a loose end at the time, with nothing definite to do. I replied that nothing would please me better. I set off within a fortnight.

Asciano proved to be a cheerful little red-brick town, hidden away in the clefts of that strange desert of clay hills situated south of Siena. Edward Hutton tells us in his *Siena and Southern Tuscany* that "Asciano is to be loved for her own sake, and strictly for what she remains to-day, one of the most charming of all the delightful towns that lie like flowers on the skirts of Siena." When I had spent a few days there I felt he did right to describe the situation as "delicious, cosily hidden among the vineyards in the billows of the desert". Like this author who has written so many books about Italy I found that her people "are honest and courteous and bid you welcome". I arrived at Asciano late at night after a long journey from England, very tired, cold and hungry. As my uncle had not yet landed in Italy I took up my quarters at the little inn, which, like Mr. Hutton, I found "clean and humble, and knowing nothing of strange comforts, is all for home". The following morning I discovered that Asciano has "treasures that many a place more famous might envy". I was lost in wonder at the beauty of the altar piece by Sassetta in the *Collegiata*, depicting the Birth of Our Lady. I found almost equally fine examples of the early Sienese masters in S. Agostino, but the greatest treasure of all was hidden away in the usually locked-up church of S. Francesco, only a few yards from Villa del Campo, my uncle's future home—an exquisite Lippo Memmi, Madonna and Child. Mr. Hutton describes this painting as " one of the loveliest things in Italy, rare and precious, and of astonishing quality ". This masterpiece hung on the wall of a seldom used church, forgotten and neglected. But perhaps it was better even so, than removed from its proper surroundings to a Museum or Art Gallery.

Around Asciano lies a bold and rugged desert-like country made up of clay hills; full of chasms, precipices, gullies and dark abysses. In many places it is completely bare, elsewhere brought into cultivation. In summer the roads were thick with dust; in winter the mud could be so deep and soft that one really needed sea-boots to wade through it. The climate offered violent contrasts. I can recall days and nights of enervating heat in July and August, when one felt so limp and exhausted that the only thing to do was to sit about in the shady garden at the villa. I remember days in December and January when I was so cold in those big, draughty un-heated rooms, even if the midday sun did create an illusion of heat, that I would wrap a blanket round my legs and warm my frozen hands over a charcoal brazier. How the icy *tramontana* could blow sometimes, and how glad one was of the thickest clothes one possessed.

Villa del Campo was a low, rambling, two-storied house, with the plaster peeling off its walls as the result of long exposure to sun, wind and rain. It was set back from the road amid trees and shrubs, but one got a charming view from the windows and terrace over the red roofs and red brick towers of the old-world town, backed by rolling hills, planted with grey-green olives, standing in corn fields or interspersed with vineyards. Dark green, spire-shaped cypresses framed the picture, contrasting with the olives and the brighter green of the young corn—which turned to a deep gold as the spring gave place to early summer, when the harvest took place. Away to the north lay range after range of hills, the most distant a pale blue against the even paler blue of the horizon. To the south one got a glimpse of the striking outline of Mont' Amiata, about twenty miles distant. The living rooms were all on the first floor, most of them opening out of each other—rather awkward for bedrooms! Beneath them were dark stores, the wine cellars and vaults. The kitchen was on the top floor. My uncle took over the contents of the villa, which included all its rather the worse-for-wear furniture—some of it really good period pieces, but for the rest mere junk. Homely is the best way to describe Campo; there was nothing luxurious about it, and it lacked modern sanitary arrangements and a bathroom. Here it was that my seventy-year-old uncle established himself in May, 1925, and here he remained until his death some ten or more years later—a strange and solitary existence, for he never managed to speak Italian with any fluency. He occupied his time making wireless sets and gramophones. One of the attractions of staying with him were the opportunities for listening to his big collection of gramophone records, only surpassed by that belonging to Compton Mackenzie on the Isle of Barra.

My uncle used to proclaim that he was an agnostic and liked to feel that he was completely tolerant towards all forms of religion, pagan as well as Christian, Catholic as well as Protestant. But, as a matter of fact, he still retained a good deal of the Anglican mentality and outlook in which he had been brought up, and it was amusing to notice how this would come to the surface when he was roused.

He contributed generously to all the local charities and, from what I could gather from remarks made to me by the inhabitants, he was much respected. But he remained a mysterious personality whom they could not understand. " Il suo zio, è tanto buono, tanto caritatevole, ma—non mangia carne, non beve vino, e non è sposato." Such was the summing up of his character by a native of Asciano. This Tuscan farmer just could not understand this forestiere who was so good and charitable; never ate meat, never drank wine and, above all, had never married—there was something definitely odd about this elderly English bachelor!

The daily life of Asciano remained an unknown quantity to him. It was impossible to talk about what went on at Mass, the local feste, the scandal and the gossip, ecclesiastical and social, for he knew nothing of them, and was not interested. He might just as well have been living in Tooting or Tunbridge Wells as in Tuscany. There have been many other elderly Englishmen who have lived very much the same sort of life as voluntary exiles in Italy, and I suppose that it did appeal to him in some indefinable way, as there was nothing to prevent him from returning to the land of his birth.

Dear old uncle Arthur! I have often wondered if you were really happy in that self-imposed exile in Southern Tuscany, and if you would have been more at home in your native England. Like your nephew, there was a good deal of the solitary about you; you liked company, but you could manage quite well without it. You had been a rover in your youth, but you ended your life as a recluse in that none too comfortable villa, almost entirely lacking any modern conveniences, on the outskirts of a little Italian town where your fellow-countrymen seldom penetrated. Your reading consisted of the *Manchester Guardian*—how furious you used to be when it failed to arrive regularly!—and those shabby, much-worn, paper-covered novels, most of them dating from the last decade of the 19th century, which you had brought with you from Ceylon. You read them over and over again, and appeared to get a certain enjoyment out of them. Still, I think you found more satisfaction in playing with your gramophones, or latterly the radio sets, which you made yourself. What a horrible mess your living-room used to be in with all the bits of wire and other gadgets littering up every table and chair! And what weird noises the queer looking instruments made when you were experimenting with sound boxes, valves, horns, and so on. It is a blessing that you died before this war, and before Italy found itself a belligerent country. It is impossible to picture you with German troops billeted in the villa, maybe amusing themselves with your gramophones and radio sets. You had so often proclaimed yourself a free-thinker, yet you were buried according to the rites of the Church of England in the Protestant cemetery at Siena. I have little doubt that in Heaven you are playing with celestial wireless and making music more satisfying than even the best of your sound boxes and horns could produce!

*   *   *

For myself, during the many visits I paid to Asciano between 1925 and 1932, I was happy enough making sketches in and around the town, and felt quite at home in the churches, where the services were as informal and spontaneous as they had been at Gavinana. The singing at the parish Mass in the *Collegiata* on Sunday mornings was perhaps even more incredible; the behaviour of the congregation more noticeably irreverent. The few benches were reserved for elderly women, and I generally ensconced myself on the step of one of the confessional boxes, if I failed to squeeze in among the crowd of men who sat on the altar rails.

On cold winter mornings the women used to carry into church small braziers containing smouldering charcoal which they placed under their voluminous skirts after they had settled into the benches. Whatever might be lacking in the way of reverence and dignity of worship, there were compensations in the ease in which one could go to Confession or Holy Communion. At any hour of the morning one had merely to walk into the *Collegiata* where one was almost certain to find a priest, who regarded it as part of his job to hear a Confession or give Communion. It was all so simple. Men went to Confession in the sacristy, and one merely flopped down on the floor beside the priest. This confession was so easy in comparison with what one is accustomed to in this country, because all one had to do was to reply "*si*" or "*no*" to the examination of conscience fired at one by the priest, or to add the number of occasions one remembered having been guilty of a particular sin or omission suggested by the confessor. Then, having been shriven and given a brief penance, the priest would don a cotta and stole, light the candles on the high altar, if they were not already burning; meanwhile one was reciting the *Confiteor* as he took the ciborium from the tabernacle and gave Holy Communion.

*   *   *

About five miles to the south of Asciano is the famous monastery of Monte Oliveto; the mother House of the Olivetan branch of the Benedictines, founded early in the 14th century by Blessed Bernard Tolomei. It was a long walk to this great abbey, hidden away in the heart of clay hills, for the road twisted and turned as it climbed higher and higher. Then at last one came to an oasis in the midst of this desert, getting a glimpse of a great block of red brick buildings behind a screen of slender cypresses, but not until one actually arrived close up to the entrance did the full size of the abbey reveal itself. Medieval monasteries had to be built to withstand attacks by armed forces, and Monte Oliveto must have been difficult to besiege. It looks almost impregnable, jutting out into a deep gorge. This lonely fortress-like monastery commands a view over miles and miles of country—a "barren sea of clay, billow after billow rolling away to the horizon, broken only by the far hills", as Edward Hutton describes it . . . a landscape of "fierceness, terror and bitterness".

There was nothing fierce or terrifying about those red brick walls, mellowed and subdued by centuries of exposure to sun, wind and rain. I walked through the archway of the gatehouse, glancing up at the exquisite Della Robbia Madonna, placed there to welcome the pilgrim. On the other side of the gatehouse, in a similar niche, St. Benedict was seated. In his left hand he held a copy of the Holy Rule, opened at the prologue. "Hearken, O my son, to the precepts

of thy Master, and incline the ear of thine heart." With that gentle
smile which only the Della Robbias and their immediate pupils knew
how to mould in clay, the saint bade farewell to the parting guest.
I passed on, and in a few moments came to the main door. I rang
the bell, and after that delay which is so characteristic of many
religious Communities, the door opened and a monk in a white habit
greeted me. He led me through silent cloisters and long corridors,
eventually showing me into a suite of rooms which looked as if
intended for the reception of a cardinal, even if the decorations and
furniture were worn and faded. My recollections of those three or
four days at Monte Oliveto are of infinite peace and quiet. I cannot
recall any other monastery in which the silence was so marked. The
little Community which occupied this vast barrack were housed in
another wing and I never set eyes on them except in church, or when
I met them in the gardens at recreation. I took my meals in the
solitude of my rooms and not in the refectory with the monks as is
usual in Benedictine monasteries. I was free to wander where I liked.
I took my sketch book and made many drawings of the exterior of
the abbey. I studied the famous frescoes of the life of St. Benedict,
painted on the walls of the cloister by the 16th-century artist, Sodoma,
whose " joyful life and cheerful manners " have been immortalised
by Vasari.

Maybe because of the white habits worn by the Olivetan Benedictines, I felt very much at home here. When I looked at them in
choir I might have been back again at Caldey. Among the Community
were several young clerics, a proof that this once widespread branch
of the Benedictine family was taking on a new lease of life. At one
time the Olivetans had nearly two hundred monasteries in different
countries of Europe; to-day not more than a dozen are left, most of
which are in Italy. The founder of this reform movement envisaged
a life of much greater severity than is laid down in the Rule of St.
Benedict. There was little or no trace of such rigid austerity in any
of the Olivetan monasteries which I visited. Both at Monte Oliveto
itself, at S. Maria Nova in Rome—where I used to call on Abbot
Placido Lugano, the learned monastic historian and editor of the
Revista Storia Benedettina—at S. Miniato al Monte, Florence, and
at S. Maria di Montallegro, on the hills above Rapallo, I got the
impression that both the observance and the spirit differed little from
that of the black Benedictines in Italy. There was a quiet peaceful family life; the Divine Office was recited in choir, a certain

amount of parochial work and teaching were carried on. Just because the Olivetans have remained an independent branch of the great Benedictine family they struck me as possessing something of the restful calm of a placid backwater on a river, undisturbed by the movement of the main stream. It was difficult to picture these monks standing out for a purely contemplative form of life or engaging in any very strenuous form of missionary activity.

*   *   *

Visitors at Harbour Head, when they lie in bed, contemplate a dozen or more water colours that help to keep up the memory of monastic wanderings in Italy which took place at intervals between 1922 and 1932. Many of these drawings were made when I was at work on a book dealing with the eremitical life in the Catholic Church, published in 1932 under the title of *The Quest of Solitude*. From Subiaco one can travel (on the walls) to Monte Cassino, Monte Oliveto, Camaldoli, the Grande Chartreuse, the Certosa di Firenze, and other monasteries not so famous but of which I have happy memories in what now seem far off times when it was so easy to move about Europe.

I remember one August when I was staying in Rome and the thermometer registered between 90 and 100 Fahrenheit during the day and the nights were not appreciably cooler. What a relief to escape from the city into the Sabine mountains in a pilgrimage to Subiaco! The train rattled along across the Campagna. Wide stretches of dried-up grassland appeared to afford little or no pasture for the sheep and goats grazing on them. We began to climb what looked like an impenetrable wall of mountains in front of us. Tivoli —with its cascades and waterfalls—appeared on the right. It was difficult to resist buying the grapes offered for sale at the station. Then we moved on again, still climbing, but through a wide valley. The mountains on either side became higher and steeper. There were glimpses of villages perched on rocky peaks, their situations chosen, no doubt, for reasons of defence. At Mandela I got out and changed into another train. The valley closed in as we proceeded— ever climbing—until at last the dusty, jolting little train steamed into the terminus.

I was glad I had not to make the rest of this pilgrimage on foot. I managed to hire a *carozza* to drive me up to the monastery of Santa Scholastica. The sun poured down mercilessly and the road was steep and dusty. It wound out from the suburbs of the city through a narrow gorge. We turned a corner by an old bridge, beside which was a ruined chapel. To the right the mountains rose up precipitously two or three thousand feet; above them, much further away, was the peak of Monte Carpineto, crowned by a cross. On the left the valley seemed to be equally precipitous, but not so densely wooded, its slopes consisting of bare rock on which grew a few scattered olives, ilexes and oak trees. Immediately above us, hanging on the edge of the gorge, was the abbey. A ziz-zag road led up to it, and until recent times when this road was blasted out of the mountain side, the only approach was a rough mule path.

A closer view of the abbey revealed that it was an immense pile of buildings, irregular in form, built in almost every style of architecture, from the 11th to the 18th century, and reared on enormous foundations. It was founded in the 5th century by St. Benedict himself but originally dedicated to SS. Cosmas and Damian. At one time there were twelve Benedictine monasteries in and around Subiaco, but only two are left—Santa Scholastica and the *Sacro Speco*. The only disappointing feature of the former was the church—a dull piece of severe Classic architecture dating from the middle of the 18th century, which at the time of my visit, badly needed redecorating and painting. It looked neglected and uncared for. There was a guest house for visitors and here I was accommodated, having my meals in the refectory with the Community as is the normal Benedictine custom. Two abbots sat at the high table—the Abbot-General of the Cassinese Congregation of the Primitive Observance to which the monastery belongs, and the Abbot of Santa Scholastica, who being an *abbot nullius, i.e.,* having the rights and privileges of a bishop, wore a purple *zuchetto* instead of the black one worn by ordinary abbots.

During the week I explored the neighbourhood, climbed over the mountains and wandered many a mile along the gorge far below the monastery where the overhanging trees gave a welcome shade on those hot August mornings when the sun blazed down so mercilessly from a sky of cloudless blue. I could quench my thirst with luscious blackberries that grew in profusion or with the ice-cold water of a stream. I wondered if St. Benedict had done so more than fourteen centuries ago. As I watched a shepherd leading his flock of sheep to the stream, it would not have surprised me if the saint, clad in his rough habit of wool, with long hair and beard, had appeared from behind a rock.

It was easier to think of St. Benedict when clambering over those bare rocky mountains than in the confines of Santa Scholastica, where his presence seemed curiously remote, and where, so I felt, he might not feel altogether at home if he were to come back again. I was far more conscious of the presence of Abbot Casaretto who had been responsible for the establishment of the now world-wide Congregation about the middle of the last century, and of which Subiaco is the most famous monastery, maybe because the Guest Master kept on reminding me that this community kept strictly to *mezza notte e magro,* in other words, that they rose at 2 a.m. for Matins and Lauds and normally abstained from flesh meat. But I noticed in the refectory that many of the monks appeared to have a dispensation from *magro* and when I once assisted at the *mezza notte* office there seemed to be a far from complete attendance of Community in choir.

More attractive in every way than Santa Scholastica was the little monastery of the *Sacro Speco,* reached by a path up the mountain, leading to a grove of dark ilex trees. Passing through this grove one arrives without any warning at the *Sacro Speco,* built on a narrow ledge beneath an overhanging cliff. It looks out over the precipitous gorge, with mountains rising up in every direction as far as the eye can see. Here is the birthplace of Benedictine monasticism, for the monastery is erected over the cave—the *Sacro Speco* itself—where Benedict—the youthful son of a Roman patrician—lived in complete solitude for three years—cut off from human intercourse, his whole mind absorbed with the things of God.

A flight of steps led down to a garden, where, so the legend relates, St. Francis of Assisi changed into roses the thorn bushes into which St. Benedict once threw himself when faced with a violent temptation. It is curious that these particular rose trees have no thorns. The six or seven monks who lived at the *Sacro Speco* lead an almost eremitical life, observing a much stricter rule than that of the neighbouring abbey of S. Scholastica.

*   *   *

Monte Cassino—to-day reduced to dust and ruin—appealed to me far more than Subiaco. When I think of this great Benedictine abbey I immediately recall that first view from the train—a mountain rising up out of a wide-stretching, fertile plain; like a headland jutting out into a green ocean, its summit crowned by a group of buildings which,

K

when seen from below, might be a fort rather than a monastery.   In
a sense it is a fort—a spiritual fortress—the cradle and stronghold of
Western monachism for more than fourteen centuries.   It is difficult
to find words adequate to convey the overwhelming majesty of this
sanctuary.   I had read plenty of books describing Monte Cassino,
but the reality took my breath away.

In former times pilgrims had to climb the 2,000 or so feet on foot,
or ride on a mule or a donkey.   Then a good road was made and
one could make the zig-zag ascent in a horse-drawn carriage, taking
an hour from the railway station to the monastery.   But by the
summer of 1931, when I made my first pilgrimage to Monte Cassino,
another means of transport was available—more rapid and exciting.
One shot up into the air in a little car, suspended on a wire rope,
and reached the abbey in a few minutes.   The Guest House was run
on the lines of a hotel; its service efficient, and the accommodation
far more comfortable than in most other Italian monasteries.

When one passed through the old Roman gateway and entered the
first of the five cloisters, around which the monastery was grouped,
one was confronted by a picture to be found in no other abbey in
Europe—Italian Renaissance architecture at its best, forming a perfect
background for flower-beds and rose bushes.   In the midst of the
central cloisters stood a lovely old Renaissance well.   How grateful I
was for the ice-cold water drawn up from the depths of the mountain
on those grilling days in August!   From morning till night came the
peasants from the surrounding countryside, balancing heavy jars on
their heads, and filling them from this well.   I liked to watch them
from my window in the Guest House.

The interior of the basilica overwhelmed me with the gorgeousness
of its Baroque decorations.   The vaulted roof was covered with
frescoes, and every inch of wall space was a blaze of intricate mosaic,
whose brilliant colours were heightened by a lavish use of gold.   The
eye was led up to the raised presbytery, in the midst of which stood
the simple and dignified high altar.   Behind it in a railed-in space,
surrounded by votive lamps, was the traditional resting place of St.
Benedict and his twin sister, St. Scholastica.   Even if Monte Cassino
could not claim to possess their bodies, for it is usually believed that
they were taken to St. Benoit-sur-Loire during the Middle Ages,
some of their relics still lay here.   No greater contrast could be
imagined than the Baroque church and the austere simplicity of the
crypt, decorated by the 19th-century Benedictine artists of Beuron

LA SPINETA, TODI, UMBRIA.

in South Germany—the style of the work being more or less Egyptian.

Before the sun got too hot I would go for walks over the mountain and again in the evening when the heat was less intense. I took my sketch book and wandered far afield, getting different views of the abbey as I climbed higher and higher, amid flowers, lizards and the humming of insects. More than once the blue sky and blue mountains changed colour to a sombre grey—then black—the prelude to a welcome thunderstorm and torrents of rain. I recall those early morning Low Masses in the cool, shadowy crypt; the sung Mass later on in the basilica, and the peace of Compline in the twilight of a summer evening. There was no lack of human interest, what with the never-ending relays of pilgrims and visitors. That courteous monk-guestmaster was a perfect *maître-d'hôtel*, never ruffled and always ready to serve them with charity. Here, in St. Benedict's own monastery, I was glad to see how the fifty-third chapter of the *Holy Rule* was being observed not only in the letter but in the spirit. "Fitting honour" was shown to all and "all guests that come were received like Christ Himself." And nobody could say that "the very fear men have of the rich procures them honour", for I noticed that the guestmaster did not forget St. Benedict's injunction, "let special care be taken in the reception of the poor"—the poorest of the poor *contadini* were received with the same courtesy as was given to the owners of a luxurious motor.

*   *   *

Another aspect of Italian Benedictine life was with the Community of *S. Paolo-fuori-le-Mura,* with whom I spent a month one winter when I was in Rome. At that date the present Cardinal Archbishop of Milan, Dom Ildephonsus Schuster, was Abbot of S. Paul's. I shall always think of that month in that huge monastery as associated with intense cold. It was an exceptionally severe winter. We had snow and hard frost. One afternoon the boy *alumni* amused them-selves at recreation with snow-ball fights; the fountains in the cloisters and well-heads in the garden were clustered with icicles. It was cold enough in the choir chapel of S. Lorenzo where the Community recited the Divine Office and where the conventual Mass was cele-brated on weekdays, but on a Sunday morning when we sat round the apse of the enormous basilica and assisted at High Mass, we were half frozen. But I remember that Abbot Schuster, who preached on more than one occasion, seemed oblivious of climatic conditions as he expounded the liturgy in his inimitable manner. A year or two later, when I wandered into this same basilica on a hot afternoon in August, I noticed that the candles on the altars were drooping with the heat. It was an oven instead of a refrigerator.

To live in a Community like that of S. Paolo, which has a history going back for more than fourteen centuries, is a curious experience. In a sense I felt I had a right to be there, remembering that before the Reformation the basilica was under the special protection of the Kings of England. The walls of some of the long corridors in the monastery are covered with Pagan and early Christian inscriptions, removed from the original basilica, burnt down in 1823. They reminded me of the venerable lineage of the monks who were my hosts. At S. Paolo-fuori-le-Mura one was in actual contact with the long history of the Catholic Church.

*   *   *

No greater contrast to the fourteen-hundred-year-old abbey of St. Paul's-outside-the-Walls could be found than the International Benedictine College of S. Anselmo on the Aventine, founded in the latter years of the 19th century by Pope Leo XIII. Here is a great block of red brick buildings, up to date and planned for their special function as a college, spacious airy cloisters, big rooms, and lovely gardens. Palm trees grow in the cloister garths and the gardens are gay with roses, lemons and oranges. In normal times S. Anselmo houses a Community made up of about 100 Benedictine monks, belonging to almost every nation. It is completely cosmopolitan, and when one watches these monks making their way into the church or refectory, hardly two of them are wearing quite the same variation of the Benedictine habit. Most of them are dressed in black, but there may be some in white habits. There are scapulars with hoods, others without hoods; leather belts or cloth cinctures, some black and a few scarlet . . . unity in diversity; the same spirit but infinite differences of spirit. For, strictly speaking, there is no such thing as Benedictine *Order*. The sons of St. Benedictine are better described as a loose federation of self-governing monasteries, themselves linked up in fourteen independent Congregations. There are, moreover, other monasteries unattached to Congregations and as well as independent branches of the Benedictine family, *e.g.,* Camaldolesi, Olivetans, Vallombrosians, Sylvestrians, Mechitarists. There are black, white, blue and brown Benedictines, who make up this world-wide family, to-day numbering close on 12,000 monks.

I look back on visits to S. Anselmo between 1922 and 1932—the last time I was in Rome. Memories of being invited to dinner on some *festa*—my host an English monk from Caldey, Downside or Ramsgate, or a Belgian from Saint André. The mental strain of trying to keep up a conversation in Italian, French, German and English—including transatlantic English! How I used to wish that silence had not been dispensed in that great refectory! At last the long and elaborate meal would be ended, and then we dispersed from the refectory to a common-room, where coffee was served. Here it was usually possible to pair off with a group of monks who were able to carry on a conversation in the same language. I could manage English, French or Italian by themselves, but it was more than I could stand trying to talk several languages at once. I was never any good as an interpreter.

There were other occasions when I called at S. Anselmo to pay my respects to the Abbot Primate—Dom Fidelis von Stotzingen. This kindly old German monk, formerly Abbot of Maria-Laach, always seemed able to find time to chat with me for an hour or more. His English was fluent, though he spoke with a strong German accent. I can see him singing pontifical High Mass in that bare austere church, with its grey granite columns; the choir filled with young monks, rendering their Plain Chant more perfectly than it was possible to find in almost any other church in Rome, except perhaps with the Franciscan Conventuals at the SS. Apostoli. At S. Anselmo the atmosphere was more Teutonic than Italian, as the majority of the Benedictine students were German or North Americans of German origin.

*   *   *

On a cold, raw morning in December, 1922, I was standing outside the Basilica of S. Paolo with half-a-dozen Benedictine monks, waiting for a tram to take us into Rome, for we were going to catch an early train for Fara-Sabina; our destination being the Abbey of Farfa. More than 1,000 years ago Farfa seems to have been the most important monastery in Italy—immensely rich and very magnificent. The morals of its monks were not all that they should be. Had our visit been in 922, instead of 1922, we might have met Dom Hildebrand and Dom Campo, who poisoned their Abbot, and divided the wealth of Farfa between them. Poisoning seems to have been a recognised way of getting rid of tiresome superiors at that date, for not long after Alberic, Prince of the Romans, had secured the help of St. Odo of Cluny to clean up Farfa and other not too well-run monasteries in Italy. Abbot Dagibert also met the same violent death as his predecessor, apparently because he would not allow the Community to sell the altar vessels and church ornaments to pay for their vices. Again and again Farfa was attacked—Vandal, Lombard, and Saracen armies destroyed the abbey, which had been founded early in the 5th century, but it rose once more, and monastic life blossomed anew. But for the past four centuries poor Farfa had been reduced to the status of a cardinalate *in commendam,* its revenues going to swell the wealth of more than one great Roman family. Since 1842 the title of Abbot of Farfa had been borne by the Cardinal Bishop of Sabina. The great monastery was abandoned, and, at the date of my visit, it was occupied by one of the Community of San Paolo who acted as parish priest; Farfa being one of the three parishes at that time under the jurisdiction of the *abbot-nullius* of St. Paul's-outside-the-Walls.

Having read much about the history of this venerable abbey in the heart of the Sabine Mountains, the opportunity to see it could not be resisted, even if it did involve getting up before dawn on a winter morning, and an uncomfortable journey. My companions were a cheery crowd; they laughed and joked as we sat huddled together in a third-class carriage, and made merry over the way in which a pre-historic motor bus shook us to bits as it careered round the hair-pin bends on the narrow roads after we had left the station and were climbing the mountains. Beneath a lowering sky that hinted we might expect snow, the country looked grim and forbidding. When at last the bus had dumped us at Farfa and I looked up at the buildings of the abbey, there was no doubt about their antiquity. The parish priest, and a lay-brother who shared his solitude, welcomed their brethren from St. Paul's, and I was introduced. Having had a very early breakfast of coffee and dry bread, we were glad to sit down to a substantial dinner. We explored the empty buildings—the cloisters, library and church, admiring its granite and marble columns. The best way to describe Farfa is to call it a fifteen-hundred-year-old monastic palimpsest. No matter where one glanced one could discover traces of some even more ancient detail beneath an ornament or decoration that was in itself many centuries old. That night after supper we sat round a blazing log fire, roasting chestnuts on the

embers.   The wind shook the window frames.   As I lay in bed,
unable to sleep because of the intense cold, I tried to picture what
Farfa must have been like in the days of its glory—when the Community owned nearly 700 churches and were the overlords of more
than 300 villages, even sea ports and salt mines.   But all this was
so long, long ago that even the ghosts of the monks seemed to have
abandoned the place.   One was merely conscious of being in an empty
shell.   On Sunday morning we sang High Mass in the basilica, a
few peasants merely emphasising the feeling of abandonment and
desolation.   Our voices could not fill that great church as we took up
the *Introit, Kyrie* and *Gloria*.   The Byzantine painting of Our Lady
of Farfa was enshrined behind the high altar—regarded as a
miraculous Madonna by the inhabitants of the neighbouring villages
and still resorted to in times of need or distress.   If she could speak,
what stories she could tell!   The following morning we returned to
Rome by the same rackety old motor bus and slow train by which we
had made the outward journey.   I shall always be grateful to Abbot
Schuster for having given me the opportunity to visit this now little-
known monastery in the Sabine Mountains.

                        *   *   *

Italy is scattered all over with empty or half-empty Benedictine
abbeys.   There is the barrack-like pile of S. Pietro dei Cassinesi at
Perugia, where I found three choir-monks and two lay-brothers.
There was always a more cheerful, not to say lively, atmosphere about
the Abbey of S. Pietro at Assisi, for it was the House of Studies for
the Cassinese Congregation, and it was usually occupied by a few
young clerics besides the two or three priests who formed the permanent Community.   S. Maria del Monte at Cesena, where on two
occasions I was the guest of the Prior and Community, was far more
typical of normal Benedictine life.   The Community numbered about
thirty, and there was an alumnate, a dozen or so little boys who were
being educated in the monastery.   From this great abbey, founded in
the 10th century, there was a wonderful view northwards over the
distant Adriatic, but how fiercely the winds used to blow in February,
and how very unlike the conventional picture of "sunny Italy" it
was when, for several days during my visit, the roads were blocked
with deep snow and S. Maria del Monte looked down on an endless
white plain.   I was grateful for the fire which the Prior—Dom
Celestino Mercuro—ordered to be lit in my room, but there was no

heating in Bramante's domed church, and one shivered in its great empty spaces, kneeling on marble pavements, when assisting at Mass and Office, but Cesena was equally hot when I returned there some months later. S. Justina at Padua and S. Georgio at Venice are two other venerable and famous abbeys which, when I visited them, were occupied by a mere handful of monks, all of whom belonged to the numerous Community of Praglia. The Abbey of S. Giuliano at Genoa seemed quite flourishing, and it was good to find more than fifty monks in the Community.

* * *

During the summer of 1931, when I was collecting data for my book dealing with the eremitical life, published under the title of *The Quest of Solitude,* I visited Camaldoli for the first time.*

The *Sacro Eremo* is situated at the far end of a long valley in the Tuscan Apennines, about twenty miles east of Florence and about 4,000 feet above sea level. I took the train from Arezzo to Poppi, where I hired a car for the rest of the way; the road climbing up into the mountains and then descending into a valley, whose slopes are covered with dark pine forests. It was mid-August and how welcome was the cool shade of the overhanging trees after the heat of the train, not to mention the dust. Passing the hospice at Fuontebuono, which became a separate monastery in the Middle Ages and where the monks lived in community and not as hermits, the winding road continued further up the valley until it came to an end at my destination.

A high wall surrounds the actual enclosure at the *Sacro Eremo,* and within it are the cells of the hermit monks—some thirty or more— each with its little garden. Close to the main entrance is a group of buildings which includes the *foresteria,* or guest house for men, where I was received by a genial guestmaster and soon felt at home. Adjacent

---

* The Camaldolesi, which are an independent branch of the Benedictine family, were founded by St. Romuald about 1009. They wear a white habit and scapular, and are now divided into two Congregations: (1) *The Monks and Hermits of Camaldoli,* who either follow the eremitical life in the seven or more hermitages in different parts of Italy, or who live in community like ordinary Benedictines. They are governed by an Abbot-General. (2) *Hermits of Monte Corona*—a 16th century reformed branch of the original stock, with about 150 members and a " Major " residing at Frascati.

to the *foresteria* are the church, kitchen, refectory and lay-brothers' quarters, for the latter do not occupy separate houses like the choir monks. The cells are best described as fairly spacious four-roomed bungalows. They are arranged in rows, divided by broad paths paved with stone slabs. Entering one of the doors that give access to each garden—gay with flowers when I saw them that August—I found myself before a loggia or porch, facing towards the south, so that it got every ray of sunshine. Within was a small hall or lobby, which, so I was told, serves as a place of exercise when deep snow prevents the hermit from walking in his garden, not uncommon during the winter months. There was something very attractive about the living and sleeping room, with its bed built in an alcove, like a bunk on board ship; an open fireplace, and a small table for meals, above which was a hatch through which the food is passed by a lay-brother who brings it from the kitchen in a specially constructed wooden box. Next to this room was a tiny study, with a writing desk and book shelves. On the other side of the actual living room was an oratory, fitted with an altar and prie-dieu, the walls decorated with religious pictures.

Such is the home of a 20th-century hermit at Camaldoli. Some of the bungalows appeared to be larger than others—for instance that occupied by the Prior—but in plan and furnishing I found that all were much alike. The novices' cells are situated in a separate enclosure apart from the rest. The entrance is kept locked, the key being in the hands of the novice master. During the five days I stayed at the *Sacro Eremo* I discovered that the normal routine was as follows: at 1.30 a.m. I used to hear the bells of the campanile rousing the hermits from their slumbers. I could picture them getting off their beds, where they sleep fully dressed, and putting on their heavy cloaks, hurrying down the stone paths in the darkness, and making their way into the church. One night I got up and assisted at Matins and Lauds—it was the Feast of the Assumption of Our Lady. The Office lasted about an hour and a half. I watched the hermits returning to their cells and, like them, went back to bed until 6 a.m. when once more I was awakened by the bells just above my head. A few minutes later I was again in church taking part in a Low Mass, meditation and the recitation of Prime. Then I got my breakfast—coffee and dry bread. On that morning of the Assumption there was a noisy clanging of bells before High Mass at 9 o'clock, preceded by Tierce and followed by Sext. The interior of the church is a gorgeous Baroque affair, cream and gold being the chief colours in its scheme of decoration. The function that morning was characteristically Benedictine—superb Plaint Chant and stately ceremonial. Gazing at the white-habited monks in the choir stalls I was transported back to Caldey. Normally the hermits have their meals in the solitude of their cells, but on twelve days in the year they dine together in the great refectory. Meat is never eaten, but if the food is as good as what was served up to me, the hermits do not starve. An hour's siesta followed dinner. I was told that some of the hermits spend the time in study or prayer. Vespers were sung at 3.30. On certain occasions permission is granted to the hermits to leave their enclosure and take a walk in the forests, silence being dispensed. About an hour before sunset the bells rang again—this time for Compline, and, after the Office, the Litany of Our Lady was sung. Then the hermits made their way back to their cells for supper. Soon afterwards I supposed they were asleep, for everything was quiet. Not even the whisper of a breeze in the pine forest broke the greater silence after Compline. The letter, as well as the spirit, of the forty-second chapter of the Rule of St. Benedict was being kept. But how different it must be in winter! Clouds hang over the mountains for days on end, shrouding the Sacro Eremo in a raw, clammy mist. Snow storms are not infrequent, and there have been many occasions when the solitaries have been imprisoned in their cells until the paths were cleared from the drifts.

* * *

A few weeks later I spent a few days at the Sacro Eremo, Frascati, belonging to the Monte Corona Congregation. I recall the hot walk from the tram terminus to the Eremo; the relief it was to catch the first glimpse of its twin towers as I turned a corner, and how at last I pulled the bell and was admitted within the enclosure by a bearded lay-brother in a white habit, and taken to a cool and spacious guest room.

The Camaldolese Hermits of Monte Corona are a reformed Congregation founded by Fra. Paolo Giustiniani in 1523—and were known at first as The Company of St. Romuald. During those few days I spent at Frascati I got the impression that these hermits had retained far less of the Benedictine spirit than those at Camaldoli. Their spirituality and their observances reflected the age in which this Congregation had been born. The choir of the religious is hidden away out of sight behind the high altar—a poky little place, hardly in keeping, so I felt, with St. Benedict's injunction "*nihil Operi Dei præponatur*".

One of the special features of the services in the churches of the Monte Corona Congregation is that the entire Office is always monotoned; *never sung,* and only twice a year is High Mass celebrated—on the Vigil of Pentecost and Holy Saturday. Strange to say the Conventual Mass is always a Low Mass. In no other Order in the Catholic Church does one find such a stark simplicity in the externals of worship.

The most striking feature of the church was a double row of *prie-dieux,* one behind the other, facing the high altar. When I watched the kneeling figures of the hermits making their three daily half hours of meditation in common, I got the feeling that this corporate act of silent worship had been raised to an almost liturgical status never dreamed of by St. Benedict, though quite in keeping with the teaching of the great mystical writers of the post-Tridentine age. It was both supernatural and super-Benedictine.

The daily *horarium* at Frascati does not differ very greatly from that at Camaldoli, except in certain unimportant details. A hermit of the Monte Corona Congregation wears heavy wooden clogs instead of shoes, and instead of the ordinary Benedictine cowl he has a white cloak, fastened with a small piece of wood.

It has often occurred to me that there might be room for a Camaldolese foundation in England. Their spirit and manner of life might suit the British temperament better than that of the Carthusians, and there must surely be vocations for the solitary life in these days?

*   *   *

The Camaldolesi were not the only hermit monks whose hospitality I enjoyed in Italy. On two occasions I stayed with the Carthusians at Galluzzo on the outskirts of Florence; my first visit being in midsummer, the second in mid-winter. The Certosa di Galluzzo was founded in the 14th century by a wealthy Florentine nobleman, Niccolo Acciauoli, the friend of Petrarch and Boccaccio. Like so many Italian monasteries, it might be a fortress when viewed from a distance, but for sheer magnificence nothing could surpass the Renaissance decorations of the church and some of the chapels. The great cloister, around which are situated the cells of the choir-monks, has its walls adorned with seventy-seven medallions of prophets, sibyls and saints; the work of Giovanni Della Robbia and his school.

The Certosa became a National Monument, and a small Community were allowed to remain there on condition that they acted as custodians. Twelve years ago the Novice Master was an Englishman —Dom Sebastian Maccabe—formerly a member of the Community at St. Hugh's Charterhouse at Parkminster. It was he who invited me to stay at Galluzzo. It was no small cell that was allotted me, but a suite of rooms, in which I felt quite lost. My diary for 1932 contains the ejaculation "Fog!" on almost every day of that week I spent at the Certosa. I was there for Christmas, and what a curious Christmas it was! I looked out of the windows against a dense white mist, visibility being confined to no more than a few yards. It was cold enough to make a fire welcome, though the smoke from the green logs in that big open grate made my eyes smart and almost choked me. Life in an Italian Charterhouse seemed to be much less rigid so far as external observances than that with which I was familiar in Sussex. It was odd to find the choir stalls filled with laymen, mostly peasants from the neighbourhood, at the three Masses on Christmas morning. They were quite at home reclining in those stalls, decorated with carving and intarsio work! They were indifferent to the white-habited monks sitting next them. The Carthusian rite—so different to the Roman—did not appear to puzzle them —it was the Mass that mattered, even if the details were not the same as they would have found in a parish church. The choir offices had to be fitted in at hours when the Certosa was not open to visitors, swarms of whom, both men and women, used to wander round the cloisters with one of the lay-brothers acting as guide. The Prior told me that at first it was rather distracting living in a National Monument, but one got used to the tourists. Moreover, once inside the cell there was complete privacy. There was no need to venture into the cloisters unless to go to church. But it was not quite what one visualised as the ideal form of eremitical monasticism, even if the Italian Government relieved the Community of financial worry by paying them as caretakers and guides!

Not all the cells at Galluzzo were built on the same plan. Some were no more than a small self-contained flat; others were more spacious. I made several drawings of the Prior's little house, which contained two short cloisters, with trellis work over which vines clustered, a garden full of flowers in bloom, a private oratory and the usual living rooms. The whole place recalled the backgrounds in some of Fra. Angelico's paintings.

CHAPTER VII

SOME FRIENDSHIPS

" What a lot of pictures you have got!" remarked one of my neigh-bours the other day. She went on to tell me that she herself liked " lots of pictures ", but in deference to her daughters, had discarded most of them. These young ladies had impressed on their mother that " pictures have gone out of fashion ". She looked just a little enviously at my overcrowded walls and wanted to know who were all the people whose photographs collected dust on my mantelpiece. They record relatives and friends, some still alive, the others no longer living. Glancing up at the photographs I recall how much I owe to some of these friendships. There is the gentle nun-like face of a middle-aged woman with much the same expression in the photo-graph of my mother alongside it. As they were sisters this strong likeness is explicable. A complete contrast is the photograph of a remarkably handsome shingle-headed young lady, seated at a desk, with a fountain pen in one hand and a long cigarette-holder in the other. A plaster statue of St. Bruno and a telephone reveal two aspects of her life; a spiritual solitude in the midst of her career as a busy Catholic author and journalist. Above this photograph is that of an elderly cleric, who from the buttons on his cassock and the piping round the edges, appears to be an ecclesiastical dignitary. He has remarkably sensitive hands and an enigmatic smile reminiscent of Leonardo da Vinci's famous portrait of Mona Lisa. As Walter Pater wrote of Mona Lisa, so might one write of this priest: he " lives in the delicacy with which it has moulded the changing lineaments, and tinged the eyelids and the hands ", but it would be hardly true to say that he has " been dead many times, like the vampire ", even if he has " learned the secrets of the grave ".

A contrast! A bearded figure in what seems to be a grey smock, without a collar; a nearly burnt-out cigarette in a long holder; eyes that look through you, from behind spectacles; an untidy mop of straggly grey hair; the camera recording the sitter in the act of writing a letter or perhaps an article. Rather out of focus in the background are what seem to be drawings and stone carvings on a wall. There are photographs of two Benedictine Abbots, both in white habits, each with an inscription recording long friendships. Beneath them is a Dominican friar with a French bluejacket on either side. I cannot catalogue all this gallery, so let me return to the first picture—the portrait of one of my maternal aunts, Morna Ross.

*   *   *

It is hard to realise that we shall never again turn into the drive facing St. Helen's Park Crescent, Southsea, to visit Aunt Morna. The typical mid-19th century houses, with their faded paint, peeling stucco, and rusty iron balconies, may survive our lifetime as they have survived four years of bombing. But if we mount the steps of number fifteen, her dusty, soiled visiting card will no longer indicate which bell must be rung, should her door be locked and the key not in its usual place beneath the mat. We shall listen in vain for the sound of her footsteps as she ran down the stairs to open the door; for the cheery greeting, expressed in that shrill, high-pitched voice, with something that was between a laugh and a giggle.

There was the drawing-room, with its greenish-grey flowered wall-paper; the pastel portrait of herself as a girl; the Indian water-colours painted by her father, Horatio Ross; two others painted by myself; and innumerable framed photographs of relatives, some revealing their age by the fashions worn by the sitters. There was the upright piano with its rosewood case, seldom opened in later years. In an adjacent stand were photograph albums, and bound volumes, containing selections of late Victorian and Edwardian musical comedies, likewise sentimental ballads of the same period.

Apart from an inlaid French escritoire, the furniture was of little value or interest. It belonged to the householders. There were usually a few ferns and aspidistras in pots, perhaps a hydrangea, spiraea or geranium plant. For Morna liked flowers, just as did Granny Ross—lots of them about the place. On wet days the pots were put out on the balcony to get a good soaking. I always wondered why one of the large window panes was never repaired. The crack across its face remained there for well-nigh twenty years. It managed to withstand the blast of the blitz, so I noticed on my last visit. The view of the red-brick terrace opposite the window was hidden by leafy chestnut trees in summer. Behind them came the queer, grinding shriek of the trams as they rounded the curve of the crescent.

A more prosaic view greeted you from the window of the little dining room; neglected gardens, and the almost indecent brick behinds of another mid-Victorian terrace, with peeps into the domestic secrets of their owners and lodgers. This seldom-used room was usually very untidy. Its chairs and sofa were littered with brown paper, bits of string, old letters and bundles of parish and missionary magazines, waiting to be distributed. Upstairs were two bedrooms; Morna's and the spare room. The latter was always at my disposal for several years when I was more or less homeless. Then, not to be forgotten, were the diminutive kitchen, rightly termed kitchenette, with its gas stove, and the bathroom, with its spluttering geyser.

Such was the background against which Morna lived her own very individual life for over twenty years; a life made up very largely of unselfish and ungrudging acts of charity to all and sundry who came her way. A lonely life, perhaps, but less so than that of many another middle-aged unmarried gentlewoman whose annual income was not more than about £300. The secret of her happiness in the last two decades of her life lay in the fact that she spent so little on herself. She was invariably overdrawn at the bank by the end of the quarter! Where all the money went to is a mystery. She did not care to reveal details of her expenditure.

*   *   *

My earliest recollection of Morna is a mental picture of a tall, rather gawky girl, with long hair down to her waist. It was the occasion of her thirteenth birthday party; the scene, the drawing-room of the Bank House, High Street, Portsmouth. After tea there was dancing on the polished floor; the music being provided by an elderly lady-pianist. I can see Morna dancing the polka, and as a contrast also see her lying prone on a mysterious sloped wooden contraption, known as a back board, with a round hole at one end for her head. Her health was never robust as a girl, and this daily hour on the back board was supposed to be good for her. This frail health, when she was young, accounted largely for her scrappy and somewhat desultory education, conducted by several governesses. She never had a fair chance to develop her intellect.

There is little doubt that Morna was repressed during her youth. She was far too much tied down to her mother—she was the youngest of a large family. I cannot recall that she went to any dances after she had grown up. She was never presented at Court, as in the case of her two older sisters. She remained a sort of Cinderella. No fairy queen came to take her to the ball, so she never got the chance to meet the prince! She lived in a narrow little world, the result being a warped and stunted character, which in some ways never found the right outlet for its emotional side, at least, not until Morna was well into middle age.

Did she ever dream of getting married, I wonder? When I look back I can recall countless and quite harmless passions for not a few actors, singers and other musicians. For Granny had an insatiable love of the stage, which took the form of regular attendance at the weekly matinées at the Theatre Royal, Portsmouth, when I was still a boy at school. She and her tall daughter were familiar figures in the two end chairs of the second row of the stalls. Musical comedy was their favourite form of entertainment.

When each summer came round, there was the attraction of the concert parties on South Parade Pier—"The Scarlet Musketeers", "The Mr. Es", and others which I have now forgotten. I recall many a hot night when the windows of the crowded pier pavilion were open to let in a breath of cool air off the sea. I can still hear the siren of a late incoming excursion steamer, back from Cherbourg or Torquay, or else the roar of escaping steam; the noisy voices of their passengers mingling with the music on the stage. Bertram Wallis warbled about "The night has a thousand eyes" and outside the stars twinkled. Herbert Clayton soothed us with "Sing Me to Sleep", or related what happened "Under the Shade of the Sheltering Palm". "Jimmy" Blakney made Granny almost choke with laughter, while Morna giggled at his jokes. Victor Marmont played Chopin and Chaminede "divinely", so that gushing young woman felt. "He's got such a sad face," Morna remarked one evening, "and such a delicate touch. I always feel he must be a *real gentleman.*" How far, far away are those glamorous summer nights of the first decade of the present century!

Such was the world in which Morna grew up. She could not be described as pretty; she never looked really smart, and needed some one to dress her properly. The big cartwheel-shaped hats, the hair piled up on the top of the head, the long dragging skirts, the blouses and belts, never suited her. The Edwardian fashions only tended to make her look a conspicuous scarecrow, for she was over six feet in height: which she definitely need not have been, as witness

L

the transformation in after years, when short skirts and small hats took their place. She was not the trailing or languorous type! Her life went on more or less uneventfully. Still, Morna " did her bit " in the last Great War. She trundled a barrow round the dockyard several mornings each week, as one of the lady workers in a canteen. Otherwise she now had plenty to do at home.

Then, at last, Granny died. 39 South Parade was sold, and after four or five years drifting about from one lodging to another, Morna rented the flat which remained her home for the rest of her life.

Looking back a quarter of a century I recall her keen love of certain types of fiction. Her choice of authors was eclectic. She was fond of music, played the piano indifferently, and tried hard to master both the mandoline and the banjo. But these two string instruments were set aside after some years, likewise the auto-harp, which had been a forerunner. Water-colour painting had been an earlier accomplishment, but she lacked the talent of her elder sister, Evelyn (my mother), and despite regular lessons from a local artist never succeeded in producing anything original, though the copies she made of some of his own water-colours were quite effective. Picture exhibitions were always a pleasure to her. She would go round the galleries, marking and underlining the catalogue most conscientiously. Her standards of criticism were peculiar and quite individual. But what she liked most was a nice " soft " landscape, preferably a water-colour. Any artist who could produce a smudgy effect was sure of her praise and a pencil mark. This irresistible attraction of softness in all forms of art embraced music as well as painting. Morna loved soft melodies and luscious harmonies, with plenty of pastel tones—Grieg, Rubinstein, Raff, bits of Tschaikovsky (even the 1812 Overture, by way of contrast, I suppose?), and Mendelssohn's *Songs Without Words* and the *Midsummer Night's Dream* music. But I think that musical comedy was the natural expression of her artistic emotions. Jazz she never absorbed, though she revelled in the earlier forms of rag-time. It was always interesting to go to a picture exhibition or a concert with Morna, just because the expression of her views was so utterly personal and entirely uninfluenced by anything she had read or heard. She knew what she liked and didn't like, and had no fear of saying so!

*   *   *

It was not until a year or two after Granny's death that Morna began to play a prominent part in the parochial activities of St. Simon's, Southsea; that barn-like yellow brick Gothic Revival church of extreme Evangelical doctrines and practices which became her Mecca for the rest of her life. Before this she had shown no particular interest in religion, so far as I remember. Her knowledge of theology was vague and undefined. I much doubt if she had any clear conception of the nature of the Church according to orthodox Anglican standards. Her religion in those later years might be summed up as an intensely personal relationship with *God*. She talked about *God* in just the same tone of voice as she used when discussing the vicar or the curate of St. Simon's, and sometimes she knew quite well that God didn't altogether approve of what they said in their sermons! She consulted God in the most intimate affairs of her life, and seldom failed to get an answer.

So, little by little, Morna became absorbed in a round of parish work. She attended Bible Classes, Prayer Meetings, and never failed to assist at Mattins and Evensong every Sunday. She distributed parish and missionary magazines. She helped at the club for working girls several nights a week for many years. She kept the parochial Baptismal Roll, which involved writing hundreds of birthday letters as well as personal visits to the children's parents, who resided in all parts of Southsea. She helped with the services for children that took place on the beach during the summer months, playing the harmonium if I remember rightly. She supported Mr. Kensit's Wycliffe Preachers, collected signatures for a parochial protest against the proposed revision of the Book of Common Prayer, which (so the clergy of St. Simon's feared) was likely to encourage the spread of Popish doctrines and practices within the Church of England. She became enthusiastic about an organisation which was connected with Colporteurs, and pronounced this word with the accent on the first syllable—I believe the Colporteurs distributed Bibles, but I am not quite sure. More than once she went off to take part in Evangelical Conferences at Keswick or elsewhere, where she got in touch with persons of the same way of thinking. She was sufficiently tolerant to have no scruples about attending Methodist or other chapels belonging to Noncomformist sects. In fact she often told me that she felt more at home in them than in Anglican churches. She enjoyed listening to sermons, but it was essential that the preacher had a nice voice.

In later years her eagerness to be of service to anybody, no matter

what were their religious views, moved her to send regular supplies
of books, papers and magazines for me to distribute among the crews
of the vessels of the Royal Navy and Mercantile Marine which,
throughout the war, came and went in the fishing port on the north-
east coast of Scotland, which was now my home. It was paradoxical
that a Service Centre of the Apostleship of the Sea should receive
its only supplies of reading matter from a devout Evangelical
Protestant! More than once she sent a parcel of woollies for distribution among the fishermen and sailors; a welcome gift that none
of my Catholic friends ever thought of.

Morna held strong views on ritualism within the Church of
England, and could make scathing remarks on the "goings on" at
St. Matthew's, and other centres of Anglo-Catholicism in Southsea.
But never do I recollect her saying anything uncharitable or even
critical of Catholic beliefs and practices, so far as she knew anything
about them. I doubt if she ever attended a service in a Catholic
church except when she once came to visit me on Caldey Island in
1919; where, rather against my wishes, she insisted on being present
at Pontifical High Mass on Whit Sunday. She told her fellow-guests
afterwards that she was much shocked at the abbot wearing "a
funny little hat" during part of the service, for was it not written in
the Bible: "For a man indeed ought not to cover his head when
praying"? She did not seem to object to anything else in what must
have been an almost incomprehensible function, it was merely this
flagrant act of disobedience to St. Paul's injunction to the Corinthians
that offended her, she could not understand why it was disregarded
at Caldey! But she admitted that the incense made her feel a bit
sick, which I could well appreciate, for the fumes of the special brand
used on great feasts were somewhat overpowering.

During that visit to Caldey Island, Morna revealed to me that
she had made up her mind to offer herself to the Church Missionary
Society for work in Central Africa. She was absolutely convinced
that God wanted her to do this, and quite certain that she would
be accepted. But, much to her disappointment, she was turned
down. The doctor who examined her maintained that her health
would not stand the tropical climate. So she had to resign herself
to missionary work beside the shores of the Solent instead of beside
Lake Victoria. Uganda became an unrealised dream, though ever
afterwards she contributed generously towards the support of such
foreign missions.

She was an amazing correspondent, and her letters were quite unique, due to her passion for filling them with minute details of what she had been doing. Some of the recipients found these letters rather boring, but personally I always revelled in their wealth of detail. It fascinated me to know that she had left the house at 9.55 a.m., walked to the Strand, posted some parcels, waited five minutes for a tram, got out at King's Road, bought some needles at such and such a shop, lunched at Kimball's, where she had eaten roast mutton, apple tart and cream, walked across the Common (where the wind was very cold); how the vicar had called and discussed this or that parochial matter, and then how she had gone to a week-night service. Or she would tell me what had been the text of the sermons of the previous Sunday, that the curate had a nasty cough, or that his wife had had another baby. Nothing was regarded as unimportant or not worth recording, and the result was that one got a vivid impression of a life spent in unexciting activities, which were of absorbing interest to the writer. These long letters became a revelation of her character, as clear as a mirror. They possessed much the same literary quality as Parson Kilvert's now famous Diaries, though I am sure that Morna never thought of her letters as literature!

*　　　　*　　　　*

After I came to live in Scotland nine years ago, we had few opportunities for meeting, but we kept up a regular correspondence. I seldom went back to Southsea, but on January 5th, 1945, I met Morna for what was to be the last time. I called at the flat, received the same demonstrative welcome, was distressed to discover her now almost complete blindness, but amazed at her courage and cheerfulness. She insisted on coming out to lunch with me. She ordered mince, explaining that this dish would save me cutting up the meat, but I had to add the salt, also lead her to a table. She discussed her private affairs, and told me that God had made it quite clear to her that He did not want her to have a paid companion, as some of her relatives had insisted on, much to her worry and annoyance. She explained that as she could no longer see to read, and could only do plain sewing and knitting, she was glad to fill in the hours cleaning the house.

Then she said she would like to come with me to visit the ruins of Old Portsmouth. But first of all, was her hat on straight and was her face clean? So we went off together and took a bus to High Street. She tapped on the pavement with her white stick and *felt* her way rather than found it by sight. We stopped again and again while she revived memories of this or that house and the people who had lived there during the past half-century. We stood and peered down into the now roofless cellars of the Bank (her childhood home), and she was able to distinguish the leafless branches of the trees in its garden against the sunlight. I piloted her down the steps into the cathedralised parish church, where she was afraid to go further than the nave because of the many new steps with which she was un-familiar. We continued our pilgrimage to the far end of High Street, and walked back again up its entire length. At one moment she nearly crashed into an air-raid shelter built on to the pavement. She insisted on my leaving her by the Grammar School, fearing that I might miss my steamer to Ryde if I waited to put her on to the next bus. " I shall hear it coming," she explained, " and they all stop here." So I said good-bye, and the last glimpse of the brave old lady was a tall figure standing alone on the edge of the pavement at the top of the street where she had been born and where she had spent her childhood. She died suddenly and quite peacefully less than a month after.

*   *   *

Then comes the second portrait—the boyish-looking young lady with the long cigarette holder—the late Cecily Hallack, whom I first met in 1929. I had known and admired her books since coming across *Beardless Counsellors* when chapters of this story were being serialised in *The Month*. I can recall a discussion with my friend, Mgr. Croft-Fraser, who was certain that these tales of Wops and his Boy Scout companions were the work of Fr. Martindale, both of us being convinced that they could not have been written by a woman and that " Cecily Hallack " was merely a nom-de-plume. But further investigations proved that we were wrong and that the author was a woman convert. Eventually I was introduced to Cecily Hallack, our first meeting being at a small Italian restaurant in Soho, where what was lacking in the quality and quantity of the half-a-crown lunch was more than compensated for by her brilliant conversation and charm of manner.

We discovered that we had many common interests, as both of us were Franciscan Tertiaries. An invitation to tea at her flat was the immediate result of this luncheon, and thus started a friendship which deepened as we got to know each other better. The flat proved to be one tiny room on the top story of a large block overlooking Lords cricket ground—a lovable room which expressed the personality of its temporary occupant. But as another friend once remarked to me, Cecily had the womanly gift for making a home anywhere; she would have made it on a three-legged stool in an attic! She loved this so-called " flat ", high above the roar of London traffic, and wrote in one of her books that " here, as well as in the country, one can have solitude, for one's neighbours have no time for minding anything but their own business. And beside the high building lies a Catholic church, like the Lion of Judah ". A small statue of St. Bruno used to stand on her desk, as if to bless her solitude in the midst of the world.

Such were the surroundings in which Cecily produced most of her best literary work for a few years. But she was always desperately hard up, and began to realise that she could not afford to go on living in London. She wanted to find a " labourer's cottage in Sussex ", so she wrote to me one day. No such residence could be discovered. However, in the end she managed to rent one of the lodges on Lord Cowdray's estates at Paddockhurst, between Crawley and East Grinstead, which the Benedictines of Downside had just bought, and whose palatial mansion they were transforming into what is now Worth Priory. Not only had she the Benedictine monks and their church within a few minutes' walk; Crawley and its Capuchin friary was in easy access by bus. So, spiritually, she was well provided for. It was Cecily's intention that " East Lodge " should become a refuge for anybody who was in need or distress—particularly those who had had any sort of mental breakdown. This was the particular sphere of Franciscan apostolate she visualised for herself. For various reasons the scheme did not prosper, mainly because Cecily was always far too generous and hospitable, and I much doubt if she made any profit out of those who were supposed to be " paying guests ". More likely than not she lost on them.

It is not easy to describe Cecily, but here is an impression of her recorded by Fr. J. P. Murphy which appeared in *The Tablet* after her death, which conveys just what I always felt about her myself. " She was intrepid, gay and debonair. She had a sort of shining courage, manifested in such details as her carriage, the straightness of her glance, her knack of coping with any little *contretemps* of life;

and in such big things as facing up to all the world with the armour of the Faith and to her great physical ordeal with the memory of the Passion. And yet so gay and debonair. Cecily was tall and handsome, with the finely chiselled features of the Celt. She always insisted that she was a Celt. She was one of those women born to wear clothes with an accomplished air. How she managed it is a mystery beyond my mere masculinity, for her poverty was always dire. She had none of that solid way of life that belongs to those whose income, however small, is well assured. Her life in this respect was an exhilarating adventure in the providence of God, and she walked entirely remote from anything harsh or unfeminine in her nature, so her gaiety was at the furthest point from vanity. It was all a sort of riot of humour, as if being a Catholic made one irresistibly happy. She had such ability as well, in all sorts of directions; from such things as ferreting out the most obscure points of information at the British Museum, to knowing the names of every plant and bird in the England which she loved. . . . And there was this special quality of hers in social ways: she invariably gave the impression that it was she, and not you, who would benefit by a conversation. She gave immense value to anything you had to say. It is only now that we all realise that the truth was the other way about; that it was she who was giving all the time. I say ‘ edifying ’, for it was impossible to be her friend if one did not set the things of God above all other things. Those who take the trouble will find that in all her writings she detests the mere complacency of controversy, and that above all things is herself ascetic and profoundly serious. She would have abhorred the idea of being a successful Catholic writer without attending to one’s own soul. She would, and did go to any length to sanctify herself.”

This, as all her many friends will agree, is the fine woman, the Tertiary of St. Francis, that we knew, loved and admired; the Cecily who lived on a supernatural plane far above anything we could hope to attain. She had dreamed of finding a refuge from the world in that “ late 19th century Tudor ” half-timbered lodge in the Sussex Weald. She loved her garden with its flowers and vegetables. She revelled in the silence and solitude of the woods that surrounded her, perhaps even more the unbroken views to the south, with the long rolling outline of the Downs in the far distance. Sometimes I would protest that this was not *real* country, but merely an artificial playground created by a millionaire having bought up as much land

CAMALDOLI . S . EREMO .

PFA
1931.

CAMALDOLI, SACRO EREMO.

as he could lay hands on to safeguard his own privacy. Cecily agreed that I might be right, but anyhow, it was *Sussex*—that was all that mattered, for she loved her native county quite as much as Hilaire Belloc or Sheila Kaye-Smith, and it was seldom that she did not make it the scene of her novels and short stories.

Once a month she would go to Crawley to assist at the meetings of the Franciscan Tertiaries. She had a special affection for this little friary and its Community. However, owing to circumstances over which she had no control, she had to leave East Lodge after four years. She looked for another cottage in Sussex, but could find nothing suitable that was within her limited means. Finally she decided to return to London, and discovered a top-floor flat in Pimlico, not far from the Thames, of which she wrote soon after she had moved in with great enthusiasm. Within a stone's throw was the chapel of the Franciscan Missionaries of Mary—an added attraction.

Gay, cheerful letters used to arrive, telling me about her life in London, but one could read between the lines that Cecily was far from well, and that her financial position was as uncertain as ever. Few of her friends knew at the time that much of what she wrote —especially for missionary magazines—was a labour of love, and editors of such periodicals were only too ready to take full advantage of her reckless generosity. Any profits she made from her novels were given away in charity, but one day she wrote: "I now realise that I must waste no time now in making some safe niche for myself if the future and old age are not to be imprudently Franciscan. It is dull to be prudent, but there it is! It is hard to know what to do. There is no material security anywhere to-day. The only thing is, I'm game for anything."

Her busy, active life was fast drawing to a close, though I wonder now if she realised it. Letters became less frequent; more often it would be a hurriedly scribbled post card that she was "too tired to write more". When she was able she loved to work at the Santa Maria Hostel for destitute street girls which had recently been opened in London by the Legion of Mary. "I feel I have left my heart in the Santa Maria sink," she wrote one day. Then, at last it was discovered that poor Cecily had a tumour on the brain, and that only an immediate and dangerous operation could save her life. The operation was performed, but it left her paralysed and deprived of the power of speech. After four months of torturing pain, such as

few are called upon to suffer in this world, she died at the Mount
Alvernia Nursing Home, Guildford, on October 23rd, 1938, having
been looked after by Franciscan Tertiary sisters. Her body was taken
to Crawley, where it was carried to the grave on the shoulders of
the friars, and where it now rests in the peaceful cemetery adjoining
the Capuchin church—always her spiritual home and where she had
asked to be buried.

A mental picture of Cecily Hallack indelibly fixed in my memory
is watching her sailing through a crowded restaurant, having spotted
me at a corner table where I had been waiting somewhat impatiently
for about twenty minutes, wondering what business had detained
her. There was something about her appearance that compelled
people to look round and pause in their conversation. That day
she was wearing that pathetically familiar fur coat, which, despite
its age, always managed to look smart. There was just the right
amount of lipstick and make-up, but no more. When she sat down
and removed her coat, I noticed that she had donned another already
familiar garment—the famous black frock, suggestive of an exclusive
design by Lanvin or Molyneux in its illusion of expensive simplicity,
but which she had got made for almost nothing when she was last
in France. Altogether she was perfectly turned out, chic and dis-
tinguée. Having apologised for keeping me waiting, she said she
must have a cocktail and produced her long cigarette holder. So I
ordered the drinks and she went on to explain that she felt this
was obviously an occasion when she must "celebrate", for had she
not managed to persuade Methuens to publish her latest novel,
Lady Georgie's House, and how splendid it was to feel that, at last,
she would be in touch with a wider circle of readers than if this book,
like all her previous ones, had been issued by a Catholic firm.

"I thought there must be some reason for all this glamour business," I remarked. "You look so definitely the professional novelist
this morning!" She laughed, adding: "Well! I hope it's all for the
greater glory of God!". As she sipped her Martini and toyed with
her cigarette holder, it struck me what a shock it would have given
people sitting at the adjacent tables if they had been told that my
companion was living under the three vows of religion—poverty,
chastity and obedience, and that her outward appearance was no
more than a mask, put on to hide a life of heroic sanctity unsuspected
by all but a few most intimate friends, and even they only got a
glimpse of the surface of what lay behind the fur coat, smart frock,

lipstick and make-up. There was nothing of the typical "*dévote*" about Cecily. If there was anything she hated it was narrow bigotry and self-advertising piety. St. Francis, when dying, saw nothing odd in asking Lady Giacoma to bring him some of her home-made marzipan—even if it was in bold defiance of the conventional death-bed of a saint. Cecily—like a true Franciscan—saw no reason why she should not enjoy other good gifts that God had provided.

She was always indifferent as to whether she would eventually be regarded as a great Catholic author. Some critics maintain that she failed to produce anything of permanent value. Yet at her best Cecily Hallack is vastly superior to most of her contemporaries. A sufficient proof of the popularity of her novels and stories is to be found in the statement made by a Catholic Truth Society librarian that " her books are never on the shelves: there is always a waiting list."

*   *   *

Johannes Jorgensen, the much more famous Danish convert writer, is another Franciscan Tertiary whom I am proud to number among my spiritual brethren. About twenty years ago, thanks to a letter of introduction from our mutual friend, Dom Pedro Suber-caseaux, the artist monk of Quarr Abbey, I called at the Villa Santa Maria delle Rose in Assisi, where Jorgensen had made his home for some time. A lovely little house, with a wonderful view over the brown-grey tiled roofs of the city of St. Francis and across the valley of Spoleto to the distant mountains. Here I was made welcome, conversation being carried on in an embarrassing mixture of Italian, English and French, according to the rapidly changing moods of my host. He often used to joke that I must be of Scandinavian origin— was not my name Anson, merely that most common Danish " Hansen " with the spelling slightly altered? And, of course, there was my love of the sea—an obviously Scandinavian hereditary influence! As readers of his autobiography will remember, Jorgensen's life has been sad and stormy in more ways than one, spiritually and from the domestic point of view. His conversion to Catholicism has cost him much, though his writings have brought him world-wide fame.

Again and again I revisited the Villa of Our Lady of the Roses during later years when staying in Assisi. He used to plan tours for

me in his native Denmark, which I had not then visited, telling
me about the ports and harbours, ships and sailors, with which he
was so familiar. Then he would talk about Franciscan Italy, and
compare notes of the different friaries we knew. He struck me as
being a lonely and rather unhappy man, glad of sympathetic company, and when I said good-bye and stood at the door, he would bid
me return as soon as possible. We have kept up an irregular correspondence ever since, and the last letter I received from him was
from Vadstena in Sweden, where he was living under the shadow
of the famous monastery founded by St. Bridget.

*   *   *

Now we come to the elderly priest with the mysterious and elusive
smile! From 1919 to 1934 I was always sure of a welcome at two
houses in Edinburgh whenever I found myself at a loose end and
nowhere else to go. I have lost count of the times that I availed
myself of the hospitality of Canon John Gray or his life-long friend
and fellow convert, André Raffalowich. John Gray was received into
the Catholic Church as a youth. After making a name for himself
as one of the most brilliant young poets of the " naughty 'nineties "—
he contributed to the *Yellow Book*, together with the artist, Aubrey
Beardsley, whose letters he afterwards edited—he astonished London
society by going off to Rome and studying for the priesthood at the
Scots College. He was ordained in 1901, and his priestly career was
spent in Edinburgh, first as a curate of the slum-church of St.
Patrick, and then as pastor of the new mission of St. Peter, Falcon
Avenue, Morningside.

The church which he had built from the designs of the late Sir
Robert Lorimer owes a good deal to his own suggestions, and is perhaps the most striking ecclesiastical building erected in Scotland
since the Reformation. It is filled with artistic treasures—a magnificent painting by Frank Brangwyn forms the altar piece, while John
Duncan's Stations of the Cross, and Glyn Philpott's painting of St.
Michael are among other notable features, not forgetting the stained
glass windows which are the work of Maurice Meredith Williams.

I loved staying at the adjacent presbytery, not only for the exquisite
hospitality of the Canon, but for the pleasure of living in such surroundings; every room was filled with paintings and drawings by his
favourite artists. There was also a fascinating library. Canon Gray
bought the first marine water-colour I ever sold, and it was largely due
to his persistent encouragement that I concentrated on this branch of

art. He shared my love of the sea, ships and sailors. He quite understood, unlike most people, why I should always insist on wandering off to the docks at Leith whenever I found myself in Edinburgh.

André Raffalowich was a Russian Jew, whose childhood and early
youth had been mainly spent in Paris. Brought up more or less as
an agnostic, he became a most devout Catholic and a Tertiary of
St. Dominic. His friendship with John Gray dated from the days
when they both were " young men about town " in the London of the
'nineties. He eventually followed him into the Church, followed him
to Rome during the years of study, and then back again to Scotland,
where he bought a house in Whitehouse Terrace, about ten minutes'
walk from St. Peter's Church. Every morning you would see this
very Jewish looking little man kneeling in the front pew at Mass,
praying with intense devotion. Those who had the privilege of
being his guests will remember the early hour at which the bathroom tap would be turned on, so that André got plenty of time for
private devotions before he started off to church on the stroke of
7.15! In his own very individual way, André Raffalowich was an
ardent apostle. He collected people quite definitely in order to help
them. His Sunday luncheon parties became a recognised feature of
social life in Edinburgh. He selected his guests with the utmost
care, and took equal pains to arrange them round his table, often
shifting the cards with their names on them a few minutes before
lunch, having had an inspiration during High Mass that so-and-so
might get on better if placed next somebody else! I recall one such
Sunday when he remarked to me on our way back from church:
" Peter! I have decided that you are not to *sit* next ....
(a young actress who was playing in Edinburgh that week). She
is so beautiful that I am sure you would prefer to *look* at her across
the table than to have her beside you!" André was such an elusive
personality that I find it almost impossible to make a portrait of him
in words. I hope that Lady Margaret Sackville, who was one of the
most regular visitors to the house, will not mind me quoting some
reminiscences of our mutual friend which she sent me shortly after
his death in 1934.

" Is it fantastic to find the same curious delicacy shown by André
Raffalowich in his sensitive grouping and arrangement of flowers,
repeated in his dealings with the more difficult material of men and
women? His treatment of flowers was somehow symbolical of his
hospitality. Every week small, exquisite blossoms were grouped

together in permanent masterpieces. He possessed the genius the flower painter so often lacks—that is to say, he really *did* make flowers *pictures!* And every week he gathered round his table guests as well-contrasted—and various as flowers. The flowers he chose were always small flowers, and many of his guests were quite 'ordinary' people. He disliked anything showy and boisterous, whether in nature or in art. He loved to analyse with much subtlety and precision the shades of motive and the more intricate side of human complexities. (It is easy to understand his admiration for François Mauriac.) Yet, unlike the 'moderns' who 'know all things but the truth', his standards were clear and unfaltering, expressed with sometimes startling common-sense. These qualities helped to make his hospitality unique.

" He found almost everyone interesting—not only those labelled as such, who often on becoming stars ceased to be men. A celebrity who was *only* a celebrity, might be invited once, treated with due deference, but never asked again. People were welcomed for their own sakes, for some gift of heart or mind which he alone may have been fine enough to discover. And all these guests so ingeniously contrasted were held together, enveloped, made one, by their host's watchful, interested, all-pervading personality. He was conscious of each individual—as a conductor is conscious of each separate member of his orchestra. His admirable talk would flash, skim, dart, with the swiftness and accuracy of a dragon-fly, over the whole—turning from books to vivid personalities, with none of the awful creaking as of cart-wheels, which so often at British lunch-tables announces a change of topic! The conversational shuttlecock was never allowed to fall, or if it *did* touch earth for a moment was soon in the air once more. Not even the clumsiest player could spoil the game.

" He was too skilled a host to permit dangerous topics. After all, a lunch-party is not a debating society! The guest who sinned by being in any way egregious was reproved—if so heavy a word can be used in connection with anything so light—by an intonation, a word, a glance, an expression, which though amounting to no more than a faint change of atmosphere, yet could not, by the delinquent (however obtuse) be mistaken. These gatherings—'parties' has too many banal connotations—would have been unique anywhere in the world, but were especially so in Edinburgh, where they formed a much needed focussing point. Here men and women of strangely differing personalities, circumstances, talents, professions and races, met and became for a few hours one, united by André Raffalowich's overflowing sympathy, and in some cases, almost fatherly solicitude. Where he admired, his generous praise was bestowed like a gift treasured. To many the moments spent at Whitehouse Terrace will remain for ever in memory as when first enjoyed—like something seen through invisible glass—in appearance part of the to-and-fro of daily life—yet actually distinct from it and set a little apart."

Such then was the atmosphere of that often-visited house in Morningside, Edinburgh, where like so many others I found what Lady Margaret so rightly describes as " overflowing sympathy and almost fatherly solicitude ", in a hard and difficult period of my life. Is it to be wondered that I went back again and again? André Raffalowich died peacefully in his sleep, and a few months later he was followed by his friend John Gray. It was almost impossible to think of the latter remaining in this world without the former. Their friendship was so deep yet so undemonstrative. A stranger who saw them together for the first time would never have suspected it from the polite and formal manner in which André treated the Canon, due, I always felt, to André's intense consciousness of the priesthood and its privileges. This little Russian Jew convert, who always talked with a pronounced guttural accent and foreign intonation, lived on a high spiritual plane, far above what most of us can understand, much less reach. " He walked with God " and it was this close touch with a supernatural world which was the secret of his influence over " men and women of such strangely differing personalities, circumstances, talents, professions, and races ".

As Fr. Bernard Delany, O.P., remarked in his panegyric at Canon Gray's Requiem Mass : " John Gray and André Raffalowich were two friends with one common faith and one devotion to the same Divine Master. St. Peter's Church is the standing symbol of their friendship ". How intense was John Gray's love of the beauty of nature. He knew almost every hill and glen, river and road of Scotland, over which he loved to roam in solitude on the rare but regular occasions he allowed himself to take a brief holiday. It is not revealing a secret to mention that whenever the Canon was away on one of these holidays never a day passed without a telegram arriving for André Raffalowich, just to mention that all was well. " Ah! here is a wire from the dear Canon! " André would exclaim as the parlour maid handed him the eagerly-awaited yellow envelope. He would open it and inform me that the Canon said he was enjoying good weather or some such obvious fact. When John Gray was in Edinburgh he neved failed to call at Whitehouse Terrace every day, even if the visit was merely for a few moments. He might have been a very great poet, but as Fr. Delany expressed it: " It is the songs and poems he did not make that give him his real and royal greatness. Good things must go for the sake of the supremely good. How many songs just die that the supreme song of self-dedication may live?" Instead of becoming a world-famous poet he became what many of his contemporaries regarded as the ideal priest; quiet and aloof, yet always ready to spend himself in the service of others. Some people were put off by John Gray's ascetic reserve. It was difficult, if not impossible to gain access to that inner sanctuary of his soul. There was a mask-like quality behind his smile. If anybody liked a " hidden life " it was John Gray; a life hidden with God.

    *   *   *

Lastly, there is the bearded lay-man wearing the curious looking smock. I first met Eric Gill in August, 1917. For a long time before that I had known and admired his lettering, sculpture and wood-engraving. I had also subscribed to that lively little magazine, known as *The Game,* which was hand-printed on hand-made paper at Ditchling, where Gill was then living as a member of a community of Dominican Tertiaries, most of them being married men with families. So I asked if I might pay him a visit. I received a cordial answer to my request, and one summer afternoon I found myself at Burgess Hill station.

Twenty-six years ago, Folders Lane, which leads from Burgess Hill to Ditchling Common, was a real country lane. There were fields on either side, and no jerry-built bungalows had then begun to transform it into a typical suburban high-road. It was easy to realise why Eric Gill and the Community had chosen this rural spot for their home. It was still unspoilt Sussex.

Having reached a cross-roads where the Common begins, I noticed an old purple-red brick farm-house set in an orchard. From directions at the station I guessed this must be where the Gills lived. When I arrived at the gate, any uncertainty about this not being my goal was dispelled by the sight of big blocks of unhewn stone lying about in what had once been the farm-yard. There was also a large stone crucifix and an austere looking Madonna.

M

On looking back after more than quarter of a century, I find that
my memory has retained very few clear-cut impressions of that first
visit to Ditchling Common. What I remember best is the " atmosphere " of the place. I fell in love with the setting—the people whom
I met there, the kindly welcome and the homeliness of everything.
People were either charmed or repelled by Eric Gill. I was in the
former category. Even if I never became a whole-hearted disciple,
I realised that afternoon that this man could hardly help becoming an
influence. There was something irresistible in the logic of what
he had to say about so many subjects.

The following year I returned to Ditchling Common and spent a
few days with the Gills. It was the first of many subsequent visits,
repeated almost every year until they moved to South Wales in 1923,
and then onwards until Eric's death in 1940. Life in that household was unlike any other I had come across. There was a certain
spartan simplicity about the domestic arrangements, and a complete
lack of what are known as " modern conveniences "—of which at
that period Eric strongly disapproved. He failed to see the necessity
of a bathroom. Water was drawn from a pump. Meals, though
the food was abundant, were somewhat erratic, because all cooking
was done on an open fire which burned logs. More often than not
the wood was damp. I have vivid recollections of one or other
member of the family squatting on the kitchen floor, trying to get
the fire going with the aid of a pair of bellows. The rest of us would
be waiting for the meal, already conscious of hunger and wondering
how long it would be before dinner or supper would be ready. Eric
himself never bothered to leave his work until a bell was rung to
announce that the food was actually on the table.

In those years he had not acquired that broader and more tolerant
outlook on life which became so noticeable latterly. He disapproved
of most modern inventions of which the majority of us are only too
glad to avail ourselves. He looked askance at a typewriter which I
brought on one occasion, and remarked that it might be all right for
me to use a " writing machine ", for I was engaged in " active work
in the world ", but it would be wrong for *him* and his fellow Tertiaries, because they had " left the world and were trying to lead the
contemplative life in the desert ".

On another occasion, during the railway strike of 1919, he expressed his delight that the rails in the cutting close to the farm
were growing rusty. The rusty railway tracks provided the theme

for one of those long talks on the evils of modern industrialism which Eric could deliver with such devastating logic. After half an hour I was intellectually convinced that the world would be far better and happier without railways, but this did not prevent me from getting more and more impatient that I could not leave Ditchling owing to the stoppage of all trains.

Eric had an extraordinary power of convincing one of almost anything, even against one's own judgment. He was such a dominating personality. Just because he was so level-headed, and visualised everything with that same clear outline as his sculpture, it was not easy to argue with him. In my own case, the effect of a day or two in his company was to make me feel so dissatisfied with my own drawings that I had no wish to put pencil or pen to paper while I remained under his roof. On several occasions he made me thoroughly disgusted with a sketch I had made by producing an hour or two later an exquisite drawing of his own which had been " inspired " by my effort, which looked so amateurish beside his one. What I envied most was that mysterious *control* of his tools—no matter whether it was a chisel, pencil, pen or graver. There was no doubt about his being a master-craftsman. But I venture to think that, in certain instances, Gill's influence over other artists had a disastrous result, even if he never tried to force them to adopt his theories or methods. He preached to them, it is true, and almost against their will they became his devoted disciples. It was the terrific force of those beliefs—not mere opinions—which was so infectious. I can remember one artist who fell under Eric's influence, and so violent was the reaction that he made a bonfire of every drawing and painting he could lay hands on, except a few which his wife refused to part with. Some years after this incident, Eric remarked to me that it was a great pity that so-and-so had ever made his acquaintance; that he had done " good, honest painting " before his " conversion ", whereas all his subsequent work had never got anywhere—it was self-conscious and affected.

Eric Gill's conversion to Catholicism had been more whole-hearted than that of any other convert I have ever met. It had changed his entire outlook on life. It was an intellectual as well as an emotional conversion, influencing every aspect of his work. Hence his attraction to the Dominican Order and the social encyclicals of Pope Leo XIII, and the Summa of St. Thomas Aquinas. When I first visited the tertiaries on Ditchling Common they had no chapel of their own. But every evening the Gill family would gather in the kitchen and sing Dominican Compline. All those who can recall those far-off times will retain memories of the beauty of that liturgical family-worship, also the reading of the Martyrology before dinner.

It was in the early autumn of 1923 that Eric and I both happened to be staying at Quarr Abbey. He was on his way to Caldey, having decided that he must leave Ditchling and find a new home more remote from London. One evening he was discussing the possibility of settling on Caldey, or on an island off the west coast of Ireland. I remarked that I did not think that either plan would suit him, and asked if he had ever considered Llanthony. "What's Llanthony?" he enquired. So I proceeded to give him an impression of Fr. Ignatius' monastery in the Black Mountains, as described in an earlier chapter of this book. Eric was so attracted by what I told him of this solitary retreat that he went on to Caldey, not to make his future home on that island, but on renting the empty monastery which then belonged to the Caldey Benedictines. A month or two later I heard that he and his family had migrated from Sussex to South Wales.

The following year I paid my first visit to the Gills in their new surroundings. In some ways they were more uncomfortable than the old farm-house on Ditchling Common, though the south cloister provided Eric with a spacious workshop. When I watched him chipping away at one of his characteristic Madonnas, I could not help wondering what Fr. Ignatius would have thought of this type of art. I had little doubt that he would have expressed his opinions in similar language to that in which he indulged when attacking the "higher critics" of the Bible!

A chapel had been fitted up in the north cloister. There was a monolith supporting the altar slab on which stood the candlesticks and a veiled tabernacle. This altar was the prototype of the one erected later on at Pigotts and in the church at Gorleston-on-Sea, which Eric designed a year before his death. St. Peter's, Gorleston, expresses all his theories of church architecture and planning.

I went to Llanthony almost every year, and I got to know Eric much better as the result of long undisturbed talks in his workshops or in walks together over the mountains. He became a real friend, someone to whom one could always turn for advice and help in moments of doubt or difficulty.

By the time that the Gill family made their final move from the

Black Mountains to the Chiltern Hills, where they bought a farm-house some miles from High Wycombe, Eric had become world-famous, not only as a sculptor, but as an authority on economic problems and much else. In some ways his life had changed. All three daughters were married and grandchildren arrived every year to swell the patriarchal family circle—for each married daughter lived at Pigotts, with her own establishment apart from that of her father and mother. When I first met Eric there had only been one apprentice or assistant working with him. Now there were at least half a dozen men chipping stone in the big, dusty workshops. No longer did he look askance at typewriters. An ever-growing correspondence had made it necessary for him to engage a private secretary and one heard her tapping on the keys of a " writing machine " all day long. For not only were there letters to be written or answered—there were books and articles and lectures waiting to be typed. I used to feel that Eric was wearing himself out with constant journeys all over Britain for the purpose of expounding his now well-known views on art, religion, economics, and politics.

There was even a bathroom! What's more, a black marble bath with chromium plated taps. The kitchen fire smoked no more, for an ultra-modern range had superseded the open fire with the green logs I remembered at Ditchling. The telephone bell was always ringing. There were two motor cars instead of the primitive horse-drawn vehicle which used to take one to and from Llanvihangel to Llanthony. Some of the Dominican Tertiary Community who had remained at Ditchling shook their heads and felt that the " Master " had fallen away from his primitive ideals—he would not have made friends with the Mammon of Unrighteousness in so blatant a manner when he was one of them. He was now regarded very much as a Lost Leader. They just could not understand how he could design letters and numbers for locomotives and evolve streamlined motor cars. They sighed just a little sadly when they read that he had been elected an Associate of the Royal Academy and saw so many other initials appearing after his name—R.D.I., Hon.A.R.I.B.A., Hon. LL.D. (Edinburgh).

There was a chapel at Pigotts where the Blessed Sacrament was reserved; there was also a resident chaplain, and Mass was said every morning. Others might find an excuse to absent themselves from week-day Mass, but never Eric. Unless he was laid up in bed, and this was a rare occurrence until the last year of his life, he was usually

the first to get to the chapel. More often than not he served Mass.
Thus he started his long day's work. Apart from enforced breaks for
meals, it might be said that he never stopped working from breakfast to supper, and unless a friend happened to be staying with him,
he often continued his work far into the night. But he loved to sit
and talk to congenial friends, and it was often difficult to escape to
bed. He had no " recreations " in the sense that most other men
have. He found relief in turning from one kind of work to another—sculpture, wood-engraving, lettering, drawing, writing, lec-
turing. I doubt if he ever took a conventional " holiday ". He was
constantly dashing up to London or making longer journeys in connection with his work. The regular passengers at High Wycombe
station became familiar with the grey-bearded little man in a blue
beret, grey home-spun cloak and scarlet stockings, who carried a
small brown leather attaché case. The occupants of third-class
smokers who travelled to and from London every day got used to
him opening his case and bringing out his well-worn copy of the
Dominican *Little Office of Our Lady,* which he recited with atten-
tion and recollection.

During the last five or six years of his life, Eric became more and
more convinced of the evils of modern warfare, and of the urgent
need to strive for peace among nations. He was a militant pacifist,
in 'the sense that he believed that peace was about the only thing
worth fighting for. He might be a revolutionary in some ways, but
he was ever a loyal and obedient son of the Church. Everything he
wrote concerning faith and morals was submitted to an experienced
theologian before publication. He never failed to alter or delete
passages to which they objected, no matter how hard it might be to
give way to their judgment. There was nothing of the " modernist "
about Eric Gill, no matter how startling to pious ears were many of
the things he dared to put down on paper. The slackness, indifference and lack of zeal for Papal pronouncements among priests and
laity were what roused him to the greatest indignation. But I cannot recall a single instance when he expressed any doubts about his
utter loyalty to the Church itself.

The last time we met he was recovering from an illness which in
the end proved fatal. I sat in his bedroom at Pigotts, and outside the
fruit trees were in blossom. Innumerable grandchildren of all ages
and other children were playing in the garden; lambs were frolicking
in the orchard, and overhead came the drone of aeroplanes. Eric

could talk of little else but peace that May afternoon as he lay there in bed, propped up against pillows. Most other people were talking of nothing else but war. He gave me a copy of a pamphlet just issued, which, so he remarked, gave a clear idea of what ought to be the Catholic attitude towards war and peace. This was his last gift to me. I never saw him again.

I think I ought to make it clear that after Eric Gill severed his connection with the still existing Dominican Tertiary Community at Ditchling in 1923, it was a parting of the ways. From now onwards he became the centre of a group, mainly composed of members of his own family and of a constantly changing group of apprentices and assistant workmen. It was a way of life pervaded by the dominating personality of Gill. To be honest, I doubt if Eric could have remained a member of any Community—he would have crushed everybody else who belonged to it, just because he was such a " superman "! But when I look back on those twenty-three years of friendship I feel that nobody else I have ever met has summed up in his character in such a complete manner the spirit of the Sermon on the Mount. Eric's personality radiated the spirit of the Beatitudes: he was meek and merciful; always thirsting after truth and righteousness, and above all else, a peacemaker. May he rest from his earthly labours and enjoy in heaven that Infinite Beauty that he sought to reproduce here below in so far as Man is capable of reproducing no more than a far off glimpse of it.

CHAPTER VIII

LIFE ON A CANADIAN RANCH

In my previous volume of reminiscences I referred but briefly to several months spent in British Columbia after that memorable voyage from Venice to Vancouver during the autumn of 1926. Let me continue the story from that raw October evening when I had said good-bye to the Italian stewards at Vancouver station and found myself in the train en route for the Okanagan.

When I awoke the next morning I pulled up the blind beside the lower berth of the comfortable tourist sleeper in which I had passed a peaceful night after leaving Vancouver. It seemed that the train was running through a wide open valley with wooded mountains rising up above a rapidly flowing river. I opened a map and decided it must be the Thompson. Presently the rumbling and swaying of the big steel coaches ceased, and the Transcontinental Limited stopped at a station whose name I discovered to be Ashcroft—the gateway to the famous Cariboo district. I was curious to see more of this fascinating landscape. It looked so different from any part of Europe. So I got up, and was ready to answer the first call for breakfast when the dining-car attendant made his way along the train. I do not know which I appreciated most; the perfectly appointed fittings and arrangements of that Canadian National Railways dining-car with its attentive and courteous waiters, or the equally perfect coffee and hot rolls and butter.

The long train started off again, stopping at stations whose names indicated the diverse nationalities of the first settlers—Anglesey—Walhachin—Savona—Tranquille; then shunted and backed into Kamloops. Here I had to change into another train for Kelowna. After we started again I sat by the window of the car, so entranced in the beauty of the landscape that the copy of the morning paper lay unopened at my side. I wanted to jump out and start drawing, for there was something irresistibly attractive in the fresh and youthful-looking country. The great mountains and deep valleys are as yet unspoilt by works of man. There are few signs of human habitation until the railway began to descend from the pine-clad mountains into the rich fruit-growing lands around Falkland and Vernon. From now onward the scenery became even more beautiful, especially as we passed Long Lake with the vivid yellow maples reflected in its still blue waters. Five hours after leaving Kamloops, and after innumerable stops at wayside stations, the train arrived at its final destination—Kelowna.

It was my destination, too, for among the crowd waiting on the platform I immediately detected the familiar figure of " the Father ", as we used to call him in bygone years at Caldey. He was no longer my religious superior, just an old friend, and was soon to become known to me as " A.F.C." The last time we had met was in England, over five years ago, just before he had resigned his official position. Then he wore the cross and ring of an Abbot. Now all the externals of a prelate had been shed. For the first moment it was difficult to realise that the wiry, bronzed and sunburnt figure could be the same man as the tired and worried monk, burdened with the financial responsibility of debts running into many thousands of pounds.

As we walked down from the railway to the pier, where a small motor-boat was moored, I had the odd feeling that we were back again in South Wales, and that in a few moments we should be on our way from Tenby to Caldey. Yet it was not upon the often storm-tossed channel through which the Atlantic rollers find their way in winter gales that we embarked, but upon the calm and peaceful waters of Lake Okanagan, backed by its dark, pine-clad mountains. Our destination was Bear Creek Ranch, which lay four miles from Kelowna on the other side of the lake.

As the motor-boat sped over the sunlit waters of the lake I watched my former superior attending to the engine and steering his course for a low, white one-storied house which lay on the far shore. It was half-hidden by a clump of golden-tinted maples—for the " fall " colouring was at its height when I landed in Canada. I felt that the whole surroundings of this tranquil inland lake and the kindly look-ing mountains with great apple orchards at their base seemed to ex-press, as no words could have done, the great change which had taken place in his life since we had last met. There was an infinite difference between that windswept little island of Pembrokeshire ex-posed to the fury of gales and tempests both spiritual and climatic, the former of which a kind Providence had used to carry him afar, to this peaceful valley in British Columbia where he might do God's work, alone and undisturbed. How often had he not described the scene to me in his letters. It was all just as I had pictured it.

It was a new experience to find myself living on a Canadian ranch, and as the " tenderfoot " I had much to learn the first few days. Monastic training stood me in good stead, for at Bear Creek we did everything for ourselves, having only one paid man, a half-breed Indian, to help us. He was proud of his name—Donald McDougal —and called himself a Scotsman, though his face did not suggest such ancestry! I slept in a little two-roomed wooden shack which stood alone in the forest at some distance from the house where " A.F.C." and Fr. Aidan Angle lived, and next to which was the chapel. When the winter snow had begun I had to keep a path open to my " hermitage ". At night-time I sometimes heard coyotes prowling around, and in the morning saw the footprints of strange animals on the snow when I made my way to the chapel for Mass.

The days flew by with extraordinary rapidity. Alongside of much

widely distributed pastoral work, at home there was always much to
do, what with "chores" of one kind or another; splitting wood in
preparation for the winter cold, work in the garden and orchard;
cooking, sweeping, dusting, not to mention washing clothes.   We
used to take them down to the beach and scrub them in the lake.
The very day after my arrival A.F.C. asked me if I could ride.   I
replied that I had done a little when I was a boy, but had not been
on a horse for over thirty years.   "Well, you had better start this
afternoon," he announced at lunch.   "The old mare won't throw you
off, and all you have to do is to hold on."   Let me confess at that
time I knew very little about horses.   I had no idea that in later
years I should become the owner of two bay geldings and drive round
Great Britain in a gipsy caravan.   But that is another story!*   However, it seemed that one could not live in B.C. without knowing how
to stick on a horse, and therefore the only thing was to learn the
painful process as soon as possible.   So I was shoved on to the
animal's back, A.F.C. being already mounted on another and
obviously much more fiery beast than my old mare.   We started off.
My companion dashed away ahead of me, and I followed.   Before I
quite knew what was happening, my animal was charging up a steep
mountainside with A.F.C. well ahead.

"This is quite exciting," I said to myself, "I wonder what I ought
to do?   Anyhow the old lady seems quite happy, and has evidently
taken matters into her own charge."   But I am glad there was nobody
with a movie-camera there to take a comic film of me trying to
emulate the late Tom Mix or some other now almost forgotten "Wild
West" cinema star, for this was several years before the advent of the
first "talkies".   Fortunately a Canadian stock saddle has a most
useful pommel to which one can "hold on", and this I thankfully
did.   Having climbed up some hundreds of feet we reached a more
or less level stretch of ground, and here was the chance of a good
canter.   Yelling to me to "stick on and not be afraid," A.F.C. dis-
appeared among the pine-trees and I followed, or rather the old mare
did, I deciding that the only thing to be done was to try and enjoy
the view and leave matters to her, for she seemed to be quite happy
and to know where to step.   The ground was broken up into gullies,
the dried-up beds of streams, and everywhere the trunks of fallen
trees and great boulders blocked the way.   For over three hours we

* See *The Brown Caravan* by Anthony Rowe (Heath Cranton, 1935).

rode these mountains among the virgin forests where there was no sign of human life of any sort, until at last we climbed down again to the ranch, where a very sore and bruised rider had to be assisted to the ground! This rather brutal and drastic initiation had certainly cured me of any nervousness of horses, and I now felt I would ride anywhere, though I was not fit to mount a horse again for over a week.

As I picked up again the threads of my more than twenty-years-old friendship with the one-time Abbot of Caldey, I could not help feeling that he was now living and carrying out his true vocation. For Aelred Carlyle, ever since I had first known him in 1908, had always been a born pioneer, restive under restraint and convention, although always eager and ready to work under obedience and authority. This is well exemplified in his twenty years' work of "reviving" the Benedictine Rule in the uncongenial soil of the Church of England. This work provided for Aelred Carlyle almost exactly the right psychological outlet for his energies and temperament. It gave him scope for the really exceptional gifts he possessed as a free-lance leader of men, subject to no immediate authority. As a matter of fact, although the Anglican episcopate would have been glad to let him carry on in the freedom of his extra-parochial and extra-diocesan monastery, this very independence and isolation were the means of bringing him and his Community into the Catholic Church. In 1912 he felt that his own individual work was done; the task that he had set himself was accomplished, and a numerous and flourishing Community of men had been built up, subject to the Rule of St. Benedict, and within the confines of the Anglican Church. The moment had come when the position of his Community should receive episcopal recognition; and it was here that the Abbot's characteristic love of order asserted itself in trying to obtain official approval from the Anglican authorities. The refusal of this recognition, and the denial of certain Catholic doctrines of faith resulted in a sincere, whole-hearted and almost unanimous submission to the Holy See. In little over sixteen months after his conversion, Brother Aelred Carlyle had been solemnly professed as a Benedictine monk, ordained priest, blessed and installed as Abbot, and all the Caldey "spirituals and temporals" given into his charge.

It was a burden that proved too much for a raw convert. There is an essential difference between the superior of a free-lance Anglican brotherhood and a Catholic Benedictine abbot. The former can be a law unto himself. A Catholic abbot is bound by fixed and definite rules and constitutions, age-old traditions, not to mention all the provisions of Canon Law. Worn out mentally and physically, the result of trying to keep going a large and growing community which, owing to its peculiar history, suddenly found itself without any means of financial support, Abbot Aelred had resigned his position in 1921. Through the generosity of some friends in the Argentine, he and Father Aidan Angle, the companion of his travels and former secretary, were able to settle in British Columbia. Here they found congenial work as missionaries attached to the Catholic archdiocese of Vancouver. They were put in charge of a very large district, including three Indian reservations. In addition to this work among the Indians and many scattered white families, they were sent to " supply " in parishes in the interior of the province which were without pastors either through illness, absence, or the fewness of priests.

In 1930, after founding the little parish of Summerland and building the church of the Holy Child, their work was greatly enlarged. A.F.C. was appointed to the mining country of Princeton, a mountainous region which, through the death of priests in the West, had been sadly left to itself and which, in the words of one who knew the country well, " had never been baptised ". At a parish, in which the ordered round of Catholic life was being firmly established, and in addition he had a number of outlying missions and " stations " which in themselves were sufficient to tax the energies of any one man. Father Aidan Angle, his life-long friend and secretary and my own contemporary at Caldey, also had a territory in his care which covered several hundred miles of the Pacific coast and adjacent islands, with Ocean Falls as his headquarters. Their work was done joyfully, but the life was a hard one, and the mixture of nationalities, of tradition, even of rite (for many of their flock are Slovaks, Ruthenians, or Ukrainians who are accustomed to the Byzantine liturgy in old Slavonic or other languages) with which they had to deal, offered a variety of problems unknown, except perhaps theoretically, to Catholics in Europe. In recent years both these two old friends have been given other spheres of work for souls: A.F.C., despite being now past seventy, is carrying on an active apostolate in Vancouver itself among sailors, prisoners, the sick and aged; while Fr. Aidan is attached to the headquarters of the Canadian Army chaplaincies.

During my stay with them the two would go off nearly every Friday

to different places north, east, south and west, returning again on
Monday to spend the middle of the week on the ranch, where each
morning they said their Masses with myself as the sole congregation
in the little wooden chapel they had built next to the house. Sometimes I was left quite alone for the week-end with no companions
but a dog and a cat. It was a solitude far more complete and satisfying than I could experience in a Carthusian cell. Our nearest
neighbour was over a mile off, and in between lay open forests through
which one could have walked in a westerly direction for over eighty
miles before coming across any other dwelling. On other Sundays I
used to accompany Father Aidan to one of the Indian reservations of
which he had the spiritual care.

How many of us realise that a large proportion of the comparatively few remaining tribes of Red Indians in Western Canada are
good practising Catholics? The largest of the Catholic tribes in
British Columbia is that of the Okanagan. Its territory covers roughly
the whole district from Kamloops, the railway junction of the
Canadian Pacific and Canadian National transcontinental lines on the
north, right down for over fifty miles or so into the United States,
about two hundred miles in all.

To-day the Indians are organised for Government purposes into
" Bands " and their land is known as " Indian Reserve ". Indians
possess unfettered ownership of their land, except that they may not
sell it to whites, but only lease or sell it among themselves.

The Okanagan Indians were evangelised some fifty or sixty years
ago by the French religious Congregation of the Oblates of Mary
Immaculate. It is curious how little is known over here of the more
than romantic story of the pioneer missionary work carried on beyond
the Rockies by these French priests when what is now the province
of British Columbia was still quite cut off from Eastern Canada, and
a transcontinental railroad existed only in dreams.

They did their work without fuss or hope of material reward and
lived under conditions of real hardship. Yet so well and so firmly
did these splendid Oblates plant the Faith in the souls of these simple
Indians, that even when they are unable to hear Mass or approach
the Sacraments more than two or three times a year at the most,
owing to the want of priests they meet together, Sunday after Sunday,
to say the Rosary and other prayers together. It is curious to hear
these Indians singing the Plain Chant Common of the Mass in Latin
—a chant which, in the progress of years, has become crystallised into

LAKE OKANAGAN, BRITISH COLUMBIA.

something all its own. You will also hear them singing old French *cantiques* set to Indian words by the French Oblates more than half a century ago. As I listened to these Indians chanting Sunday after Sunday I could not say that I thought their language was a beautiful one, however rich and intricate it might be. It is guttural and full of the queerest little clicks and jerks, and I did not feel moved to study it. The two reserves that were in charge of " A.F.C." and his fellow priest were Head of Lake and Westbank.

In the former there were about 400 Catholics. Each reserve has its own chief, part of whose duties is to take care of the church and the spiritual needs of his subjects. The piety of the squaws is something I shall never forget; their devotion to the Blessed Sacrament is intense. It struck me that the male Indians, especially the younger men, were less religious and, frankly, somewhat slack. I regret I was not in B. C. for the feast of Corpus Christi, which is their great day. Each year it is held at a different reserve, in rotation. The Indians will flock there from hundreds of miles or more. Mass and Procession in the morning are followed by games and races in the afternoon—a regular Christian holiday.

Feathers and war paint are now relics of the past, and most well-to-do Indians now own their own Ford cars. Their villages much resemble one of those untidy gipsy encampments one sees on the outskirts of English towns, for the average Okanagan Indian has no sense of order or neatness, and prefers to live in a litter of old tin cans, broken bedsteads, rags, and a general confusion of rubbish. As I have said they own cars—but what cars! You wonder that they manage to go at all, but they do, and the Indians are good though reckless drivers. Despite the automobile and other inventions, the Indians still show amazing skill in horsemanship. It is a thrilling sight to see a young Indian blood, well mounted with saddle and bridle and chaps of leather, heavily decorated with silver. They have a passionate love of dazzling colours, and like the English gipsies to whom I have already compared them, possess a genius for making colours harmonise which would be utterly impossible if attempted according to " Art-School " principles.

One night " A.F.C." was called out hurriedly to a dying Indian girl about six miles down the lake. He went in a boat, and got to the crowded dirty Indian shack at the same time as the doctor. They found a child with appendicitis, congestion of the lungs, and elephantiasis! She would certainly have died where she was, so they wrapped her up in her bedding, carried her to the boat and thence across the lake in the darkness of the night to the hospital at Kelowna. He told me of a long missionary expedition, from which he had just returned, away in the Babine mountains to the north-west, far beyond the Cariboo and the Skeena river, in which he had covered more than two thousand miles. He was on horseback through the bush for sixty miles, and in Indian canoes for two days at a time going down the big lakes. He mentioned casually among other minor adventures without which no such trip would be complete, horses getting away at night so that the party were hung up for two days in the forest and the crank of an Evinrude engine snapping in the middle of a lake two hundred miles long, involving a long wait ashore in the bush tormented by mosquitoes while word was sent on foot to the chief at the head of the lake. Then there were pouring wet days in the mountains and freezing nights at an altitude of seven thousand feet, not to mention the continual work of wrestling with Indian guides and trying to keep to some sort of time-table, in spite of the time lost three times a day in preparing and eating food.

" But I love it all," he smilingly added, " in fact one could not do it without that nameless joy and satisfaction that the wilds always bring to those who love the ways untrod of men. I thank God for having sent me to this country."

One morning I assisted at the funeral of a little Indian girl, daughter of the chief. There were hundreds of Redskins at the Mass and graveside, and it was a pity that I could not have painted the wonderful picture it made with the early morning sun on the snow and the bright colours of the squaws' blankets. They are a reverent race, and the silence at that funeral was greatly impressive, with a calm dignity and self-restraint not always seen among " whites ". When death comes to the Indian he faces it with the calm which has been handed down to him from his forefathers. To the Indian soul the spirit world is a vivid reality, and accepted as a matter of course. Because of this philosophic attitude towards death you seldom see tears at an Indian graveside.

When I arrived at Kelowna on the afternoon of October 28 the brilliant " fall " colours of the landscape were still at their best, and I saw that it was true that, as one is always told, they surpass anything seen in Europe for sheer gorgeousness. Three weeks later the winter came quite suddenly, with a heavy fall of snow on the hills, where it rested, and then day after day it crept nearer and nearer until everything looked like an old-fashioned Christmas card. Then how one revelled in the cosy wintry sound of the wind as it " whooed " and " swished " about the doors at night and the resinous pine logs laughed as they burned on the hearth, for the comfort they bring when winter comes.

One thing that struck me greatly was that one never bothered to lock the doors on the ranch if one went off for the day anywhere. In fact they were left open deliberately, so that any chance caller could come in and make himself a cup of tea or a meal should he feel inclined. Several times I have availed myself of this communal hospitality when, having arrived at some neighbouring ranch, I found everybody out. The Indians, however they may try and cheat in selling a horse or such like business, would not dream of robbing a house. So both doors and windows of my wooden shack in the forest were left ajar until the winter snows and frost made it necessary for me to close them.

After a month at Bear Creek I went down to the coast and crossed over from Vancouver to visit my cousin, Ida Crofton, who lived on Salt Spring Island, one of the many small islands that cluster in the Strait of Georgia at the south end of the much larger Vancouver Island.

Before leaving Kelowna I had definitely arranged with the Franciscan Fathers at San Luis Rey, near San Diego in California, to go there about Christmas, having been invited to teach drawing in their college. But the U.S.A. Immigration Departments, both at Vancouver and Victoria, absolutely refused to allow me to enter the country, even with a " tourist-permit " for six months, for it appeared I had committed the unforgivable sin of crossing the Atlantic and landing on Canadian soil in an Italian ship not registered by the American Government to carry passengers! No amount of Consular and other influence in high places was of any avail. It is true that I was told I might get a " dispensation " if I appealed to the Secretary of Labour at Washington. But even here it seemed very doubtful if it would result in my being allowed across the border, and it would have necessitated long correspondence with the Libera Triestina Company in Italy, and possibly a delay of six to nine months! What was I to do meanwhile?

So, after three weeks on Salt Spring Island I returned to Bear Creek, where I remained until the end of January. Christmas was a curious experience, for I spent four days in absolute solitude on the

N

ranch. By this time "A.F.C." had gone to Europe on business, and
I had Fr. Aidan as my sole companion. He had already left for one
of his "Stations", and I had been invited to stay with friends. But,
on Christmas Eve, we had such a heavy fall of snow that it was quite
impossible for me to struggle through the deep drifts to the ferry
across the lake, some three miles off. So there was nothing to do but
"dig myself in ". Fortunately there was an unlimited store of logs,
and plenty of canned foods and fruit in the store. Our half-breed
Indian had also gone off to celebrate Christmas with his family at the
reserve. Consequently, for three days I had ample opportunities for
contemplating the beauty of the snow-covered landscape that
surrounded the ranch on every side. And as we had a good library
and a gramophone the time did not seem long. In fact I think I
probably enjoyed this solitary Christmas among the snows far more
than I should have done with a noisy house-party of people.

*   *   •

I discussed the possibility of getting artistic or literary work in
British Columbia, but I was told that my chances were poor, owing
to the fact that such jobs were few and far between in a pioneer
country at a moment of business depression. Funds were getting
low, and I did not want to be stranded in Canada. The doors of
the U.S.A. were closed to me, and the congenial work with the
Franciscan Fathers at San Luis Rey seemed beyond my reach. So,
finally, I decided there was nothing else to be done but recross the
Atlantic. On my return to Britain in March, 1927, I informed a
correspondent that I was "reduced to a really Franciscan state of
poverty ". But I added that, as several art galleries were taking my
pictures and that "Mr. Sands says he will gladly publish anything
I like to write or illustrate about Scotland, it must be merely a
question of time before I am earning a more or less regular income ".
It was not until my father decided to allow me a small but definite
allowance, that I was able to settle down to a more peaceful existence.
In July of that year I had the first "home " of my own at "Anson
House ", High Street, Portsmouth. On my thirty-eighth birthday,
August 22nd, I wrote: "I am more or less installed in my studio.
It looks very attractive, with its whitewashed walls and tarred beams
At night when the wind whistles through the tiles (it has an open
roof), and I sit here in candle-light, I have the feeling of being at
sea in an old sailing ship."

A few months later Mr. Sands commissioned me to write and illustrate another book, to be entitled *Benedictine Italy,* intended as a companion volume to my *Pilgrim's Guide to Franciscan Italy,* which had received excellent reviews, even if the sales might have been quicker. Here was an excuse to be off again to Italy. I visited numerous Benedictine monasteries, made a start on the book, but for various reasons it got no further.

In May, 1928, I moved into other quarters, this time at 12 High Street, Portsmouth. From now onwards I could never complain of a lack of paid work. Every letter mentions being " very busy with drawings ". There were commissions from the Challenge Gallery for drawings of Westminster Abbey and Christmas cards. This same firm, in the person of Miss Ethel Barton, were anxious for me to visit Oberammergau to write and illustrate a guide book for the use of English visitors to the famous Passion Play. But this scheme fell through. Early in 1929 I secured the job from the Challenge to do six pictures of Palestine. They were afterwards reproduced in colour and were used in Sunday Schools. At the same time the Catholic Association gave me a free ticket for one of their pilgrimages to Palestine, on the understanding that I supplied them with a certain number of drawings to illustrate their brochures and other publications. Thanks to the Catholic Association, or rather to my friend, the late Harry Wallack, who was at that time its Organising Secretary, there had been another extensive tour on the Continent of Europe the previous winter, during which I made drawings of famous shrines, such as Lourdes, Rocamadour, Paray-le-Monial, Bruges, Lisieux, and Rome. Then came an invitation from Dent's to write and illustrate *Fishing Boats and Fisher Folk on the East Coast of Scotland,* which was a turning point in my literary and artistic career. Of this book, and others of maritime subject-matter, I have already written in *Harbour Head.*

From the autumn of 1930 to the spring of 1934 my home was on the banks of the Lower Thames; first at Gravesend, then at Northfleet; a period of my life which is fully dealt with in my first medley of memories. Yet it was now entirely associated with maritime matters. I found time for frequent visits to monasteries and constant tours to draw churches, both at home and abroad.

CHAPTER IX

MORE MONASTERIES

Pictures of other monasteries besides those already mentioned keep up the memory of hospitality given me by many communities in Great Britain.   Stored away in shelves are drawings made when visiting these religious houses.   A small suitcase, that usually hides itself under the bed of my spare room, contains the still unpublished typescript of a " popular encyclopedia " of Religious Orders and Congregations.   A long row of books dealing with the history of monasticism indicates a field of research that has little in common with those maritime matters which I confess appeal to me much more!   But these two branches of study have been prosecuted almost simultaneously ever since I was a boy.   So there is an obvious excuse for a few more memories of monasteries.

At one time or other I have enjoyed the hospitality of many other religious communities in England and Scotland.   First on the list must come Downside Abbey, Somerset, if only because it takes precedence of the rest as the oldest Benedictine foundation.

Dom John Chapman—who was our Superior at Caldey during the year that followed the submission of the Community to the Holy See —became Abbot of Downside in 1929, so I was always certain of a warm welcome from this old friend whose scholarship was sufficient excuse for many little oddities of manner.   His knowledge embraced so many subjects, and one was never certain what would be his absorbing interest at the moment.   It might equally well be variants in the texts of the Vulgate; the right way to phrase a particular passage in a Chopin valse; the subtleties of English prose rhythm; a new game of Patience; or the higher stages of contemplative prayer. In most respects John Chapman was the most humble of men; but he fully realised that in particular fields of scholarship he need fear no rivals.   For instance, that masterly, if rather brutal, answer to Bishop Gore's Roman *Catholic Claims*—a brilliant piece of polemical writing.   He might have excelled in many walks of life; for instance, he loved drawing plans of buildings and had an encyclopedic knowledge of the country houses of England.

Another member of the Downside Community was Dom Bede Camm, like Dom Chapman, originally a monk of Maredsous in Belgium and latterly of Erdington Abbey, near Birmingham. On the closing of the German Benedictine house after the last war, both were affiliated to Downside. Dom Bede was quite a different type to his life-long friend Dom John. His chief interest was the promotion of the cultus of the martyrs who had laid down their lives for the Faith at the Reformation. He wrote many books about the English Martyrs and lectured or preached about them. As I have told in an earlier chapter, it was this pious convert-monk who hurried to Caldey on the news that the Anglican Community had decided to make its submission to Rome, and who said the first Catholic Mass in our abbey church.

I have always felt that the most attractive part of Downside is the fact that the abbey has never been completed. Like so many medieval monasteries, it is a mixture of almost every style and period of Gothic architecture. One can study each phase of the Gothic Revival, mixed up without any feeling of incongruity. The abbey church gives one an idea of what the typical English pre-Reformation cathedral must have been like. For the outward presentation of religion at Downside is intensely English, in fact some Catholics find it almost Anglican in atmosphere!

The so-called English Altars are just the same as those which in recent years have become so popular in almost every Anglican cathedral—with their dossals and riddel posts. The finest of these altars is in the Lady Chapel. It was designed by Mr. J. N. Comper about fifty years ago, and, at the time, was a complete novelty in a Catholic church.

The large resident Community is chiefly engaged in teaching, but the celebration of the Divine Office and Conventual Mass is carried out in keeping with the dignity of the setting. The ethos of Downside is somewhat suggestive of an English country mansion where family life has gone on without a break for more than three centuries, and where the present members of the family are conscious, yet unconscious of their long history. They are so sure of themselves that they do not need to advertise their social or ecclesiastical status!

There are no lay-brothers, and the domestic work of the place is performed by men servants, some of them being the sons or grandsons of men who were employed in the same way. How can one describe the hospitality shown to guests in normal times? Plates of crisply fried bacon and eggs at breakfast, and delicious coffee—and a man servant, in linen jacket with blue cuffs, whispering into one's ear at dinner: "Beer or cider, sir?" What I love to look back on more than all else are those perfectly carried out High Masses and Vespers —the Plain Chant or Polyphony, with the masterly accompaniment of Dom Gregory Murray. Here was *English* (not Anglo!) Catholicism at its best!

Ampleforth Abbey, which is situated on the edge of the Yorkshire Moors, a few miles from Helmsley, is only two years younger than Downside, for it was established at Dieulouard in Lorraine in 1608. What is more, it can claim a direct descent from the pre-Reformation Abbey of Westminster, having been legally vested with all the rights and privileges of the old English Congregation of Benedictines by Dom Sigebert Buckley, the last surviving monk of the Westminster Community, who died in prison in 1607. The French Revolution obliged the Community to flee to England in 1794. They found a new home in Yorkshire, and here around the original 18th century mansion has grown up the scattered groups of buildings that to-day make up Ampleforth Abbey. Unlike Downside, where the monastery, school and church huddle together, the units of Ampleforth straggle along a steep hillside with gaps between. At Downside the school and monastery, although in close contact with each other, are completely separate, whereas at Ampleforth a visitor in term time would form the impression that monks and over 400 boys make up one great family, or rather that Ampleforth consists of several "Communities", since each schoolhouse carries on its own corporate life as in the traditional English public school manner. Each "house" is under the charge of one or two monks who live with the boys there. There are more than 100 monks belonging to the Ampleforth *conventus*. Their work is threefold: the celebration of the Divine Office in the abbey church; pastoral work around the monastery and in about thirty parishes in different dioceses; scholastic work in the two schools attached to the abbey.

During the past five years, thanks to the evacuation of Avisford Preparatory School from Sussex to Yorkshire, where it has found temporary quarters in one of the college buildings, I have had a special inducement to visit Ampleforth. Major Charles Jennings— the headmaster of Avisford—and his wife have been the kindest and most hospitable of friends for nearly a quarter of a century (in fact, they should have been mentioned already in these pages, for they have

played no small part in my life). As their guest I have been able to
enjoy for three successive Christmases the dignified ceremonies and
rare perfection of the Plain Chant in the abbey church at Ampleforth
—a still unfinished building designed by Sir Giles Gilbert Scott on
not nearly so large a scale as the abbey church at Downside. I can
now count many monks of this Community as my friends, and their
welcome is quite in the Benedictine tradition.

The average monk of Ampleforth leads a strenuous existence, for
he has to combine his monastic obligations with the duties of a busy
schoolmaster. His vow of obedience may call him to shed his black
habit and change into white flannels to play cricket, or mud-stained
shorts for a rugby match, or a run with the college beagles. Or
you may find him in the khaki uniform of an officer of the O.T.C.
at one moment, and a few minutes later he will be transformed into
a black-cowled figure in choir, or vested in a cope at Vespers or giving
Benediction! Altogether the whole thing is utterly different to the
popular Protestant conception of life in a " monkery ", and indeed
to what is held by many Catholics.

The first Catholic Benedictine Community I visited after my reception into the Church was Belmont Abbey, near Hereford. In 1914
it was still the general novitiate of the English Congregation, and
ranked as the Cathedral Priory of the diocese of Newport, ruled over
at that time by the late Bishop Hedley. It was not until 1920 that
Belmont became an independent Community and was raised to the
status of an abbey. Like all Benedictine monasteries, Belmont has
its individual character, even if the outward observance is much the
same as in other houses of the English Congregation. I always picture
it as a peaceful Victorian backwater where life has not altered much
during the seventy or eighty years; the illusion being helped by the
faint smell of gas which still mingled with the fumes of stale incense
on the occasion of my last visit about six years ago. The comparatively
small abbey church is a perfect example of ornate Gothic Revival
architecture, dim with stained glass windows in the usual style of
Messrs. Hardman of Birmingham, and overladen with elaborate stone
carvings on columns and reredoses. It would be a pity to touch such
a remarkable period piece. Again, it was pleasant to discover that
the Community were still using the old edition of the monastic
Antiphonale, and to listen to the psalm tones and antiphons with
which I had been familiar at Caldey. But do not imagine that Belmont
is moribund! In recent years it has opened a small school, which is

conducted on quite modern lines. Those of the monks who are not occupied with teaching are engaged in parochial work.

Quarr Abbey, Isle of Wight, which I have already mentioned in earlier chapters, has always been one of my favourite monasteries, for it is unique. My first memory of Quarr goes back long before the Benedictines of Solesmes settled there in 1907, six years after their expulsion from France by an anti-clerical Government. I remember being taken over to Ryde from Portsmouth when I was quite a little boy and having a picnic in the woods of Quarr Abbey House—then unoccupied. A good many years later I first encountered Benedictine monks when I called at Appuldercombe House, nestling among the hills behind Ventnor, which was the first home of the Solesmes Community in the Isle of Wight. I have described subsequent visits to Quarr when I was still an Anglican. When I reverted to the status of a layman in 1924, and for about a year before that, while still wearing the habit of a Benedictine oblate, Quarr became my home for a considerable period, thanks to the hospitality offered me by the Prior, Dom Bouvet, that hard-headed but kind-hearted Norman monk, who became one of my most loyal and devoted friends. Among the Community at that date was the artist-monk, Dom Pedro Subercaseaux, a Chilean by birth, in whom I found a kindred spirit. To-day he is back again in his native country the sub-prior of a small Community of Benedictines near Santiago. Only last year, 1944, he invited me to come out to South America, to help him with the planning and decoration of churches. Owing to the war it would have been impossible for me to have obtained a permit to travel; otherwise I might have been tempted to accept this offer. During the months I lived at Quarr on and off between 1923 and 1927 I had a good deal to do with the designs if not the actual painting of the altar pieces in the crypt upon which Dom Pedro was engaged. This artist-monk gave me much useful advice and criticism of my own water colours and drawings.

How can I describe the buildings of this great abbey on the shores of the Solent? "What a revolution when Quarr Abbey appeared!" Here was a building built with brick in an absolutely new form. "No iron?" The engineers felt instinctively that they were to lose the ecclesiastical market. "This man is insane," they roared. "Can you imagine such a thing—a building without girders? It will fall on the bowed heads of the worshippers." The monastery at Quarr is still standing in its beautiful robe of pink brick. The building at

Quarr was at once a vindication of Dom Bellot's principles and an expression of a new freedom. Dom Bellot had leaped to freedom at a single bound, and at Quarr he found his way of celebrity.*

This same writer points out that this great monk-architect created a new form of building, deeply religious and substantially suitable for sacred worship. But at Quarr, as elsewhere, he " never forgot the advice which St. Benedict had put down in his Rule: ' Let the oratory be an oratory and nothing else, nor let anything be kept or anything be done that is incongruous ' (ch. 52). Dom Bellot believed that a church was a place for worship, a place for the hieratic dramas of the Mass and the Divine Office, where the faithful could breathe the true atmosphere of their heavenly home." Again, " he was a true Parisian with many tricks in his bag." He had an uncanny knowledge of the technique of building. He revived the Moorish parabolic arch. " Just as the Angelic Doctor had converted Aristotle for the sake of his *Summa,* so Dom Bellot later introduced Mohammed into a Benedictine monastery clothed as a black monk." Then again, he revelled in colour, not only bricks of every hue, but concrete coloured in vivid tones, even the mortar joints play their part in his colour schemes.

To quote from an article on Dom Bellot which I contributed to *Pax* shortly after his death in 1944: " When I think of Quarr Abbey on a summer afternoon, with its golden-orange brickwork rising out of the green woods by the seashore, or visualise the interior of the church, its hard lines softened down with the haze of incense, and the sun's rays making queer patterns as it shines through the tall windows of the sanctuary."

Dom Bellot's great church, which one either loves or hates, according to one's temperament, is—to my mind—the perfect setting for the perfect presentation of the worship of God; which is the only way to describe the services at Quarr Abbey.

As a complete contrast there is another Benedictine abbey—Ramsgate—which appeals to me for utterly different reasons. The only thing it has in common with Quarr is that both monasteries are built close to the sea. Quarr has an ultra-modern or, rather, ageless church of red brick; Ramsgate's place of worship is Augustus Welby Pugin's flint and stone built replica of a typical medieval English

---

*Dom Marcel Pierre Hamel, O.S.B., article in *Orate Fratres.* Vol. XIX. No. 4. February 25, 1945.

QUARR ABBEY.

parish cnurch, complete with rood-screen and windows filled with
rich stained glass. At Quarr, you feel that Dom Bellot's aim was to
let in as much light as possible, even if he mellowed it with a golden
glass; at Ramsgate, Pugin's ideal was to create a " dim, religious
light " and to make people forget the sunshine and the open air. In
the former church there is a sense of infinite space; in the latter the
feeling of the crowded page of illuminated missal, full of minute
details. At Ramsgate I seemed to recapture something of the spirit
of the Italian Community of Subiaco, and with good reason, for the
first monks who settled on the Isle of Thanet in 1855 made their
novitiate at Subiaco, and the abbey, with Prinknash and Buckfast,
now forms the English Province of the Cassinese Congregation of the
Primitive Observance, commonly known as the Subiaco Congregation
of Benedictines. Here, as at Downside, Ampleforth and other abbeys
of the English Congregation, one finds a flourishing school for boys.
Many of the monks live outside their monastery, having charge of
seven parishes in Thanet.

Buckfast Abbey, South Devon, is perhaps the best known of any
Benedictine Community in Britain, at least to the man in the
street. It has become famous because of the rebuilding of the
church erected by Cistercian monks in the 12th century on the original
foundations; the work being finally completed in 1937, thanks to the
zeal and enthusiasm of the late Abbot Vonier, who ruled over the
Community for thirty-two years. I must confess that the new church
at Buckfast leaves me cold. It suggests a machine-made copy of
medieval work and, apart from some of the furniture, possesses little
originality. I got to know the place fairly well when invited there
in 1935 to make a series of drawings for reproduction as post cards.
Buckfast attracts thousands of visitors, and every day throughout the
summer two monks are on duty in the church to conduct parties from
altar to altar, explaining as they pass by, the chief dogmas of the
Catholic religion. In fact, Buckfast might well be compared to a
spiritual powerhouse where Catholics and non-Catholics can learn
more of religion from contact with men whose lives are wholly given
up to the things of God. There is no school here, but the Community find occupation in the gardens and orchards, or in the manu-
facture of honey and tonic wine. Both these products of the
Buckfast monks need no advertising from my pen! They are
world-famous.

I have never stayed at Douai Abbey, near Reading, though often

invited there.   Fort Augustus has been familiar- to me for more than
twenty-five years and I have a great affection for this the only Benedictine monastery in Scotland.   It is associated with an important
phase in my life, for it was when living with this Community during
the winter of 1919-20 that I was mainly occupied with drawing up a
scheme for an international Catholic sea apostolate.   Moreover, there
are strong ties of heredity since both my great-grandfather, Horatio
Ross, and his brother, Edward, rented Glendoe—the shooting lodge
that looks down on Loch Ness—for many years.   I can recall my
mother talking about Fort Augustus when I was a small boy.

When I first arrived here in December, 1919, the place seemed very
empty.   The school buildings were unoccupied, and there were
many unused rooms in the monastery block.   Then, under the
dynamic influence of the new Abbot, Andrew Joseph McDonald,
who later on became Archbishop of St. Andrews and Edinburgh, the
dry bones began to live; the school was reopened; the novices
from Douai Abbey in England were sent up to Scotland for lack of
accommodation in their own monastery; a crowd of young men who
had been serving in the Forces during the last war came along to
do their preliminary studies for the secular priesthood.   From being
the sleepiest Community I had met with, the Fort developed very
rapidly into a hive of activities.   It was no place for drones.   Nobody
worked harder than Abbot McDonald himself, whether in his own
monastery or when dashing around England and Scotland giving
Retreats or preaching sermons.   If he saw that a monk was capable
of work, he made him work!   He put me on to the job of assistant
guestmaster during the busy summer of 1920, and as a sort of maître-
d'hôtel in the refectory, to keep an eye on the servers.   During
dinner and supper I had to watch that everybody in that crowded
refectory needed nothing in food or drink; that the guests' table was
not neglected and, at the same time, keep half an eye on the Abbot
himself, seated at the high table.   Not content with these jobs, my
superior for the time being ordered me to design a May Altar,
and later on a Sacred Heart shrine.   One of the more conservative
members of the Community remarked that my May Altar reminded
him of the counter in an up-to-date tea shop, and that it was not the
sort of thing he cared to see in a church!   Previous to this I had
designed a very primitive looking mitre for the Abbot, of soft
materials and light to wear.   It was made by the Dun Emer Guild
in Dublin.   Abbot McDonald always maintained that he knew

nothing about Art, but he liked wearing this cosy little mitre because it was as comfortable as a Glengarry bonnet! Lastly, I was asked to design a new throne for the monstrance at Benediction, and this piece of liturgical furniture is still in use.

I have returned to Fort Augustus as a guest again and again in the past quarter of a century. Since I made my home in the north-east of Scotland I have often gone there for Holy Week, or some of the greater festivals. It is always a pleasure to get back to these familiar surroundings. The community can claim a direct continuity with the venerable Scottish monastery of St. James, Ratisbon, founded in the 12th century, and whose last surviving monk eventually joined the new foundation established in 1876. Its observance, apart from a few small differences, is not very different from that of either Downside or Ampleforth. The majority of the resident community are engaged in teaching. Manual work is carried on by the twenty or more lay-brothers.

For the past twenty years I have kept in close touch with my old Community of Caldey Abbey. Seldom a year has passed when I have not visited them, whether on their island-home off the coast of South Wales or latterly at Prinknash, that picturesque Cotswold manor-house whither they moved in 1929, now far too small for the number of monks which has been almost doubled in the past sixteen years. Prinknash Abbey is, indeed, the most overcrowded monastery with which I am familiar, despite temporary additions which have been made to the original house in the shape of concrete or wooden shacks. But even these have not solved the housing problem, and two years ago my one-time Anglican novice-master, Dom Wilfrid Upson, who to-day rules this Community as the first Abbot, found it necessary to move a dozen of his monks to Bigsweir House on the banks of the Wye, not far from the ruins of Tintern. At the time of writing the monks are moving to another temporary home in Shropshire. I hope that it will not be very long before I have some of my former monastic brethren installed at Pluscarden Priory, Morayshire, where they will be much nearer of access than they are in Gloucestershire.

The Prinknash monks do not go to the world: the world comes to them. There is a Guest House, nearly always occupied by priests, men in the Forces, and other laymen, who go there to spend a few days and find a renewal of the things that really matter, and to escape, if only for a brief spell, from the materialism and paganism of to-day. Some of these visitors are Catholics, others are not. All are equally welcome. As has already been stated in earlier chapters, the chief work of these monks is corporate prayer, and the carrying out of the Church's liturgy with all possible dignity and solemnity. To spend about six hours in church daily demands a greater output of mental and physical energy than most people realise. It means a big slice out of a working day.

Strenuous manual labour also forms an integral part of the life. Visitors may be rather startled at the medieval, more correctly the age-less, atmosphere of the monastery, especially the picturesque white habits and tonsured heads. They might well expect to find methods of husbandry and craftsmanship which belong to the same period as this " get-up "! But this is far from being the case. There is an up-to-date dairy, fitted with electrical milking machines, electric saws in the carpenters' shops, the most modern equipment in the stone quarries, electrically operated kilns for making stained glass and pottery, not to mention the last word in modern cooking ranges in the kitchen. The silence of the house is broken by the tapping of typewriters or the frequent ringing of the telephone bell. Even the clocks are synchronised by electricity. On their looms—now moved to the daughter house—the monks weave the material for their white habits and cowls, also silks for vestments.

Practically all available land at Priknash has been brought under cultivation since the war. One will find monks, both priests and brothers, without distinction, ploughing, digging, hoeing and quarry-ing. Some of them may be tramping round and round their silo; others may be at work in the gardens. There is room for every type of man. Some are painters or sculptors, others writers or wood-carvers. Vestments, incense, stone and wood carving, and pottery, are among the many industries. Whatever criticisms are made of these Benedictines, nobody can accuse them of idleness or sloth! They live within the precincts of their monastic enclosure, but they are very much in touch with the outer world. Neither Priknash nor its daughter Community could be described as " static "!

To visit these two Communities is always rather like turning on an old and familiar gramophone record. For in most ways the life has changed little, both in spirit and in outward observance from what I knew at Caldey. A new generation of monks behave in much the same way as I recall my contemporaries doing thirty-five years ago; there is still that same atmosphere of

fraternal charity, mutual tolerance, strenuous manual labour and
intensive prayer. Even to-day, although the Community has reached
middle-age so far as the number of years since its foundation, it has
not stopped growing. Perhaps it is largely due to this buoyant
youthfulness that Prinknash attracts such crowds of postulants.

I went back to Caldey after the island had been taken over by
a Community of Cistercian monks from the Abbey of Chimay
in Belgium. It was strange to find another type of monastic
life in the buildings which I had known so well for over
twenty years; and rather amusing when, on my ringing the bell on
the occasion of my second visit, a monk came to the door and asked
if I wanted to be shown round the abbey. I smiled and told him
that I had watched these same buildings being erected; that I had
known Caldey before they were even planned, and that I thought I
could quite well do without his help! I have also stayed at the
Cistercian Abbey of Mount St. Bernard's in Leicestershire. The
now completed church is, in my opinion, the most entirely satisfactory monastic church in Britain, with its utter simplicity, practical
planning, and simple furniture, some of which was supervised, if not
actually designed, by Eric Gill.

I know most of the Dominican houses in England and Scotland,
especially Woodchester, Hawkesyard and Laxton, where I have been
the guest of the Friars Preachers on many occasions. I am familiar
with the insides of Jesuit houses, for I have stayed at Manresa (Roehampton), Stonyhurst, and Heythrop; of which I made a set of
drawings for post cards. What is more, I have had the rare privilege
of entering the enclosure of several Benedictine Communities of nuns;
here again on the pretext of making drawings of the buildings. In
a Community that has what is known as a Papal Enclosure, the
act of entrance is quite a solemnity; the door has to be unlocked by
the portress, in the presence of other officials, and carefully locked
again the moment one is inside. But once inside, one is allowed to
wander more or less where one wills, given reasonable discretion.
Having completed my drawings I was let out of enclosure with the
same formalities.

This list does not exhaust the religious houses in Great Britain
which I have visited, but it would take too long to mention them
all and to describe the lives of their inmates. A friend once remarked
to me that although I had never succeeded in becoming a permanent
member of any Community, yet in the course of years I had become

an honorary member of most of them! In a sense he was correct, for I have really no idea how many such institutions have made me welcome in the course of my life. They include not only Communities that claim allegiance to Rome, but others in communion with Canterbury, and even with Geneva! Community life—outside the Catholic Church—is a fascinating study. I wrote about it at some length in the long introductory chapter to my *Benedictines of Caldey*, published in 1940.

That same year the chance came to gain a closer insight into the life of the Iona Community in which I had been interested for some time. It was a curious experience for a Catholic layman to be invited to give a series of conferences on the History of Christian Worship and the Monasticism to a Presbyterian Brotherhood! The Iona Community was founded by the Rev. George MacLeod, D.D., to-day one of the best known ministers in the Church of Scotland, both as a preacher and as a pioneer. In itself the Community is a sufficient proof that traditional Presbyterianism is moribund in Scotland. Its founder—or leader as he prefers to be called—is never tired of driving home the fact that the old relationship between the Kirk and the people is fast disappearing, and that old ways of worship are no longer adequate for men's spiritual needs. In other words, it looks as if the Church of Scotland may yet find itself bankrupt unless something is done to reorganise its parochial machinery and methods of worship on different lines to those which have become so deeply embedded in both town and country.

The Brotherhood consists of ministers and laymen. The former are pledged to work for two years in the Home Missions, more especially in the big housing estates and industrial parishes. The latter consist of artisans who, in the summer months, together with the ministers, are engaged on the restoration of the 13th-century Benedictine monastery on Iona. It is intended to make it the head-quarters of the Community which, in the first years, spent three months every summer in a large wooden building which has been erected alongside the abbey.

But the outbreak of war in 1939 necessitated a change in these arrangements. Every summer the Community House has been occupied by groups of ministers and laymen, who flock here in increasing numbers for a week's Retreat or conference. My own conferences were given to the members of the Community who had reassembled on the island for a fortnight. We lived a common life, and the day was spent in study, manual work and prayer—everyone being given his particular task in keeping the house clean and tidy, washing up after meals, and waiting at table. During the afternoons the ministers, most of them quite young men, shared in the jobs done by the artisans, either in the gardens or on the building operations.

There were two daily services in the abbey church, morning and evening. The form of worship was definitely liturgical, although brief and simple. Of course it was not possible for me as a Catholic to take part in this worship, but I would often sit at the back of the nave, and look on from afar! The evening service in particular was what would be called very devotional. Two rows of candles flickered above the choir stalls. Two branch candlesticks of wrought iron stood in the sanctuary, casting a glow of light on to the high altar; now furnished in such a manner that it might well fill some of our own liturgical enthusiasts with envy, except that they might protest at the Cross standing on a wooden box-affair behind the Holy Table—a compromise to placate Presbyterian prejudices! But lest the word "furnished" should convey a wrong impression, I should explain that the great marble altar is entirely bare, except for its linen cloth and an open Bible.

On Sunday mornings there was a choral celebration of the Lord's Supper, performed according to a rite, based more or less on primitive traditions, but which, it must be confessed, was somewhat eclectic. It was certainly very different to the Sunday morning worship in the average Scottish Presbyterian kirk. The officiating minister wore the usual black cassock, Geneva gown and white bands, the effect from a distance being not unlike a Requiem Mass with the priest vested in a very full black chasuble!

It must be made clear that Dr. MacLeod and his disciples are not attempting to revive monastic life. The Iona Community is best described as an experiment in collectivism. It is a fellowship of ministers and artisans, some of whom are married.

Two years later I went back to Iona and spent a week at the Community House. This time the conferences (on Prayer) were being given by an Anglican clergyman who had been a missionary in India, and who himself had founded a Brotherhood, with a rule of life inspired very largely on that of St. Francis; its members being both natives and Europeans. Dr. MacLeod asked me to be present in order that I might be able to answer questions from the Catholic

o

point of view! And what unexpected questions they were! I wished I had gone armed with the sixteen volumes of the *Catholic Encyclopedia!* I found I had been put down as one of the four orderlies at tea time. Differences of belief were forgotten for the moment when a Catholic layman, the minister of one of the leading Presbyterian churches in Edinburgh, a Baptist minister from the Highlands, and a Newfoundland corporal belonging to the Canadian United Church, were faced with a pile of greasy dishes, dirty cups and saucers, and not always enough hot water to wash them. Waiting on this undenominational tea party took on the nature of an agape. It was indeed a case of reunion all round when we were made up into parties to hoe potatoes or tidy up the paths of the abbey grounds.

During those two experiences of sharing the life of the Iona Community I was often reminded of the words of Fr. Vincent McNabb, O.P., to be found in his C.T.S. pamphlet *Catholics and Nonconformists.* "We Catholics must try to understand with joy that a certain logic of life is urging many Nonconformists to modes of thought native to us. It is not merely that detached débris of Catholic doctrine finds a welcome in the life of the Free Churches. It is almost the complete Catholic spirit that is being taken back again, covertly and with conditions." During those weeks on Iona I might have paraphrased the last paragraph of this pamphlet by Fr. McNabb, for I was, as it were, one of God's spies in the land of those who have been against us in the past. Perhaps in my own small and very amateurish sort of way I was hastening the day when these men will be no longer against us, but will stand at our side, chanting our common Creed to our common Father?

CHAPTER X

THE PILGRIM ARTIST

There was another interlude in my life, best described as the Pilgrim Artist Period, dating roughly from 1929 to 1936. During those years I spent much time wandering around Europe, making drawings which were reproduced each week in *The Universe.* I sketched churches in France, Italy, Belgium, Holland, Denmark,

Norway, Sweden, Palestine, Egypt and Ireland, likewise taking countless photographs which have been of untold value to me since a ban
on travel was enforced after the outbreak of war six years ago.
Readers of *The Universe* will now know how I can still go on giving
them weekly drawings of foreign churches! I also wandered around
England, Scotland and Wales, and I find I have had over eight
hundred drawings published in this paper since the Pilgrim Artist
series started.

In the summer of 1933, after over two years spent on the writing
and illustrating of a monumental volume entitled *Fishermen of
Britain,* never published, I felt I wanted to get right away from the
sea, ships and sailors, at least for a time. One day I decided to buy
a horse-drawn gipsy caravan and tour the roads of Britain in this old-
fashioned and leisurely manner. How this dream materialised is
related in a racy style by my devoted companion, Anthony Rowe, in
his entertaining book *The Brown Caravan* (Heath Cranton, 1935).
The story of our long journey from the Thames Valley to the far
north of Scotland, and back again as far south as Yorkshire, can be
found in my own book, *The Caravan Pilgrim* (Heath Cranton, 1938).

Two frames, each containing three photographs of gipsy-caravans
and horses, bring back our wanderings. There are two pictures of
an elaborately built caravan with panelled sides; in one case standing
on a village green, suggestive of the South of England; in the other
the van has stopped in a country lane. In the third photograph, a
young man and two horses are staring at the camera. The second
frame contains photographs of another caravan with a canvas roof,
drawn by two sturdy horses. In the first picture the caravan is
turning off along a moorland road beside a sign post indicating that
Ugthorpe is one mile distant and a board stating that teas are provided at the Black Bull Inn. The second snapshot is a close-up view
of the caravan outside a church; the third appears to be taken at
Gretna, to judge from the notice: " Over 10,000 Marriages Performed
in this Marriage Room: Established 1830."

*   *   *

On looking back over this gipsy existence, so utterly different to
any phase of my life either before or since, I am glad I had this rare
opportunity to acquire a close-up view of rural life in England and
Scotland before it was too late. For, had I put off these tours much
longer, I doubt if it would have been possible to have travelled with

a horse-drawn caravan. As it was, we realised again and again, that our method of progression was out-dated. In many parts of Britain the roads had such slippery surfaces that they were a positive danger to horses; quite apart from other dangers of motor traffic. Then there was the constant difficulty of finding land on which to graze the horses; the lack of shops where harness could be repaired; the numerous blacksmith's forges which we found closed; even the fewness of corn merchants. Yes! We discovered that the internal combustion engine has ruined the roads for horses; a proof of which was to be found in the number of gipsies who had already taken to motor cars!

As I wrote in the preface to the *Caravan Pilgrim:* " Those wanderings through Great Britain were one of the happiest times in my life. The pleasure was derived not so much from seeing the country, or from visiting certain places, for the route we covered was already familiar to me, if not to my companion, but in the chance meetings with all sorts of strange types of humanity—tramps, tinkers, gipsies, farmers, shopkeepers. Again, there was the insight gained into the daily life of the Catholic Church, for, in almost every place in which we stopped for more than a day, we were entertained by priests, monks or nuns."

Neither must Jack and Bill be forgotten, for with never a complaint these two horses dragged the caravan from the South of England to the Highlands of Scotland and back to the Yorkshire moors, where, to my great regret, I had to part with them. These horses were the means of introduction to many people, for, thanks to the splendid condition in which they were kept by Anthony Rowe, they never failed to arouse admiration and comment on the roads.

For about nine months of 1934 I made my home, when not moving about in the caravan, at the Black Bull in the village of Ugthorpe, high up on the moors behind Whitby. From the windows there was a distant North Sea. The brown caravan, named the Portiuncula in remembrance of St. Francis' Little Portion, that is, the Church of Our Lady of the Angels, Assisi, rested in a yard behind the inn. Ugthorpe is still a lonely enough spot, more or less cut off from the outer world. This is, perhaps, the main reason why its inhabitants stuck to the Old Religion at the Reformation. With the neighbouring village of Egton Bridge, it forms a little Catholic oasis on the windswept moors. Picture it as a straggling village built of greenish grey stone; low pitched roofs, with mellow red tiles. Winter storms cannot penetrate those thick walls. Here one finds a real native type of English Catholicism, redolent of the soil. The outward expression of the religion of these farmers and country folk is as natural and spontaneous in its own way as that of a Breton peasant or an Italian *contadino*. Here in Ugthorpe one found a genuine Nordic Catholicism, practised by sturdy Yorkshire folk who have never ceased to be in communion with the Holy See. Romanism, in the form that one finds it in Ugthorpe, is most emphatically a type of religion that seems to suit the English temperament. It is as much a part of the background of the people as are the solid stone houses and the rolling moorlands.

In many a farmhouse it is still possible to find the family saying the Rosary together before going to bed. On a Saturday night the bar of the Black Bull used to be crowded with men and lads who had come on there after going to Confession, enjoying a pint of beer or a game of darts. These men were as proud of being Catholics as they were of being Yorkshiremen. It is not untrue to say that they rather looked down on anybody who did not share these privileges!

The caravan was sold; the two horses were also disposed of. My next mode of transport was a side-car attached to a highly temperamental motor-bike, by means of which my ex-caravan driver sped me round England. We had so many breakdowns that I became convinced that a horse was more reliable than a worn-out internal combustion engine. I could be fairly certain how long the caravan would take to reach its destination, whereas it was no good relying on the motor-bike to keep to a schedule!

*   *   *

No more violent contrast in religious atmosphere could have been found than the two villages of Ugthorpe and Walsingham; the former a stronghold of indigenous Roman Catholicism from pre-Reformation days; the latter a centre of an exotic form of Anglo-Catholicism, with no past history or roots deep down in the soil. This little village, about five miles from the coast of Norfolk, lying north of the town of Fakenham, became my next home.

The editor of *The Universe* asked me to visit Walsingham to make some sketches of the ruins of the Priory and of the Slipper Chapel, situated in the adjacent village of Houghton-St.-Giles. After being in

Catholic hands for over thirty years, this pre-Reformation shrine was
about to be restored for Catholic worship. So I travelled to Norfolk
and was able to assist at the first Mass celebrated in this lovely 14th-
century chapel, dedicated to St. Catherine. During the few days
spent in Walsingham I met James and Lilian Dagless, then pro-
prietors of the Church Shop. I was much struck by the work of
these two craftsmen, and as it happened that I was anxious to find
a firm who would be capable of carrying out my own designs for
ecclesiastical decoration, so I suggested that we might come to some
sort of working agreement. After some discussion it was agreed that
I should become their " liturgical adviser ", and I decided that it
would be better for me to transfer my residence to Norfolk. Jim
Dagless mentioned that he had an empty cottage which needed
repairs, but which could be ready for occupation within a few months.
I liked the place and decided to rent it.

Like most visitors, I lost my heart to this romantic village at first
sight. It is redolent of the past and its old houses are perfect
specimens of East Anglican domestic architecture. Warm red brick
predominates, with pantile roofs, either glistening black or deep red
in colour. Some houses are built of flint, others cream washed. On
every side are reminders of the fact that, during the Middle Ages,
Walsingham was the greatest pilgrim shrine in England. The
ancient parish church had been stripped of its rood-screen at the
Reformation, but since 1921 when the parson whom I had chanced
to meet in Assisi had been appointed to the living, great changes had
taken place and, to quote from Father Gilbert's *What to See in
Walsingham,* " many features of a Roman Catholic character have
been added by the piety of the present zealous incumbent, to replace
some of those things which the Protestant Reformation destroyed."
Whether these " Roman Catholic features " are in the best of taste is
a matter about which there must be a difference of opinion, but as it
would seem that the rector's ambition was to transform his church
into a replica of a typical village church in France or Belgium, there
can be no doubt that he has succeeded. So numerous are the shrines,
pictures, statues, banners, lamps and other *objets de piété* that now
clutter up this venerable building that it would be almost impossible
for the ordinary visitor to guess that it was in communion with Canterbury and under the jurisdiction of the Anglican Bishop of Norwich.
Studying the notice board in the porch one noticed that the calendar
of the Book of Common Prayer had given place to that of the Roman

DOWNSIDE ABBEY.

Missal, or maybe the *Ordo* of the Catholic diocese of Northampton?
It was in a side chapel of the parish church that the Anglican
devotion to Our Lady of Walsingham was revived in 1921 by
the setting up of a statue based on that depicted on the old
Priory seal. Some years later a new shrine was built in the village
to which the statue was removed. This building was on private property and for this reason was not liable to any interference from the
bishop of the diocese, who had already begun to frown on this revival
of Mariolatry.

The claim was put forward that this new shrine was erected on the
site of the original Holy House of Walsingham, but few archæologists
were prepared to accept this theory. Anyhow, a replica of the *Santa
Casa* at Loreto was erected to house the statue and it stood within a
larger chapel. I must admit that I was fascinated by the cleverness
of the copy as well as the beauty of this new shrine. The imitation
of the original Holy House was almost perfect—but what did it
all signify, I asked myself. The dim, dark interior of the chapel,
heavy with incense fumes, and lit up with flickering candles and
many hanging lamps; ex-voto tablets encrusting the walls; the black
Madonna vested in a jewelled cope and wearing an ornate crown;
the holy well from which pilgrims could drink the water; the
Stations of the Cross in the garden, gay with flowers that surrounded
the shrine at one side—could all this display of Continental
Catholicism be fitted in to even the most comprehensive vision of
Anglicanism? It might be all right, say in Italy, Austria or France,
but was it likely to re-Christianise the natives of Norfolk? Perhaps
they were not considered, and the whole thing was conceived mainly
to appeal to a very limited section of extreme Anglo-Catholics. At
a bookstall one could purchase leaflets and pamphlets dealing with
the pilgrimages of Our Lady of Walsingham—rosaries, scapulars,
medals, and all the usual pious objects which are on sale at sanc-
tuaries abroad. Some years after my first visit to England's Nazareth
the Anglican shrine was enlarged, and fifteen altars were included
in honour of the Mysteries of the Rosary.

One may smile or even be irritated at this exotic manifestation of
Anglican piety, but there can be little doubt that it paved the way
for a revival of Catholic devotion and to the opening of the shrine
at the Slipper Chapel in August, 1939, due to the zeal of the late
Bishop Youens of Northampton. Many pilgrims have mistaken the
Anglican shrine for a Roman Catholic sanctuary, and with good

reason. There have been Catholics who have entered the Slipper Chapel for the first time, and wondered if by chance they had strayed into the wrong place. The medieval English altar with its frontal, dossal and riddels, is a feature to which most of them are unfamiliar, and even the shrine itself, gorgeous as it is with gilding and colour, is not always sufficient to convince them this is the Catholic shrine. The "ugly little statue" (a frequent comment!) was copied from the old Priory seal under the direction of Professor Tristram.

When I went to live in Walsingham during the winter of 1934 no resident Catholic priest had yet been appointed and it was only once a week that Mass was said at the Slipper Chapel by the priest from Fakenham. The village was still in possession of the Anglo-Catholic party and had not begun to feel the effects of the Roman Invasion. Indeed it was a much more peaceful place than it became a year later when the rivalry between Anglos and Romans grew intense. It was a strange world, and it was not long before I began to dislike it. Few of the natives appeared to attend the parish church, for they had been alienated by the unfamiliar type of religion introduced by the present incumbent with the most laudable intentions. The congregations, so I gathered, were largely made up of the handful of pious ladies who had been attracted to Walsingham by the opportunities it afforded for "full Catholic privileges", or by groups of pilgrims during the summer months. I remember talking to a middle-aged farm worker one afternoon and his caustic and ironical comments on ecclesiastical affairs in his native village are worth recording, though I fear it may be regarded as a lack of charity. He maintained that "a parson is a parson, no matter if he dresses up in long skirts and wears a furry hat", whereas "a priest is a priest even if he goes about in trousers, a short jacket and no hat." My neighbour—who had equally decided opinions on history—was also convinced that "them priory ruins ought to be given back to the Roman Catholics, for didn't old Henry VIII steal them?"

I talked with other natives of Walsingham and found that they held very similar views to those expressed so crudely yet so clearly by my farm-labourer friend, though they put them less bluntly and more politely. When I went to live in Walsingham I was fully prepared to find that nearly fourteen years of intensive Anglo-Catholic apostolate might have begun to take root and that the younger generation, at least, would be a solid mass of Anglican Papalists. But it was not so, and unless they happened to be members of one or other of the Nonconformist chapels, the farm lads and most of the village youth appeared to be more or less pagan in their outlook.

Altogether it was a strange, unreal world, difficult to convey in words to anybody who has never visited England's Nazareth. The little Norfolk village, once known the length and breadth of the land as the most frequented pilgrimage shrine in this country; desecrated and abandoned at the Reformation; forgotten by the outside world for nearly four centuries, and now at last galvanised from its long sleep.

The polite aloofness of the Anglo-Catholic towards their Roman brethren showed signs of developing into open hostility within a few months of my settling down in the village, due, it must be admitted, to a certain lack of tact on the part of the Romans, whose zeal sometimes outran their discretion, at least in the case of individuals. I was often reminded of that tense atmosphere which I had noticed in Palestine where Latins and Greek Orthodox, not to mention other dissident Eastern Churches, wait side by side, like cats with their fur standing up, all ready to start fighting with dogs!

On the whole, I think I am correct in saying the Anglo-Catholics did not resent the establishment of a small Community of Capuchin Franciscans half so much as the arrival of a secular priest, a year before. For this secular priest happened to be a convert, and what is more had lived at Walsingham as a member of the Anglican Benedictine Community of Nashdom. So it was rather hard when he returned to the village as its first " Popish " priest, especially as there had been no other cleric to compete with the Anglican parson until this moment. The bearded Capuchins were not converts. Their brown habits and sandals added a new note of romance to the already over-romantic Walsingham, and, after all, there had been Franciscans here before the Reformation, so there was a logical reason for their return. But it was quite out of order, so the Anglicans would argue, for there to be two *secular* parish priests living in a state of rivalry; one in full communion with the Holy See, the other praying hard that he might be, sooner or later.

The friars took over a charming old red-brick house which had been bought by the Bishop of Northampton; his original intention was to occupy it himself for at least part of the year. Previous to the arrival of the Capuchins, the parish priest had used this house as his presbytery, either saying Mass in the chapel fitted up in a bedroom, the decoration of which was supervised by James and

Lilian Dagless under my direction, or else at the Slipper Chapel. But from now onwards he retired to the cottage adjoining the Slipper Chapel, and the village of Walsingham was left to the friars.

Some queer and inexplicable disturbances took place in this house during the first year of its Catholic tenancy. There were fairly convincing proofs of the presence of a poltergeist, horrible sounds at night—clanking of chains, and mocking laughter. Fr. Thurston, S.J., was consulted, but this famous authority on ghosts, real and fictitious, was unable to form a definite opinion as to the genuineness of the apparent haunting of the Bishop's house. Then, almost as suddenly as they had started, the mysterious noises ceased, and so far as I know, have never been heard again. Behind the old-world charm and beauty of this Norfolk village one was always conscious, so it seemed to me, of an invisible, yet quite positive sinister influence. I do not claim to be the least psychic myself, but I can recall moments at Walsingham when for no reason whatsoever I was filled with an unaccountable terror of some unseen evil presence. On one occasion a friend of mine happened to be staying there, and I took her into the parish church. We had not gone more than a few yards up the nave when she gripped my arm and whispered: " Peter! Get me out of here at once; I can't stand it!" Imagining that she was feeling faint, I piloted her into the churchyard, where she turned round and smiled, saying: " I'm all right now! It was just that building. I don't know *what* it was, but it made me afraid of something. I'll never set foot inside it again!" At first sight it all seems rather ridiculous, but when one recalls those thousands, if not millions of pilgrims who made their way to Walsingham during the middle ages; how those venerable stones must be permeated with their personalities—or whatever you choose to call them—some good, some bad; others criminals and notorious sinners, it is possible that certain people, even to-day, find themselves in tune with waves or emanations of these long-dead pilgrims—who can tell? It is just a theory of a mystery that baffles explanation on purely material grounds.

One may prefer a much more simple explanation: that *if* Walsingham is really a holy place, sanctified by an outstanding devotion to the Mother of God in past ages, which our own generation is trying to revive, then how obvious it is that the powers of evil should show their displeasure by trying to frighten people away.

Not only the invisible power of evil tried to stop the revival of devotion to Our Lady that summer; there were likewise Mr. Kensit's Wycliffe Preachers, who arrived with a motor-caravan and stormed and harangued the inhabitants on the evils of Mariolatry and idol-worship. There was no doubt about the fervour and conviction of these Protestant evangelists, but I doubt if they cut much ice with the natives. They merely gathered round the preachers hoping to be entertained with some indecent revelations of the Maria Monk type, but they were disappointed.

As a contrast to these 19th century admirers of Wycliffe, were the devout layfolk; women, old and middle-aged and young, with their sky-blue cloaks and veils, together with the very sacerdotal-looking parsons who made up the Anglo-Catholic pilgrimages. There were processions to the Priory ruins and holy wells with banners, and the singing of litanies and hymns in honour of Our Lady; the rattle of rosaries, and what I gathered must have been stately and ornate functions at the Shrine. It was not easy to discover just what went on within this building, for it was considered more diplomatic, in view of possible interference from the Bishop of Norwich, not to advertise any public celebrations of Mass. The Shrine was not officially recognised as an Anglican church, and to celebrate the Communion Service openly would have been a defiance of the law of the Church of England. So, like the early Christians in the catacombs, these 20th century witnesses to the Faith worshipped more or less in secret within the Shrine.

Even before I left Walsingham there were signs that it might soon develop into another Lisieux, Loreto or Lourdes, and that the piety of pilgrims would be put to commercial profit. House property increased in value; new cottages were being erected, and new shops of the art and crafty types were opened, some under Roman auspices, others Anglo—and the rest more or less neutral. The Anglicans already had a Pilgrim's Hospice, run by the Sisters of St. Peter. The Catholics followed suit and established a Hostel of St. Clare, for women only; St. Francis' Hostel for men, and lastly, the Hostel of St. Benedict Joseph Labre, intended for very poor pilgrims. In one of these hostels was the office of the Catholic Bureau which arranged the pilgrimages. The Second Spring came in with a rush, and two years after I had departed, there was a great Catholic pilgrimage organised for the youth of England, led by Cardinal Hinsley. Plans were prepared for the building of a large pilgrim church in the village, where the Franciscans would celebrate the Divine Office in choir and sing Conventual Mass. With the outbreak of war in 1939, all these schemes came to a stop. Walsingham found itself in a banned area, and all pilgrimages had to cease!

*   *   *

I loved England's Nazareth in many ways. I was sorry to leave that charming cottage built of flints with its red-tile roof which was my home for just over a year. On the whole, I think I should have been far happier in Walsingham if it had been just an ordinary Norfolk village with nothing special in it to attract such crowds of pilgrims, whether Anglican or Catholic. I am certain it could never have become a permanent home. It was all too extraneous; too supercharged with religious emotionalism, and even worse, ecclesiastical controversy.

Nevertheless, those twelve months in Norfolk were an interesting experience. My brief professional association with James and Lilian Dagless as their liturgical adviser resulted in our collaborating in the decoration and furnishing of several churches in England and Scotland. I was responsible for the design of that elaborate shrine in the Slipper Chapel which houses Professor Tristram's Madonna. We worked together on the complete redecoration and a new high altar in the church of the Benedictine nuns at Talacre Abbey, North Wales. Other jobs were the redecoration of the Catholic churches at Portsoy, Banffshire, and Aboyne, Aberdeenshire. Also the Shrine of Our Lady in St. Peter's, Aberdeen. Had it not been for the war, our partnership might have effected the redecoration of many other churches up and down the land, including St. Thomas of Canterbury, West Cowes, Isle of Wight, and Stonehaven, Kincardineshire, for both of which plans had been prepared.

Out of these jobs came the inspiration to write and illustrate a big book dealing with the planning and furnishing of churches. After rejection by several publishers on this side of the Atlantic, it was finally accepted in America. So, in one sense, I am grateful to Walsingham.

CHAPTER XI

HARBOUR HEAD

There could be no more violent contrast between the religious atmosphere of England's Nazareth and that of the north-east coast of Scotland, which became my home in 1936. All around that village in Norfolk where one was already in danger of being blown sky-high by a sudden collision between the rival groups of Anglo and Roman Catholics, lay wide stretches of countryside where the Church of England, in its most traditional and unexciting manifestations, reigned supreme. Its only rivals were an occasional Nonconformist chapel that bore witness to the presence of Dissenters from the Established Church.

In the north-east of Scotland the religious background was utterly different. Presbyterianism was the established form of belief. At the same time there happened to be isolated pockets of Catholics and Episcopalians in parts of Aberdeenshire and Banffshire; each a proof of the conservative mentality of the people, who in the first instance had been opposed to any change of religion at the Reformation, and who, later on—at least in some districts—had preferred to adhere to Prelacy rather than adopt Presbyterianism in the 17th century. There was little evidence of any violent antagonism between the small groups of Catholics and Episcopalians and the otherwise almost all-powerful Established Kirk. Nobody could accuse either the Papists or the "Piskies" of being aggressive or militant. These remnants of religious systems discarded by the majority could not be described as Christian soldiers, marching on to war!

Even before I came to make my home in the north-east of Scotland I had a fairly intimate knowledge of the country. I had visited most of the forty Catholic parishes in the enormous diocese of Aberdeen, which includes the Orkneys and Shetlands as well as practically all the mainland above a line drawn W.N.W. from Aberdeen. I was already acquainted with the majority of the fifty or so secular priests who serve these often lonely churches. I had made a long study of the history of these missions when working on my *Catholic Church in Modern Scotland,* which was eventually published in 1937. There was something curiously attractive about this simple, austere and undemonstrative type of Catholicism. Indeed, one might say that it contains the essentials without any superfluous trimmings. In the long run oatmeal porridge is more nourishing than cream-filled chocolate éclairs. Walsingham had provided the latter (spiritually, I mean!) without stint. Banffshire offered a more wholesome diet, even if less tasty. There would be no danger of any more ecclesiastical indigestion! In *Harbour Head* I gave the impression that it was merely an urge to find a home that "commanded a close-up view of shipping, with seamen all round me as well as the sea in front of me" which was the reason for my flight to Scotland; actually the motives were more complex and not quite so simple as might be concluded from my previous volume of reminiscences.

Eventually I found myself a domiciled Scotsman in a busy little seaport of about 4,000 inhabitants, with two places of worship belonging to the established Church of Scotland, a Congregational Chapel, a Salvation Army Centre, and no less than three meeting houses of different groups of The Brethren, each in a schism with the other. There were not more than half a dozen practising Catholics. Most of this infinitesimal leaven was made up of Italians! The nearest Catholic church was about two miles distant. The Episcopalian chapel ("in full communion with the C. of E." as it proclaimed on its notice board during the war when spiritually-starved Englishmen and women serving in the Forces might be looking for a church where the worship would be familiar) was also a good half-hour's walk. But this little Early Victorian chapel—invariably called The English Kirk by the natives—made no effort to convert its congregation to even the mildest expression of Anglo-Catholicism, unlike some Episcopalian churches in Scotland, which are very High indeed. So, it will be realised that I now found myself in a completely different world to that which I had been accustomed for the greater part of my life; whether in my Anglican childhood and youth, or in the next twenty-five years as a member of more than one Catholic religious community, and latterly as a Catholic layman, who, more often than not, lived in Catholic countries abroad.

As regards the public worship in the Catholic churches of the north-east of Scotland, they are not yet out of the catacombs when compared with other countries where the Old Religion managed to hold on after the Reformation. So slowly do old customs and traditions linger on that, even to-day, it is rare to find a church in the country districts or smaller towns where there is an early Mass

on Sundays, except once a month.   Yet the Episcopalian chapels
invariably have an Early Celebration of the Communion service
every Sunday.   It is difficult to induce the older generation of
Catholics to give up devotional habits which they and their ancestors
have been accustomed to for centuries.   Even monthly Communion
has only been achieved after many years of effort on the part of the
clergy.   Only in perhaps three or four out of the forty parishes in
the Aberdeen diocese is it possible to assist at the ceremonies of Holy
Week.   In the average parish church there is no service of any kind
from Mass on Wednesday morning until Easter Sunday, except for
Stations of the Cross on Good Friday afternoon.   It should be mentioned that neither Christmas nor Good Friday are holidays in
Scotland, and there is no legal obligation for shops to be closed on
these days as in England.

In some churches an interesting relic of bygone times is the
recitation of the " Prayers for the Intentions of Mass " before the
one service on Sunday morning which usually takes place at 11 o'clock.
Almost unknown is the *Asperges,* i.e., the blessing of the congregation with holy water, carried out in nearly every church in other
countries throughout the world.   In few places does one find the
prescribed processions on Candlemas Day, Palm Sunday and Corpus
Christi.   The Litanies of the Saints are not recited publicly on either
the feast of St. Mark or on the three Rogation Days preceding
Ascension Day; at least I have never come across these functions.
Perhaps it is feared that open-air services would stir up strife, but
the Plymouth Brethren and Salvation Army boldly sing hymns and
preach sermons in the streets of many towns on Sunday evenings
in summer; admittedly with few or no persons listening to their
efforts at evangelisation!   The funeral ceremonies at the graveside
are invariably performed by a priest wearing his ordinary clerical
suit, the only mark of his office being a narrow stole round his neck.
Unlike the Presbyterian minister, he does not usually add solemnity
to the function by donning a shiny lum hat!   Yet the Episcopalian ministers are often courageous enough to walk through the
streets at the funeral vested in cassock, surplice and purple stole—
even with a biretta in some places!

The Irish immigration that brought new life to the Church in
the industrial towns and districts of the Lowlands of Scotland never
reached the north-east.   So the outward expression of religion has
not been affected to any perceptible degree by the warm individualistic

piety of the victims of the potato famine and of earlier and subsequent
enforced exile from Ireland. These good people had to fight for the
Faith when they settled in Scotland, whereas the Catholics in the
north-east and in the Highlands had been fighting for three hundred
years in peril of dungeon, fire and sword. When, at last, the Catholic
Emancipation Act was passed in 1829, they were more or less
exhausted. " I have fought the good fight, I have finished my course,
I have kept the faith," St. Paul wrote to Timothy. Such an epitaph
might well have been cut on the tombstone of many a Scottish
Catholic throughout the Penal Times. For the past hundred and
sixteen years their children and grandchildren have asked nothing
better than to be allowed to live in peace. They have no urge to
proselytise.   There are in consequence few evidences of what
George Blake describes as a "rapid growth in stature of that scarlet
and interesting woman, the whore of Babylon " in the north-east of
Scotland. The Presbyterian majority has no need to raise the cry
" No Popery!"

The churches themselves are an outward expression of the type of
Christianity found in the Catholic remnant of the north-east. They
are, almost without exception, kept in good repair and an example to
those in many other countries so far as cleanliness, neatness and
general adornment. Seldom occupied by a body of worshippers for
more than an hour or two on Sundays, there is little chance of their
showing signs of wear and tear. Most of them are as spick and span
as are the drawing-rooms or best parlours in the homes of the average
fairly well-to-do member of the congregation, and made use of about
as often. It would be rather embarrassing for a workman to turn
up at Mass in dungarees. A beggar would feel conscious of his rags
in such surroundings. The bare-footed urchins with their grubby
hands and faces who are so completely at home in their Father's
House in Ireland would think twice before they dared run in and out
of our churches. In other words, a church is a building mainly used
for Divine Worship once a week, not a spiritual refuge where, at any
hour of the day, one brings all one's joys, hopes and sorrows, knowing
full well that there is Somebody there who will understand what lies
in the depth of the heart and soul. Except in the larger towns few
persons attend Mass on weekdays. It is quite common to find the
priest's housekeeper as the solitary congregation, and taking the place
of a server. The life of a priest in such surroundings can be a lonely
one indeed.

P

There can be few countries in the world where Catholics have so completely lost the idea of corporate participation in worship as in Scotland. There is little to suggest that the Liturgical Movement, now making such strides in England, is taking root in this land. In most towns and villages in the north-east of Scotland the principal Sunday morning act of worship consists of a Low Mass during which a mixed or female choir do their best to drown not only the Canon, but also the parts of the rite intended to be audible by the congregation by singing bits of things—that practice which the late Dr. Adrian Fortescue regarded as " too dreadful to be described " in *The Mass: A Study of the Roman Liturgy* (p. 191 note).

In England there was usually a religious house, if not a parish church, within fairly easy distance, where I could take part in either Vespers or Compline on Sundays or the greater festivals. But once I settled on the north-east coast of Scotland I could indulge in this form of liturgical worship in only *one* of the 480 public churches in this country—the Benedictine abbey at Fort Augustus, and this involved an eight-hours' journey! By way of paradox, the *Scottish Catholic Directory* informs its readers every year that " the evening service of the Church is contained in the Vesper Book ", and goes to the trouble of providing a most complete calendar to enable one to take part in a service which cannot be found in any of the churches served by secular clergy!

It would be difficult to find words in which to express my respect and admiration for the secular clergy of the Aberdeen diocese, most of whom have long since become personal friends. To be a mission priest in a small town or country district where almost every form of Catholic Action, apart from keeping a fatherly eye on a small, scattered, and often dwindling flock, is non-existent; to say Mass on week-days in an empty church; to live isolated and alone in the midst of a Presbyterian majority, needs great faith and a heroic vocation. For positive opposition is infinitely easier to endure than negative indifference. To some of the younger priests I have in mind, the war was a blessing in disguise. It brought them new and untried fields of apostolate—among evacuee children, members of the Army, Navy and Air Force, and prisoners, both German and Italian. The accommodation of some of their little churches was taxed to the uttermost.

Ecclesiastical affairs, once I had cut myself adrift from old friends and interests in England, fell into the background. I formed a new circle of friends, some of whom were prominent in the Scottish Nationalist movement. Sir Alexander MacEwen, at one time Provost of Inverness, became a regular and frequent correspondent. I forget how many times Lady MacEwen made me welcome in that attractive house at North Kessock on the Black Isle, with a view of Inverness and the mountains beyond. This friendship with Sir Alexander, based on many common interests and ideals, only ended with his death in 1941. There were Neil and Daisy Gunn—the former one of Scotland's most famous novelists. Our friendship was bound up more with our mutual interest in the sea fisheries of Scotland than in literature. I was always sure of a welcome at the Gunn's house in Inverness, and latterly at that tiresomely inaccessible farm outside Dingwall. I had often admired the paintings of Keith Henderson long before I came to live in Scotland. Here again I wish he and his wife had not insisted on making their home in a remote corner of Lochaber, otherwise I am sure we should have met more often. It was a chance visit to Compton Mackenzie on the Isle of Barra that decided my own migration from England to Scotland. The war prevented more than one visit to Eric Linklater in his equally far-off home in the Orkneys. It was not so difficult to stay with another author—George Scott-Moncrieff—for he lived within easy reach of Edinburgh. So also did the sculptor, Hew Lorimer, who, like Scott-Moncrieff and his family, became a Catholic later on. In Edinburgh I was always certain of the hospitality of two architect friends—Reginald Fairlie and Ian G. Lindsay. I collaborated with the latter in the designs for a small Catholic church at Invergarry, near Fort Augustus. Ian Lindsay and his wife introduced me to Dr. George MacLeod, the Leader of the Iona Community, the most loyal of friends, despite (or maybe because of) our persistent arguments on points of theology, liturgy and ceremonial. Frequent disagreements never prevented some most enjoyable visits to the Community House on Iona, where I met numerous Presbyterian ministers and laymen, some of whom have since become intimate friends and whose manses have offered me hospitality.

Priests of the Aberdeen diocese, most of whom owned cars, frequently called on me before the war. Not far off was Rothiemay Castle, where I was often welcomed by its Catholic laird, Colonel Ian G. Forbes. Two of his sons were Benedictine monks at Ampleforth and two daughters nuns. In England it never struck me that the profession of a Catholic author-artist was anything unusual—

I was merely one of a crowd.   In Scotland it was quite different.   So
far as I could discover I was the only Papist earning a living by literary
and artistic work in the vast diocese of Aberdeen!

*   *   *

Then came the war, and with it a ban on travel from September,
1939. As much from necessity as from choice I seldom left the fishing
port which was now my home. I became much more of a recluse
than a rover! Yet there was no chance of getting bored. I can now
reveal, without the risk of any breach of official secrets or of imparting
valuable information to the enemy, that there were many types of
vessels in the harbour besides the local fishing fleet. Grey-painted
auxiliary craft of the Royal Navy—most of them converted trawlers
or drifters—were a common sight. Later on many minesweepers were
laid down on the slips and fitted out within sight and sound of my
house. Others came back for an overhaul or a refit. Grey-painted
coasters, armed with guns and fitted with balloons, added a picturesque note to the crowded basins and quays. All day long an
examination ship patrolled the entrance to the harbour—what a
boring existence her crews must have had, yet some of them seemed
happy enough. For a year or more, in expectancy of an invasion, two
converted steam-drifters were ready to be sunk and thus block the
harbour. At the shipbuilding yard and in the engineering works,
men were working overtime and on Sundays. The town was full of
seafarers of all types and nationalities.

Soon after I bought " Harbour Head " my parish priest had
nominated the house as an Apostleship of the Sea " Service Centre ".
Not long after it became one of the regional headquarters of this
organisation in Scotland. But for about a year this status was more
or less nominal—there were few opportunities of carrying on any
definite apostolate for seafarers. From September, 1939, and for the
next five years, it was otherwise. As a Founder and Promoter member of *Apostolatus Maris,* the least I could do was to keep open house
for the crews of the varied classes of vessels that came and went. For
there was no canteen or similar institution in the port. Many sailors
seemed to find " Harbour Head " a congenial *rendezvous;* if nothing
else there was always a fire and a comfortable arm-chair on a cold
night! I had become the owner of a registered fishing boat, and had
my fishing permit. Other visitors drifted in and out of my door
besides   seafarers—shipwrights,   engineers, . farm-servants,   shop-

assistants, men and lads home on leave from the Forces, and last but not least, a cheery gang, whose ages ranged from ten to twenty. No longer could I write as I did on Caldey in 1916: " I feel I cannot become a member of a family ". Without any deliberate effort on my part I had become a member of a very big family; a community in fact, but not the sort of community in which I tried so hard to take root in earlier years.

Just as my friend and fellow-writer, Neil M. Gunn, discovered " not only the salt of the sea, but also the salt of the earth " among the crew of an east-coast herring drifter, so did I find that same " kindliness and friendliness, best called disinterestedness. And not consciously on the part of these fishermen as a decent or moral thing to do, but naturally as one might tell a joke or pass the time of day " (*Off in a Boat*, p. 327). Yet I fear it is a case of wishful thinking for Fr. Anthony Ross, O.P., to tell the readers of *Blackfriars* (July, 1945) that this fisherman's cottage beside the harbour has " become a centre of the Apostleship of the Sea strikingly kin to Fellowship Houses and to the Houses of Hospitality established by the Apostolate of Christ the Worker ". But I must admit that the result of living in such close contact with seafarers of many types and having been accepted by this small maritime community has been to modify my ideas as to the lines on which a Sea Apostolate can best develop. A quarter of a century ago I dreamed of a world-wide, centralised organisation. To-day I rather incline to think that this is putting the cart before the horse, so to say. Apostles are more needed than an Apostolate; men rather than machinery.

Actually there were not many Catholics among the seafarers who came and went during the war, except in the case of French and Belgians. So far as the purely local members of the loosely-knit community are concerned, most of them have no allegiance to the Kirk of their fathers. Scotland, more rapidly than England, is relapsing fast into a confused but not yet convinced secularism. As Dr. George MacLeod points out in his stimulating and provocative book, *We Shall Re-Build* (p. 37): " We have rejected an earlier discipline and discarded its Reformation alternative, and left our youth with nothing. Thus and thus have the outward disciplines broken down."

There is so much that I would like to write about those men and lads who have haunted Harbour Head in the past six years that I would not know where to stop. I must content myself with a few

memories of one local youth, the son of a fisherman, for a brief period
a boy-seaman in the Royal Navy. This was Campbell Cowie, who
was certainly the most remarkable member of my family while he
was with me.

*   *   *

One afternoon, early in the year 1939, I was walking along the
shore. I noticed an old fisherman coming towards me. He was
accompanied by an overgrown lad in Naval uniform; at least he was
wearing a Naval overcoat beneath which I detected bell-bottomed
seaman's trousers. But what struck me as odd was the absence of
the regulation cap. An untidy shock of dark brown hair emphasised
the dirty pallor of his face. As we passed, the old man made some
remark about the weather. The lad smiled. I continued my walk
and wondered who they were. Perhaps visitors? Maybe staying here
with relatives or friends? Probably the young seaman was on sick
leave after an illness or operation? My curiosity was aroused, and
one day I mentioned this overgrown youth to a friend, who immediately replied: "That's Campbell Cowie. He was discharged
from the Navy. The old man is his grandfather. You ought to see
his ship models—they're great!"

After several weeks this mutual friend arranged to bring the model-
maker down to see me. One evening they appeared at my door. It
was only when Campbell Cowie got inside my low rooms that I
realised his size. When he collapsed into an armchair it did not
seem big enough to hold his unwieldy body. In appearance he suggested some primitive type of man, for his arms were abnormally
long, his jaw projecting, and his hands gigantic. His chest measure-
ment (so I discovered later) was 55 inches. The disease was
acromegaly, i.e., trouble connected with the pituitary gland; diagnosed
during the brief period he spent as a boy seaman in H.M.S. *Caledonia*,
the Naval training ship on the Forth. I learnt that Campbell had
been a patient in the Royal Infirmary, Edinburgh, for several months
under a famous neurological surgeon; that he had not been cured,
and that eventually he had been invalided out of the Navy.

When I paid my first visit to his home I found him at work in
the kitchen, making a model of a three-masted sailing ship, without
any notes or plans to aid his memory. The delicacy and details of
the work fascinated me; it was quite up to professional standards.
It was hard to believe that those huge hands could create such minute

shapes. Even harder to recall that the model-maker was not yet seventeen years of age. Then he produced other models—an ocean liner, a destroyer, and finally a large lifeboat, made, so he told me, when he was only twelve years old. I realised that I had discovered a genius in his own line. Thus began my friendship with Campbell Cowie which lasted until his death little more than two years after our first meeting.

From now onwards he came down to visit me daily. It struck me that there was very little space for either the maker or the models in that kitchen " up the brae ", where everybody got in his way and he in theirs. So I suggested that he might as well carry on his work in the loft at Harbour Head. He jumped at the idea, brought down his tools and some of his unfinished models, and usually turned up every afternoon, remaining until it was time for him to return home to bed. Life at home was not too easy for Campbell. His mother was in hospital and he missed her care. One day, when we were visiting her together, I remarked that it might be a change if Campbell were to stay with me for a bit, pointing out that it would save the daily climb up the steep brae, which he found such an effort. She gave her consent readily, and thus it was that Campbell came to live with me. Two months later his mother died. Henceforth Harbour Head became his second home.

Now that Campbell was living under the same roof with me, I got to know him intimately. I realised that he had an abnormal brain as well as an abnormal body. There appeared to be no subject in which he was not interested, and about which he could not carry on an intelligent conversation or argue. When talking to him it was difficult to remember his age. He had the mind of a highly educated man, instead of a boy of seventeen. His whole outlook on life was mature, though one could not describe him as precocious, just because he was so utterly simple and natural. I learnt that he had done brilliantly at school. He showed me the prizes he had won, and his certificates; proving that he had been first in almost every subject for three successive years. He would explain with a sort of blasé indifference that he never *had* to work. It was quite easy for him to memorise anything once he had glanced at a book. I proved this statement again and again. Sometimes it could be rather awkward! He remembered too much!

His chief interests lay in the direction of nautical history and everything connected with the sea and ships. He seemed to know all that

"HARBOUR HEAD."

could be known about any famous ship, past or present.   His
geographical knowledge was equally extensive.   At the same time
he was equally at home in science, mathematics and engineering.
He could turn his hand to any practical job that needed doing.   Not
long after he came to live here he began to paint water-colours of
fishing boats and other types of craft.   Here again, it did not take
him more than a day or two to master the essentials of water-colour
painting.   One of his first efforts now hangs on the walls of my
kitchen—a drifter hauling in her nets.   I always doubt if the many
people who admire this picture believe me when I tell them that it
is the unaided work of a seventeen-year-old boy and not one of my
own paintings.   I feel fairly certain that it would be accepted and
hung at the New English Art Club or any other well-known exhibition if I chose to submit it!

When Campbell had lived at Harbour Head for about a month he
noticed the inconvenience of not having water laid on inside the
house.   There was merely a tap in a very dilapidated shed outside.
He was constantly bumping his head against its low roof, and one
day, after some highly abusive language, he asked if I would like him
to build me a proper scullery with access from the kitchen.   He
seemed convinced that this would be quite an easy job, and sat down
to draw plans, sections and elevations, with alarming professional dex-
terity.   Then taking another sheet of paper, he proceeded to work
out the cost of materials.   The plans had to be approved by the Burgh
Surveyor, and I am quite sure this official doubted my word when I
assured him that I had had no share in the drawings that were submitted to him.   So the day after war had been declared we began
to pull down the old shed, and for the next three weeks the two of
us were hard at work building the scullery, Campbell doing most
of the actual labour, while I acted as a rather inefficient mate!
Most of my neighbours shook their heads and told me that I ought
to have got a proper builder to do the job.   But when it was completed they were unsparing in their praise.   Finally he wired the
scullery and put in electric light.   Campbell Cowie began to make a
name for himself.   People came along and asked him to do similar
building jobs for them.

Campbell was now free to get back to his model-making.   That
autumn was produced, among other things, a lovely water-line model
of a tramp-steamer, ploughing her way and dipping her bows into a
realistic putty sea.   Then he started work on a big model of an

old-time "Zulu" fishing boat (without any plans to guide him), upon which he was engaged for over five months, but which was never completed. I forget how many thousands of small nails were used in this built-up model, all complete with ribs and timbers. It was to find a home in the Liverpool Museums, but it remains at Harbour Head.

It was in the spring of 1940 that my architect friend, Ian G. Lindsay, who was then engaged on the restoration of the monastic buildings at Iona, asked if Campbell would be capable of making a model from his plans and elevations. I had sufficient confidence in my young companion's uncanny gifts by this time, that I felt sure he would be able to turn out what was needed, even if this was the first architectural model he had tackled. It was left to me to do the painting, for I had already visited Iona and made notes of the colours of the stones. The work was started in April and completed in six weeks. What added to the difficulty of the model was the fact that, as in so many medieval buildings, the planning was highly irregular. The church was slightly off the straight, and the cloister garth, around which the monastic buildings are grouped, is not a perfect square, none of the corners being right angles. Campbell cut out the elaborate Gothic tracery of the windows of the church with a fret-saw, and how his elephantine hands managed to achieve such minute and delicate details was a mystery. When all the separate parts of the buildings were completed we fitted them together on a large board, covering it with hard-wall plaster, so as to give the correct rise of the ground. Into this the buildings were set, and finally the plaster was painted green to represent grass. Last of all were added two minute Celtic crosses, close to the west door of the church. A vast crate was made to transport the model to Edinburgh, where the following year it was exhibited at the Royal Scottish Academy.

Other big models were to follow on after Iona, including one of the new church at Prinknash Abbey, and fishing boat models for the Liverpool Museums. Indeed, it seemed that Campbell would be kept busy with such work for the rest of his life. But the last model to be completed was a destroyer, which was bought by a friend of mine in British Columbia and sent out to Vancouver via the Panama Canal.

So his days at Harbour Head were fully occupied. He was an omnivorous reader, and when he was too ill to work, would lie in bed, devouring books borrowed from the London Library or from the local

branch of the County Library. When I first met Campbell he had
no time for fiction; his only desire was to fill his mind with yet
more *facts*. By this he meant history, especially maritime history,
travel and biography. But later on he developed a highly critical
taste for novels, new and old.

Campbell could be safely trusted to revise or correct any literary
work of mine. He never failed to detect mistakes in spelling or
grammar. For those two years I never dared send off an article
to an editor without letting him look through it. He was equally
helpful in correcting proofs. As to drawings of ships, he was certain
to discover inaccuracies and make me rub them out! Almost the
last job of this kind he did for me was to revise the typescript of
How to Draw Ships. He was now almost blind, so I had to read
what I had written. He made drastic criticisms; in fact, I re-wrote
most of the book as the result. It is more than likely that the amazing success of this little book is largely due to Campbell, for he
must be given the credit of having dictated, if not actually written,
the greater part of the text that goes with the drawings. I regret
that his name did not appear as the real author. He was only able
to get a dim idea of the drawings, and used to peer at them with a
powerful electric light behind him, just able to make out the shapes
of the ships, but none of the details.

A visit to Iona was perhaps the greatest event in his brief life.
The two of us spent a fortnight on the island during the summer
of 1940 as the guests of Dr. George MacLeod. Campbell spent most
of those two weeks making tables, shelves, and other furniture for
the Community House.   He also designed and made the wooden
pylon behind the Communion Table in the Cathedral, on which
now stands the silver cross. He loved Iona and seemed quite at
home with the ministers and artisans of the Community, though
quite capable of arguing with them on points of theology!   His
aloofness amused me. When we were alone he would discuss individual ministers as if he was a middle-aged professor instead of a
lad many years younger than any of them! Never shall I forget
that morning when part of the temporary wooden buildings caught
fire, and how it was Campbell who directed operations to
extinguish it.

He had an idea that he would like to go back to Iona and take
charge of a boat. He discussed the scheme with Dr. MacLeod and
was told to look out for a suitable vessel.   But like so many of

Campbell's dreams for the future, this Iona boat scheme never materialised, at least not in his lifetime.

For the next six months he carried on his usual jobs at Harbour Head, proving among other things that he was a most efficient cook. He had a crowd of friends among the fishermen and the employees at the shipbuilding yard and engineering works, likewise in the Naval Reserve crews of the examination ships then stationed here. These men and lads, also the crews of the many coasting vessels then discharging their cargoes here, were always dropping in to see him at all hours of the day, or he himself would disappear for an afternoon or evening to go aboard a ship. So the house became a real Sailor Centre, thanks to Campbell's personality. During the past year he had grown even more gigantic. His strange slouching figure was now a familiar sight as he dragged his body along the shore or round the harbour.

Campbell was not a peaceful individual to live with. His brain was far too active. He had a quick temper, not to mention a rich and lurid vocabulary when he was roused to anger. Yet there was something very stimulating in having an argument with him. It involved bringing up the whole of one's mental reserves, and in the end I was generally laid out flat and had to admit myself beaten. But these verbal battles gave us a chance to sharpen our wits, and never resulted in any lasting quarrel.

In *Harbour Head* I have told the story of how we bought our boat *Stella Maris* and how we put a motor into her and then took it out again. Campbell's dream of becoming a professional inshore fisherman remained a dream. We never used the boat for more than a few pleasure trips that first summer. When the autumn arrived she was laid up, and the following year he was far too ill to venture out in her, except once.[1]

Early in 1941, Campbell was back in the Royal Infirmary, Edinburgh, for purposes of observation. Here he remained five months, writing to me almost daily. Finally he was discharged as incurable, and I brought him back to Harbour Head. It was during

---

[1] This 15 ft. dinghy remained an infinite source of enjoyment for the next four years. Every evening during the summer months I was out rowing, sailing and fishing whenever the weather permitted. She was smashed to bits by a collier entering the harbour in a strong gale on September 23, 1945. Campbell would have mourned the loss of *Stella Maris* as much as I did!

those five months in Edinburgh that Campbell suddenly decided to become a Catholic. We had often discussed religious matters, but I had come to the conclusion that his whole outlook was far too critical and analytical for him to accept the claims of Catholicism. So far as I could make out, he had no attraction towards the institutional aspect of Christianity. Yet his interest in the Catholic Church went back to when he was a boy seaman in *Caledonia*. The Catholic chaplain, Mgr. Dewey, used to visit him much more often than the Church of Scotland minister. This kindly old priest left papers and magazines for the patient to read, among which was *The Universe*. Campbell told me that long before he knew that I was living in his home town he had studied my drawings in this paper, little thinking that sooner or later he would be living under the same roof as " The Pilgrim Artist ".

I never made the least effort to persuade Campbell to join the Catholic Church. I realised that he was groping after some kind of religious belief, but I could not see in what direction he was moving. About a month after our return from Iona we paid a visit to Fort Augustus Abbey. Campbell had said he would like to see what a Catholic religious Community was like in comparison with a Presbyterian Brotherhood. This brief contact with Benedictine monasticism did not make a very favourable impression. During those four days at the abbey, Campbell seemed rather bored. Had it not been for the chance to get out in a boat on Loch Ness, I think he would have been even more bored, although he liked browsing in the big library.

One day I got a letter telling me that he had asked the Catholic chaplain at the Royal Infirmary to start giving him instruction, for he had definitely made up his mind that he wished to be received into the Church. What were the motives that lay behind this decision were never revealed to me. The chaplain, Fr. Capaldi, S.J., told me later on that what struck him was the entire absence of intellectual difficulties: this eighteen-year-old lad simply came into the Church like a tired child coming home. " For a person of his intellectual capacities," wrote Fr. Capaldi, " I consider this fact to verge on the miraculous. Do you know, he never once asked me to explain anything, or how this or that truth could be: he just accepted everything. Moreover, it may surprise you to learn that I gave him just *one* short talk on Catholicism, and that towards the end of his stay in the infirmary. Perhaps he himself solved his own difficulties, but I incline to think he simply didn't have any, at least during the period that I knew him."

Campbell's reception into the Catholic Church was carried out in a somewhat unconventional manner. He was determined not to return to Harbour Head before he was a Catholic, and when he heard that the doctors and matron had decided to let him travel with me the following morning, he ordered me to get hold of the chaplain, even if it involved bringing him up from the Sacred Heart Church in Lauriston Street! Fortunately this was not necessary; I soon ran him to earth in another ward. I explained the situation, and within a few minutes the three of us had retired to the nearest dispensary, where amid the incense of iodoform and disinfectants the brief function took place.

On his return home this great giant was very helpless owing to his almost total blindness. Feeling that the end might not be far off, it was decided to give him the Last Sacraments. I stood by the bed while he was being anointed, and as he held up his huge hands to be wiped with the drops of oil, I wondered if they would ever make models again, or if those dull eyes would regain their sight. The windows were open and in the distance were the blue sea and the harbour. But Campbell could not make out any objects save as in a glass, darkly. Then he received Holy Communion, and when all was over thanked the priest for having taken so much trouble on his behalf.

This proved to be one of those occasions when the Last Sacraments effect what seems to be a cure, as was the original intention of the anointing with blessed oils. In less than a week, Campbell got up and went out for short walks.

That last month Campbell spent at Harbour Head, now that I look back on it, was curiously like making preparations to leave home for a long journey into a distant country. In his case, the *viaticum* was quite literally a supper partaken of by a traveller before setting out on a journey; metaphorically speaking, the provision for his passing out of this world into the next. I am convinced that he knew he would not return, and that was why he made such careful preparations beforehand. He gave me instructions what to do with his tools and other personal possessions. He wanted all the theological information I could give him about this unknown land for which his ship was likely to be sailing. He had no fear of death: he talked of it as an exciting adventure. It often seemed as if his spiritual self was already detached from his body; that he was looking at this body from outside it. As Father Cuthbert says of St. Francis of Assisi: "full deliberately would he die, even as he had lived", and so it was with Campbell Cowie; he would have saluted Death with St. Francis' own chivalrous salutation had he ever known the Canticle of the Sun and read the story of those joyful farewell scenes at the Portiuncula. "Welcome, Sister death! She is to me the gate of life." Like Francis, he would make merry of his infirmities; laugh at "Brother Ass", his great cumbersome body, and just as Francis bade Lady Giacoma di Settesoli to bring him some of his favourite sweet-cake made with almonds and sugar, so did Campbell, more than once ask me to buy him a bottle of sherry or cider!

He had already bidden me write to the neurological surgeon to ask if he would perform a risky operation that might partially restore his sight. One day a telegram arrived, stating that there was a bed vacant in the Royal Infirmary, and that Campbell was to go to Edinburgh as soon as possible. There was nothing more for him to do, except to say good-bye to his relatives and friends.

We set off together the following morning. When I was taking the tickets he interrupted my request for two returns: "No! Take a single for me. I don't suppose I shall need the other half, and it would be a pity to waste the money!" When we were settled in the train, he gave me definite orders that I was not to return home for a month, no matter what happened to him. "If I should get over the operation, you can pick me up in Edinburgh; otherwise there's no need for you to come back from England to bury me!" I promised to obey these orders—and did so. We parted at Dundee, for I was to stop first with friends in Fife. Five days later, having got as far south as Leicestershire, I received a telegram from Bangour Hospital, outside Edinburgh, that the operation would take place the next morning. Twenty-four hours later another telegram informed me that he died of a cerebral hæmorrhage. Subsequently I learnt that no sooner had Campbell been moved to Bangour Hospital than he asked the Sister to 'phone to the Catholic chaplain, Fr. McIlhargie of Broxburn, to hear his Confession and give him Communion.

Campbell's body was brought back to his native town, where it now rests in the old kirkyard above the harbour, in sight of the sea and the ships which he loved so much in this life. Around his grave are the tombs of many a seaman of bygone days. Strange to say one never thinks of Campbell as *dead*—in the ordinary meaning of the word, rather that (to quote that prayer in the Canon of the Mass) he has merely " gone before us ", and that his soul has found " a place of refreshment, light, and peace." His personality still lives on at Harbour Head.

*　　　　*　　　　*

On the feast of St. Francis of Assisi, 1945, I revisited Caldey after an interval of fourteen years. It was a perfect autumn morning. The sea was calm and opal coloured. Far away in the distance, as I stood on the beach at Tenby, lay the island, veiled in a soft mist, dim and mysterious. As the little motor-boat chugged across the three miles of open water, I thought of the countless times I had made this same passage in *Firefly* and *Stella Maris,* both of them wrecked in after years. It was strange that my own *Stella Maris* should have shared the same fate only a week ago. I wondered if my life would have evolved on very different lines had I not chanced to fall under the spell of this Welsh " Sirene " as a youth of seventeen.

The island drew nearer. I began to make out familiar landmarks—the leaning spire of the Priory church; the lighthouse; the long line of roofs, broken by towers and spires, which forms the modern Abbey. The tide was low, and the few passengers had to disembark in a dinghy. The concrete slipway, covered with green seaweed, was just as slippery as in the past. Once I had reached dry land and started to walk up the rough road between gorse, bramble bushes, and tall fuchsia hedges, still in bloom, and sniffed the scent of damp grass and bracken, it seemed only yesterday and not thirty-five years since I had first set foot on Caldey. On my left was the grey-stone, red-tiled Guest House where I had spent the Holy Week of 1910. Then came the first of many shocks—a dense pine wood had vanished completely, revealing a house formerly invisible from the road. A second shock—the walls of the monastery, instead of being an almost blinding white, had turned to a dirty weather-stained grey.

A third shock—there was no sign of the village church. It was completely hidden by a dense grove of trees, which I remembered being planted. I made my way through the village, past the Hall, where I had assisted at so many entertainments and acted in the Passion Plays. It looked abandoned and neglected. Then I climbed up a steep path, once open to the four winds, now dark and over-grown. Leaning against a barrier I gazed at the interior of the Abbey church, completely gutted by fire three years ago. Nothing was left but the four walls. Gone were the gilded reredos, oak choir stalls, side altars and screen. The pavement, which I had so often polished as a novice, was split and broken with the flames. What remained of the famous high altar, made up of stones from ancient monasteries, was covered with sheets of corrugated iron. Never have I beheld such a picture of desolation. A green-leafed shrub was growing where the Abbot's throne once stood. Flowering weeds covered the other side of the sanctuary. I thought of the many events in my past life which had taken place within these four walls—my clothing as an Anglican novice, my profession a year later, my reception into the Catholic Church, and much else. This abomination of desolation drove home the transitoriness of human existence as nothing else could do. The church, which once seemed so permanent, had been reduced to dust and ashes in a few hours. Not one of us who used to spend so many hours every day beneath its roof remained on the island. The winds and currents have drifted us far apart on the ocean of life.

The fire had also gutted the adjacent row of cottages which formed the original monastery. The large room that once served as the chapel was choked with weeds and bushes. The only consolation was the discovery that the Cistercian monks had improvised such a perfect church out of what had been the Benedictine Chapter House and " Statio ".

The flower gardens on which so much money and time had been spent were now mostly given over to the produce of vegetables. How many memories were revived by sudden contacts! There was the " cell " I occupied during the years I was dreaming of and working an international sea apostolate. I wandered up to the lighthouse and recalled the exact spot on the cliffs where I had sat on that August afternoon in 1921 when designing the now world-famous badge of *Apostolatus Maris*. I pushed my way through bracken, brambles and gorse in order to look at the much-loved Sambuca hermitage. Nothing was left but the concrete foundations. Anyhow, the view eastward across the British Channel remained as I had so often visualised it in later years.

Those few hours on Caldey helped me to realise how true it is that " the best-laid plans o' mice an' men gang aft agley ". The carefully charted expedition which had been pursued by the Community to which I belonged—all of us eager to arrive at the promised land of our ambition—was by the hand of God diverted from its course. Our sailing orders were changed. As I stated in the fore-

word to this book, my own life has been not unlike a long voyage
on a choppy sea; my ship tossed about like a shuttlecock for many
a long year. This little island is now nothing more than the background of a very remote phase of our existence, nevertheless, something which helped to mould our characters.

*   *   *

Oddly enough, it was the sea—that most unstable element—which
seemed to be the only permanent and lasting feature. It was a
pleasure to examine the two dinghies which had been built by these
practical-minded and capable Cistercians who now own the island.
As I sat in the motor-boat on my return to the mainland, talking to
one of the monks mostly on maritime matters, and watching Caldey
receding into the haze, I thought of my present existence among a
very different type of maritime community far away on the north-
east coast of Scotland. The isolated bits and pieces of my career
as a roving recluse formed themselves into a definite pattern. They
were linked up, as it were, into the story of a man drawn by two
almost equally strong ideals: an ever persistent love for the sea,
ships and sailors, together with an apparently contradictory attraction for monasticism. In the long run it was the former which
proved the stronger. My only regret as I looked back on Caldey
from the cliffs of Tenby on that autumn afternoon was that, like
another Peter, I had not listened to the voice that whispered so
often—a call to "walk upon the waters", or more correctly,
"beside the waters". If you have had the patience to wade through
these memoirs you will guess what I mean!

INDEX

PERSONS AND PLACES